AN INTENSE CALLING

How Ethics Is Essential to Education

Positing that education is a movement from one way of being to another, more desirable one, *An Intense Calling* argues that ethics should be the prime focus for the field of education. The book locates ethics, education, and justice in human subjectivity and describes education as a necessary practice for ethical reflexivity, change, and becoming (ethically) different. It also situates ethics as something that exceeds subjectivity, thereby engaging ethics as a material phenomenon through topics such as aesthetics and solidarity with non-humans.

Jesse Bazzul explores various concepts in the book including power, biopolitics, the commons, subjectivity, and materiality, and draws from over twenty years of experience teaching in different countries including Canada, Ireland, the United States, China, and Ukraine. Taking a wide-ranging philosophical approach, the book entangles ethics, urgent political issues, and pressing educational contexts of the twenty-first century. In doing so, *An Intense Calling* maintains that ethics is the core of education because education involves finding better ways of living and being in the world.

JESSE BAZZUL is an associate professor in the Faculty of Education at the University of Regina.

JESSE BAZZUL

An Intense Calling

How Ethics Is Essential to Education

UNIVERSITY OF TORONTO PRESS
Toronto Buffalo London

© University of Toronto Press 2023
Toronto Buffalo London
utorontopress.com

ISBN 978-1-4875-4786-8 (cloth) ISBN 978-1-4875-5834-5 (EPUB)
ISBN 978-1-4875-5058-5 (paper) ISBN 978-1-4875-5562-7 (PDF)

Library and Archives Canada Cataloguing in Publication

Title: An intense calling : how ethics is essential to education / Jesse Bazzul.
Names: Bazzul, Jesse, author.
Description: Includes bibliographical references and index.
Identifiers: Canadiana (print) 20220440581 | Canadiana (ebook) 20220440638 |
    ISBN 9781487547868 (cloth) | ISBN 9781487550585 (paper) |
    ISBN 9781487555627 (PDF) | ISBN 9781487558345 (EPUB)
Subjects: LCSH: Moral education. | LCSH: Ethics. | LCSH: Subjectivity.
Classification: LCC LC268 .B39 2023 | DDC 370.11/4–dc23

We wish to acknowledge the land on which the University of Toronto Press operates. This land is the traditional territory of the Wendat, the Anishnaabeg, the Haudenosaunee, the Métis, and the Mississaugas of the Credit First Nation.

This book has been published with the help of a grant from the Federation for the Humanities and Social Sciences, through the Awards to Scholarly Publications Program, using funds provided by the Social Sciences and Humanities Research Council of Canada.

University of Toronto Press acknowledges the financial support of the Government of Canada, the Canada Council for the Arts, and the Ontario Arts Council, an agency of the Government of Ontario, for its publishing activities.

Canada Council   Conseil des Arts
for the Arts   du Canada

ONTARIO ARTS COUNCIL
CONSEIL DES ARTS DE L'ONTARIO
an Ontario government agency
un organisme du gouvernement de l'Ontario

Funded by the   Financé par le
Government   gouvernement
of Canada   du Canada

Canadä

Many thanks to the wondrous creatures of Treaty 4 and Ireland.

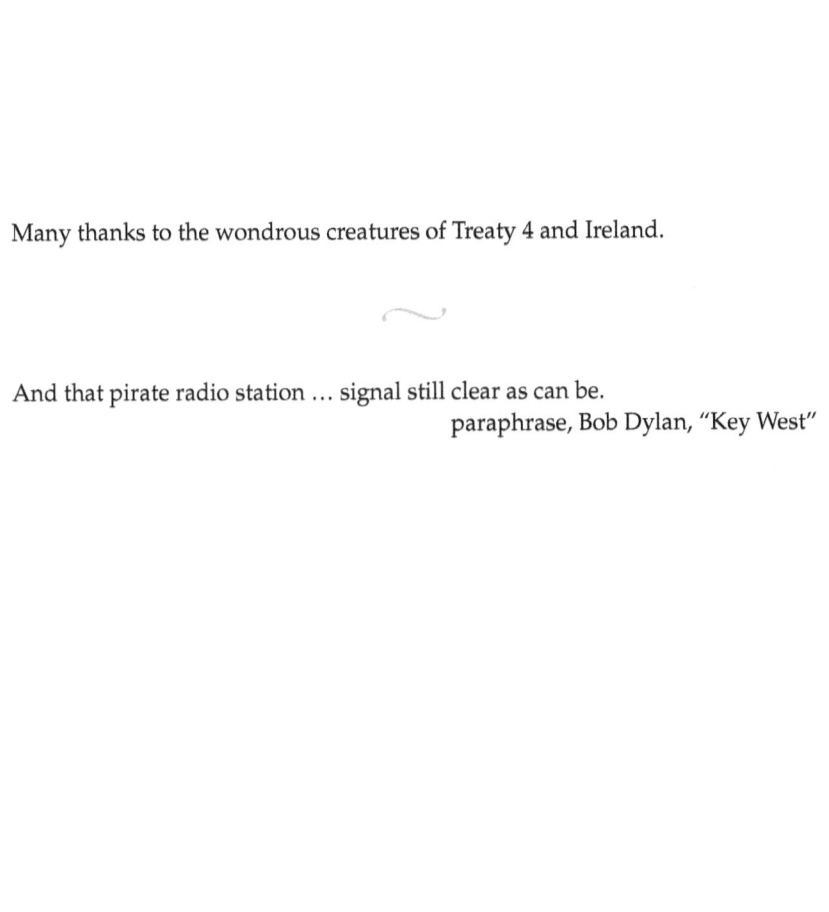

And that pirate radio station ... signal still clear as can be.
paraphrase, Bob Dylan, "Key West"

Contents

List of Figures ix

Preface: A Mapping of Education and Ethics 1

Part One: Ethics and Subjectivity

1 (Un)Disciplined: Education as an Open Work 15

2 Multiplicity and the Commons 43

3 Education Needs Politics and Imagination 61

4 Ethics and Subjectivity: The Vital Terrain of Education 73

Part Two: Ethics as Ontological Exploration

5 Outside the Subject of Ethics 93

6 Assemblages and the Emergence of Difference 116

7 Aesthetics and Environmentality 140

8 Solidarity with Nonhumans 161

Afterword: Monstrous Flesh and Possibility 177

Notes 179
Bibliography 197
Index 211

Figures

0.1 Map of this book. 10
1.1 Conducting conduct through the apparatus of education. 32
3.1 Representation of Jacques Rancière's politics of dissensus. 64
4.1 Dimensions of relations of self. 82
5.1 Gilles Deleuze's "diagram of Foucault" or "diagram of the fold" relating aspects of being and subjectivity. 96
5.2 The fold of subjectivity as forces of the social and material outside turned/folded inward. 99
5.3 A. Rhizome in relation to root-stem-flower B. A tangle of rhizomes C. Closed "Arboreal" system D. Open rhizomatic system. 108
5.4 Rhizomes giving rise to virtual and actual becoming(s). (Diagram inspired by Marc Ngui.) 114
6.1 Two hypothetical and interrelated plains of emergence: Ecological crisis and human evolution. 121
6.2 School as assemblage, with its different parts and varying capacities. 124
6.3 Assemblages can be overcoded or free-flowing in their materiality and expression. 127
6.4 Politics of HIV transmission as assemblage. 134
7.1 A depiction of Toronto occupied by a late twenty-third century imperial army in the film *Wakening*. 148
7.2 Collective life in *Psychopompolis*. 150

Preface: A Mapping of Education and Ethics

I'll begin this book the way I do most formal things in Regina, Saskatchewan. By acknowledging the spirit that breathes life into our collective futures. This spirit has many manifestations, one being the spirit of treaty between Indigenous and non-Indigenous people – past, present, and future – in the land known to many as Canada. I began writing this book as an uninvited guest on Treaty 4 territory, the homeland for the Nehiyawak, Anihšināpē, Métis, Dakota, Lakota, and Nakota communities. The final chapters and revisions were completed in Westmeath County, Ireland. I moved there thinking I might make a new life on that very green island. However, it turned out I couldn't escape the spirit I found in Regina (that pile of bones!). Ireland reminded me that it's good to have adventures, but it's also good to sit with the deep cuts they cause. This book was written in that interlude, between accepting a job in Ireland in the summer of 2019 and returning home to Regina in the summer of 2021. At a time of flight or fleeing.

I also want to begin with a funny, but useful, anecdote I picked up from a Slavoj Žižek lecture. Though I'm not 100 per cent sure that's where it's from, and I've looked everywhere. It goes something like this. There are two kinds of people in the world: idiots and morons. Morons think that the rules and norms of society are, on the whole, unproblematic and more or less the way things are supposed to be. If you were to wear pyjamas to a dinner party a moron would ridicule you to tears. How could someone wear pyjamas to, what was supposed to be, a relaxed and casual social event!? Idiots are the ones wearing pyjamas to dinner parties. Straight faced, they ask why people wouldn't attend dinner parties dressed as comfortably as possible. Ready to crash hard on the couch from sheer boredom or eating too much. In a nutshell, idiots don't respect social conventions or traditional mores very much while morons respect them too much. While basic etymology doesn't support Žižek's farce, the point it makes is important. There needs to be a balance of well-meaning idiots and morons in the world. I happen to veer hard towards the idiotic side of things – though the field of education tends to attract moronic types. So, anyone expecting this book to provide a list of best practices is going to find it rather idiotic. At least in several places. But I'd prefer to write something that leans towards the idiotic rather than the moronic. And I'm also aware that this book might not be idiotic enough!

The main thesis of this book is that ethics is the essence of education. Education's core practice involves guiding others towards what should be done. Moving them from one subjective position or outlook to a better one. This question of subjectivity, ethics, and education is the main focus of part 1. In part 2, I try to slowly move the question of ethics and education beyond human subjectivity. In doing so, ethics becomes more about nurturing difference. Something that enables rather than destroys. My original idea was to write something linking imagination and politics to education for just futures. And while this idea remains part of the book, it comes with a few problems. How much can an able-bodied white guy from southwestern Ontario say about politics or political imagination? Add to that the uncomfortable feeling that comes with writing something "non-empirical" and "non-practical" in a field dominated by the social sciences and "how-to" pedagogies. Educators are trained to value the practical and revere the empirical, and for good reasons. However, it may be that the arts and humanities hold the most promise for education today. Maybe the social sciences and practical manuals have held our attention for far too long.

First and foremost this is a book of educational philosophy and theory. Its aim is to provoke imagination in a field tasked with social and ecological renewal. What makes it philosophical is the use of concepts like biopower, the commons, correlationism, rhizomes, becoming, and so on, which can be connected to other concepts and phenomena at infinite speed and depth (at the speed of thought!).[1] This isn't a comment about the quality or usage of the concepts themselves. It's more a comment on the writing style, one that values philosophy and theory.

I view education as a transdisciplinary field of research, practice, and thought. Scholarly contributions to this field should all *feel* different. By demanding uniformity, educational institutions often alienate students and teachers from their own visceral experiences and situated understandings of the world. This is especially true for Black and Indigenous people, people of colour, the 2SLGBTQIA+ community, those in poverty, and students with exceptionalities. The work of an educator involves bringing relations of self into the foreground. In this way, education is an intensive ethical journey that moves someone from one way of being to another. Knowledge acquisition is always secondary. David Orr makes this point about the importance of ethics using the example of Germany's education system in the early twentieth century. While Germany was arguably the best place to study the natural sciences a hundred years ago, its education system utterly failed in preventing widespread destruction and genocide.[2]

Ethics doesn't just apply to codes of conduct, and it can't be learned solely through "what if" scenarios from the biomedical sciences. Rather, ethics should be seen as an entirely open field of creative enquiry. Consequently, this book cannot outline even a fraction of what ethics entails. Nor does it adequately engage the vast traditions of land-based education or moral philosophy. There are, in my view, at least two practical reasons for these shortcomings. First, this is not really a book about ethics itself. It's a book about education and ethics. More specifically, it's a book about how ethics is the core of education. Second, concepts and codes of ethics vary widely. Catholic dioceses, organized crime, professional teachers, and the corporate world all have an ethics. Ethics, essentially, pertains to how people should conduct themselves and live in the world. And as you can imagine there are an infinite number of variations of how to be. So your take on ethics will no doubt differ from mine.

Ethics on its own, however, is never enough. A book, class, or discussion about ethics is always in need of some context or direction. For example, in order for ethics to be relevant to the survival of life on a dying planet, it needs to be able to connect with a collective politics. Educating for a just, sustainable future is fundamentally an ethico-political aspiration. And the more educators situate themselves between questions of equality and basic ethical questions like "what should I do?" the more intense things become. This is because the space between collective existence and personal attachments is effectively the centre of social and political power relations. This is what makes the predicament of being an educator messy. Even though the role of teacher as ethical guide has been around for thousands of years the intense ethical work educators are called to do remains daunting and obscure.

When referring to educators I sometimes use pronouns like "ours" and "we." The use of these pronouns is inherently problematic but also useful. The kind of collective imagination needed to face things like poverty, environmental destruction, and white supremacy sometimes requires simple and easy conduits to a collective mentality. However, there is no "we" that holds together as a universal and does not exclude many beings (like nonhumans). The use of "we" as a universal erases or smooths over inequalities. Leaving them hidden and festering. The "we" I sometimes refer to should be seen as the community of this book, which I think of as educators of all kinds: schoolteachers, outdoor guides, spiritual leaders, professors, coaches, counsellors, new teachers, aspiring university students, and so on. If I could infuse this "we" with something it would be a democratic principle that affirms the equal ability of teachers and students to contribute different thoughts, interpretations, and performances to the world.[3] I'm also cognizant that I don't understand the experiences of Black and Indigenous educators who feel the intensity of power relations in ways I can't imagine. Nonetheless I still, at times, reach for this partial "we" fraught with difficulty. If just to imagine that for a brief moment, perhaps in some future sense, there might be some sort of abstract collective "we."

Education is perpetually caught between the vital tasks of conserving the world and changing it. This means it bears the ethical responsibility of doing both. Since politics always plays a substantial role in positioning educators somewhere between these two tasks it's not possible for education to be apolitical. Neutrality is a political position. Often one that condones violence. Also it is easy to hide behind platitudes, for example, to declare that education is about changing the world and simply stop at that. Educators need the freedom to fully explore and ethically engage the perplexing and often dangerous circumstances facing life on this planet, some forms of life more than others. Education involves the infinitely variable ways beings are brought to be in ethical relation with themselves and their community in the widest ecological sense. As educators, we see how ethical beings are constituted, because our work involves bringing others to better ways of living. This is not to say that educators know best. What constitutes ethical ways of living is a totally open question, and this is one of the things that makes education fascinating and worthy of rigorous study. It's okay for educators to be a little lost when trying to figure out the core of their discipline. In fact, it might be better for everybody if educators were to dwell in that realm more often.

This book also wrestles with some long-standing issues embraced by the political left. While educators have no choice but to look to progressive ideas for collective living, the left still struggles to find a coherence that appeals to the working poor and globally marginalized. Finding this coherence involves expanding creative concepts like universality, multiplicity, and fidelity. It involves finding ways of sharing our world(s) while nurturing difference. It is wrong to say that the left is split between the politics of representation and identity on the one side and socialism on the other. But it's true to say that the left has not been successful in creating institutions that effectively fight economic inequality, white supremacy, and environmental degradation simultaneously. In my view, what the left needs badly is a collective vision that seeks justice, yet offers the openness needed to nurture difference. This vision needs ethics and spirituality as much as it needs politics. Teachers now understand that treating everyone the same in a classroom often only works to cement inequality. A focus on difference can help educators resist forces that normalize and control. Students with exceptional learning needs, or who face everyday racisms, need teachers to respond differently. But does this focus on difference enable a radical sharing of what all of us (should) have in common? How do students and teachers cultivate the kind of equality needed to share the planet with all other beings? The tension between difference and commonality is similar to the tension between ethics and democratic politics. Addressing this tension is unavoidable for educators pursuing a vision of justice. I still believe in the political left. It's impossible for me to imagine how humans can confront mass extinction and growing inequality without collective institutions that enforce just and caring policies. However, people will always need ways of exploring meaning, pleasure, and creativity. In other words, to explore being. Any political vision must allow for ways of being that inspire and excite, and to encourage the connections that keep the horizon of politics open.

Education is a fascinating field because of its transdisciplinarity. Is education more like a (social) science or an art form? Should its theoretical frameworks be more aligned with psychology or cultural studies? Are the behavioural sciences or Indigenous ways of knowing most useful for teachers, students, environments, and governments? Are schools simply a tool to govern populations or are they sites of emancipation? Education as a field of study has been tied too closely to the social sciences, as if they are a natural fit for a discipline whose core is ethics. After the Second World War, nation states increasingly looked to education as a way to deal with social and economic concerns such as dutiful citizenship and human capital needs. States not only shaped curricula to meet their needs, but began investing in educational research, teacher education, and policy formation. This partly explains how education was slowly revamped as an evidence-based social science discipline.[4] Investment in institutions like faculties of education, however, have had unforeseen consequences. When given the chance, students of education often don't see the needs of the state, and their corporate partners, as the most deserving of attention. Not once they're exposed to the urgent needs of marginalized communities and the destruction facing nonhuman life. It makes more sense to me to view education as a branch of the humanities or the arts, especially if its core is ethics. And if ethics entails nurturing different, more enabling, ways of being in the world, critical reflection and creative expression (basic practices of the arts and humanities) are therefore vital to the study of education. At the end of the day, positioning education as an essentially transdisciplinary field seems to be the most pragmatic way forward, thus allowing disciplines like sociology, theology, biology, and the visual arts to all have their say.

When approaching topics like subjectivity and ethics, writers often draw from their own experiences. This can help the reader to understand where the writer may be coming from, and why they might include some topics but not others. It also makes a book that uses philosophical ideas more relatable and accessible – though from time to time complex ideas require diverse and complex terminology.[5] Teaching is often a lesson in how limited one educator can be! There are so many things a teacher will never mention to their students, let alone realize themselves. We educators are always incomplete as we set out to meet our calling. This means we need a great number of people, not to mention other species, to do our jobs effectively. We need to remain open to change for the sake of our students.

Ethics is a slippery thing. Just when you think you've figured it out, the makings of a new way of living, being, and relating presents itself.

Part 1 and Part 2

This book is divided into two parts, both of which use creative philosophical concepts to think more deeply about ethics. The first part introduces some overarching contexts for education; I also share some personal experiences that influence how I approach the field. It develops the idea that education is a crucial site of ethical formation. Subjectivity is a major theme in part 1, as are the socio-political contexts and modes of governance that work to constitute how individuals come to see themselves as ethical beings. Part 1 employs concepts like power and the commons. How are people brought to see themselves as ethical beings? How does education both constrain and afford ethical possibilities? Part 1 also explores some productive relationships between ethics and politics.

Part 2 begins by opening up the question of ethics and subjectivity to some kind of "outside." It attempts to open ethics to a world beyond subjectivity. One problem with framing ethics in terms of subjectivity is that you're then stuck with the idea that ethics only exists in human consciousness or between humans. What our current ecological crisis tells us, however, is that humans are deeply connected with different forms of life and the material world around them. In a time of ecological crisis, shouldn't ethics take things like mutual dependence and multispecies kinship more seriously? Part 2 is more concerned with these material dimensions and utilizes concepts like aesthetics and symbiosis. Ethics becomes something that emerges in assemblages of living and nonliving entities, something that includes but exceeds human-human relationships. Does ethics exist even when there are no humans around? The answer depends on how far beyond anthropocentrism we're willing to go. While part 1 takes a more critical poststructuralist approach, part 2 follows the "ontological turn" in social theory and philosophy. This movement in contemporary (Western) theory focuses more on the nature of reality or "how things are" than its immediate predecessors. I do my best to avoid an "onto-theology" in that I don't hold too closely to any one set of ontological concepts. The concepts in this book are intended to enable connections. They are not intended to establish any one framework about the nature of reality. That would run counter to the task of opening education to new ways of thinking about our shared world.

Overall, the book follows my pedagogical and academic interests in chronological order, which is also a geographical order. I'm thankful to have had the chance to leave Ontario and think differently about myself in the world. Perhaps that's how this book should be read: as an effort to think differently.

Reading and Writing

I've tried to resist jamming this book with unneeded references. I've also dispensed with APA citation and style – which is better suited for writing that wants to fit within an already determined field of knowledge. I also hate serial citation. Unless you're a scientist or psychologist it makes more sense to introduce sources when necessary and in a more comprehensive way. The advice from the editor at University of Toronto Press was to forget that small group of academics that direct so much of our writing. Instead, I was told to imagine an interested undergraduate student that wanted to change the world. Maybe it was just run-of-the-mill advice but nevertheless it made an impression on me. Writing a book means trying to let go of the performativity that would please (or enrage) my academic colleagues. Reducing a certain kind of performativity in writing means taking the risk of seeming naive, uninformed, or parochial. It's difficult to write an academic book without some pretension, but it's even more difficult to put academic jargon in plain language. And while it's almost always best to write in a straightforward way, I don't think it's possible to avoid words that describe the reality of our situation today, words like extinction, inequality, white supremacy, colonization, capitalism, emancipation, anthropocentrism, heteronormativity, genocide, justice. Using "softer" or more generally accepted terms like privilege or sustainability can sometimes obscure systemic violence as well as collective politics. As if it were enough for educators to recognize that some students have inherent advantages or that humans need to do less environmental damage.

It's been twenty years since I began teaching and I still believe education is a wholly fascinating endeavour. Educators spend a lot of time writing about things that can easily be put into practice, and not enough time writing about ideas. As a teacher, I find myself regularly looking for an "outside" to conventional wisdom, the semblance of some new thought, which usually involves those ineffable things that "professionals" often don't seem to value. The integrity of the undergraduate students at the University of Regina made me want to write something I could share with people from places like Southey and Kelliher, Saskatchewan. I've always disliked those educational know-it-alls. You know the type. Everything they say somehow comes out perfect for the moment. But someone who has all the answers, or tells you what questions to ask, can never replace the people who pose unexpected questions. To say that educators should be sceptical of "sages of learning" is not going far enough. The danger of relying on people who claim to have all the answers is stultification. The stakes come down to whether students and teachers are set on a path to think and do things differently or reproduce what's already being done.

Teachers and books have at least one thing in common: they grab you or they don't. Some you hate and some you love. Sometimes it's a mysterious detail that determines whether a person or piece of writing resonates with us. A late family member of mine, Sean McEvenue, who was a theology professor at Concordia University in Montreal, was often troubled when he didn't like books other people revered. While Sean disliked the poetry of Emily Dickinson and the Book of Revelation (two things he thought he should have liked), he loved hard-boiled detective novels and real-life encounters with quirky strangers. His research on truth and the Bible taught me that all texts and people have this quality of *expectancy*.[6] A set of expectations that a person has for the world and themselves – what they hope will happen. At this gut level we either embrace a text or person or feel turned off. Teachers should be sensitive to how they come off to other people, even when they can't do much about it. I hope some of the ideas in this book resonate, but they likely won't if the expectation is that it will tell teachers and school systems what to do. Enough with the gurus already! Maybe the best this book can do is distort expectations. Like when we encounter something strange and reality wavers just a little.

Overall, I take a materialist view of texts. Their production is more an extension of discourses already circulating, as well as the material arrangements that enable them. They are more representative of the wider social world than the unique voice of their authors. Considering the materiality of a text means thinking about the larger socio-historical and ecological forces that "move" through them. They make sense only within specific social and historical backdrops (some backdrops being more specific than others), although each text will have elements that make them unique and special.[7] From this perspective, what a text means is less profound than what it *does*.[8] It also makes writing a very messy process, something much less refined than many would have us believe. The positioning of a text draws attention to what philosopher Fredric Jameson calls "the problem of getting started" in writing.[9] The problem of getting started has less to do with how to say something than with determining what needs to be articulated at this particular moment. Getting started on a paper or book or curriculum document is therefore a distinctly ethical and political problem. I think this preface is a case in point.

Mapping the Book

I decided it would be best to map the book out using my Sketchbook™ app. I sometimes use basic sketches when I feel a picture might express something words can't.[10] Figure 0.1 is a basic map of the book, laid out like a footpath through its various parts. Let me describe this topology.

One of the main points of chapter 1, and this preface, is to cast education as an open transdisciplinary field. The biggest threat to education, and its ethical calling, is stultification, that is, the stifling of our collective (and equal) powers of creation. Education today is situated within the violent forces of modernity. Colonialism and capitalism continue to drive an ecological crisis that has radically changed earth's biological and geological make-up. Education is always a site of contest, one where power is exercised over bodies but also resisted 'from below' by students, community members, and teachers. Chapters 1 and 2 situate education as one of the many strategies of modern governance or *biopower* – the power exercised over all life through institutions, policy, and the distribution of material resources (*bio* referring to both biological and social life). However, education also offers a mode of resistance

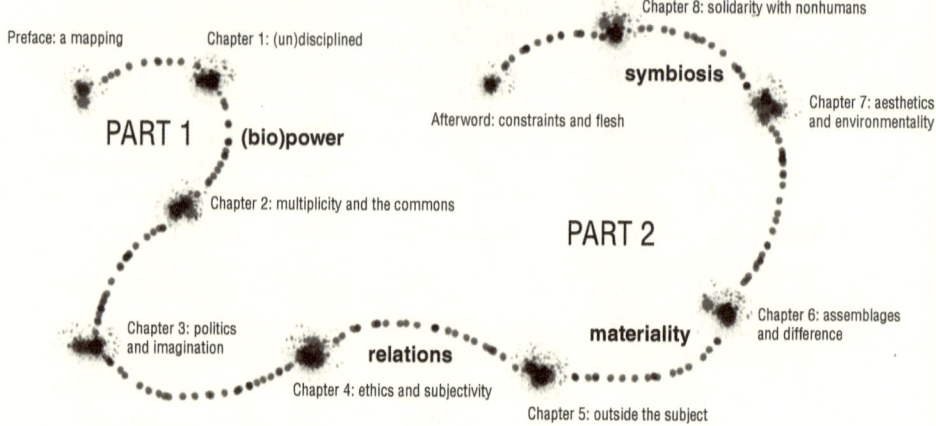

Figure 0.1. Map of this book.

to biopower through ethical reflexivity. Creative concepts like "the commons" and "multiplicities" can help educators think through what ethical resistance to biopower might entail. While concepts emerge from particular social and historical contexts, they also have atemporal and acontextual features – a point Noel Gough and Warren Sellers emphasize in their efforts to expand the horizon of curriculum theory.[11] Following Gilles Deleuze and Felix Guattari, Gough and Sellers emphasize that all concepts assume the existence of a pre-conceptual material world. But this pre-conceptual world is not just material in the actual sense. It is also virtual, existing along an infinite (and immanent) plane of reality and thought.

In the first few chapters I rely heavily on the work of Michel Foucault, a prominent social theorist who can also be described as a formative and trusty philosopher of education. Right from the beginning of part 1, the productive tension between ethics and politics becomes a major theme of discussion. This is because, in my view, neither ethics nor politics, on their own, provides a viable alternative or resistance to biopower. Education needs to engage both ethics and politics to be relevant.

Chapter 3 is a bit of a sidestep, a plea for educators to think about politics and imagination in education. It was originally written as a standalone paper that focused mostly on the interplay of science, politics, and imagination. However, I feel it has a place among the other chapters. Its overall aim is to emphasize the importance of (re)imagining a political horizon to our ethical work in education. Chapter 4 ties together ideas of subjectivity with the biopolitical contexts discussed in previous chapters. Its goal is to consider ethical reflexivity, exploration, and resistance as the primary terrain of education. Chapter 4 ends part 1 and its engagement with the movement of thought that anchors ethics in human subjectivity.

Chapter 5, the beginning of part 2, reconsiders ethics and subjectivity in relation to an "outside," that is, an outside to human subjectivity. The outside consists of a world or materiality that cannot be divorced from an "inside" (subjectivity). Once it is possible to imagine ethics outside of human subjectivity it becomes easier to see it as an emergent phenomenon. It arises among diverse assemblies of things, or assemblages, the vast majority of which are nonhuman or nonliving. Indeed, there's a spiritual-materialist dimension to this kind of imagining in that it requires us to behold a mysterious and fascinating world beyond human perception. This is also one of the first lessons of Indigenous education as I understand it.

Chapter 6 explores the idea that ethics encompasses nonhuman elements. One elephant in the room, and there may be many others, is that Indigenous ways of living already include nonhuman elements in their ethics. This leaves two viable options. The first is putting much of Western thought aside to pursue Indigenous ways of living. This is happening to some extent, especially in classes related to teacher education. Western thought, and its ethical potential, cannot remain unchanged in light of our shared ecological crises and the inequalities created by colonialism and capitalism. If anything about Western thought is to be salvaged it must reinvent itself. This, in my view, is the second viable option and the one taken in this book. If Western thought and philosophy fail, or more accurately continue to fail, then all the better they be abandoned.

The final chapters of the book emphasize the importance of aesthetics and its relation to ecological thinking. Chapter 7 explores how educators might start thinking about the aesthetic dimension and the uncanny nature of reality itself. Part of the problem is that Western thought and culture have left modern societies with an impoverished view of how infinite and wondrous the world really is. This impoverishment was gradual and involved slowly cutting relations with other beings and their worlds, that is, anything that didn't seem immediately important to things like making cities and storing food. For too long science has dominated all serious thinking about nonhuman and nonliving beings. It is time for the humanities and social sciences to also consider the world "outside." This will involve rethinking the idea that humans can only consider reality through human perception and human-human relations. Chapter 8 discusses the ethical stakes of moving beyond anthropocentrism and establishing solidarity with nonliving things. This solidarity entails a fuller realization of our symbiotic existence and promises a deeper sense of connectedness, responsibility, and pleasure. The end of the book might offer a brief glimpse into what an ethics that can engage the reality of the Anthropocene might entail. What might education look like in a more "symbiotically real" world? Probably a lot different than it does now.

A dear colleague named Audrey Aamodt has taught me a lot about ethics through her mishaps and misgivings with settler colonial identity, "being good," and colonialism. Perhaps the greatest thing she's taught me is that "being good" is completely elusive. You may grab hold of it, but it'll eventually wiggle free. This is a good thing, because everything must eventually change. How else would the world continue to be different? If we could grasp the absolute right way of being, education would come to a halt. The good news is that things will always change. This is the one thing about existence we can be sure about – which means people can always be different and think differently. Differently from last year, or even last week. And that is an encouraging thought.

PART ONE

Ethics and Subjectivity

who is in charge of the ethics police   whose frames matter   whose are expendable
who holds the reins   and whip   the keys to the dungeon   the drawbridge
this too   is the stain and cut of ethics.

– Peter Cole, *Coyote and Raven Go Canoeing*

1 (Un)Disciplined: Education as an Open Work

The divine tape recorder holds a million scenarios, each perfectly sensible. Little quirks at the outset, occurring for no particular reason, unleash cascades of consequences that make a particular feature seem inevitable in retrospect. But the slightest early nudge contacts a different groove, and history veers into another plausible channel, diverging continually from its original pathway. The end results are so different, the initial perturbation so apparently trivial.

– Stephen J. Gould[1]

Opera Aperta

Let's begin with the overall theme of this book. The essence of education is ethics. The most important work an educator does involves moving people from one ethical perspective or way of being to another. One of the things that makes education so fascinating is that there's no prescription for how to do this. There are an infinite number of ways to be in the world just like there are an infinite number of possible people, species, ideas, and universes. Having said this, education still bears the responsibility of finding and guiding us towards better ways of living together. Especially in times of crisis. And it would seem obvious that some ways of living are more conducive to facing things like mass extinction and social inequality. In this way, education has never been a more relevant field of study and practice. Rather than be disheartened at the never-ending task of finding better ways of being in the world educators can take heart in the expansive possibilities for ethical "becoming" and self-creation they nurture in students.

When I was an undergraduate biology student at Brock University, Stephen J. Gould's *Wonderful Life: The Burgess Shale and the Nature of*

History was recommended to me by a wonderful ecology professor named Miriam Richards.[2] Two things from Gould's work stayed with me over the last twenty-five years or so. First, I was impressed that a prominent scientist would be so interested in connecting the biological sciences with their social and historical foundations. As science students we were implicitly taught that any academic pursuit that wasn't scientific was of lesser quality or importance. Such interests were not relevant to the "real research" at hand. Second, Gould's work proposed the astonishing notion that if Earth's natural history were "replayed" the forces of randomness and contingency would lead to very different evolutionary pathways for life. This idea is not just a profound comment about the nature of biological life, history, and time. It also has big implications for ethics and creativity. It means that the emergence of different forms of life – social, educational, biological – is possible at every turn and scale. It also means no way of living is inevitable. In other words, there is no ultimately correct way things should unfold. Educators can take the fact that life is mostly unforeseeable as an encouraging sign. Becoming ethical in/with the world, whatever that might mean, is completely dependent on the many different relations, contexts, and material conditions of the here and now. It's heartening to know that if I were to write this book a few years from now it would look very different. Sometimes all educators can do is breathe and fall forward.

Ethics resides at the core of education because many of the intense experiences that lead to a different way of being are pedagogical in nature. Who or what constitutes a "pedagogue" remains open to interpretation. Parents, neighbours, and friends can all be wonderful teachers. Attending public school in places like the United States or Ireland, places with relatively well-functioning institutions, means learning to meet the demands of a community. It also sometimes entails learning to be critical of these demands. At some point between kindergarten and post-secondary education the idea that people should live differently than they are now percolates through. These different ethical aspirations, of duty to a community and living differently than people in the past, constantly intertwine. This is because at some fundamental level both are necessary. When someone considers teaching, parenting, or mentoring work, they piece this role together from past experience. They immediately infuse it with various ethical aspirations. They may want change, preservation, or both.

When I started my bachelor of education degree at the University of Toronto my goal was to enlighten youth through science. I wasn't interested in challenging a social order I found non-threatening as a young, white, able-bodied male. If I were to capture my teaching philosophy in a slogan it might have read: "Learning to live life through the truth"! That slogan also characterizes my religious upbringing to a T. Strange how two very different forms of truth can generate a similar ethic of education. So, even before my first students arrived at Earnscliffe Senior Public School in Brampton, Ontario (shout out to 7-E/7-F), I'd already figured out the ethos of my life's work. Basically, I was a walking billboard for scientific realism and the Canadian state's narrative of multiculturalism and continuing colonial rule.

Thank goodness overly simplistic outlooks can't last long. Sooner or later they give way to complexity and consequences. Through the labour of other educators, I slowly came to see education as a way to challenge truth: truth as knowledge, truth as morality, truth as the political order of things. Despite the stock images of classrooms depicting docility and order, education is also a space for dreamers and lunatics. As time went by the challenge became less about holding on to the ideals that brought me to education and more about finding different ways of thinking. It's crucial to remain open to difference, which is a big step up from keeping an open mind. It is true that our thoughts, conduct, and identities are largely shaped by power, for example, in the way social norms exist in every aspect of our lives. Schools play a starring role in exercising power as they establish these norms through material spaces, practices, and discipline(s). Despite this control, life always holds the potential to diverge from the expected. Even when suppressed, difference emerges eventually. The consistency and variably of queer relationships (friendships or otherwise) are a testament to this fact.

Possibility and variability are available to educators every day through their students and extended communities. It's through these differences that educators, in turn, nurture deeper ethical relations with the world and its inhabitants. They bear the responsibility of changing destructive ways of thinking and being – even when people (including educators themselves) are intimately attached to them. For instance, there are lots of seemingly harmless classroom practices that reaffirm heterosexuality and a strict gender binary. Activities that arbitrarily force students to identify as one of only two genders are actually quite common in classrooms. Taken together these practices work to exclude and destroy any expressions of sexuality and gender that don't affirm a rigid heteronormative view of the world. An educator's task is to make things that seem sensible and innocent, or even just practical, feel problematic, odd, or very wrong. Once teachers leave the university to engage the broader public it becomes obvious that all of us are extremely dependent on what others enable us to see.

This book tries to provoke a reimagining of the many ways educators take up their ethical role or calling. The imagination of readers is arguably more important than that of writers. Teachers who inspire others understand that the imagination of their students is far more important than their own. The Italian scholar and novelist Umberto Eco used the term "open texts" to describe bodies of work that lend themselves to ongoing interpretation and creativity.[3] The Bible, for example, can be viewed as an open text if different readings of scripture are given relatively equal weight. It becomes a closed text once a single interpretation is arbitrarily deemed superior to all others. A conventional role often expected of teachers is as a "master" of closed texts – where they alone control access to very limited readings of these texts (and therefore the world). A much more difficult task for educators is to see the world as a series of open texts, as well as to show students that closed texts can always be opened. In this spirit of openness it would be wrong for anyone to dictate an ethics for education. Instead, it would be more appropriate to position ethics, and its many embodiments, as the key question of education. The philosophical approach this book takes doesn't mean it bears no responsibility for making change. If the ideas don't elicit a different thought, inkling, or practice they will have failed. The value of this book might be measured by how much it helps educators explore different ethical questions and ways of living in precarious times.

Many educators are already challenging social inequality and the growing ecological crisis in their practice. In my experience, it's usually newer (or younger) teachers that understand the need to teach against colonialism, mass extinction, and heteronormativity. Discipline doesn't seem to matter. Justice-oriented education can happen when writing poetry, debating the nature of the divine, and conducting middle-school science experiments. Experienced teachers should look to youth for relevancy and thoughtfulness. I've devoted much time and effort trying to understand how the science education curriculum shapes ethical outlooks and possibilities of teachers and students. However, any examination of ethics in science education must be considered within larger socio-political and ecological contexts. Not because things like environmental destruction and heteronormativity are somehow "de rigueur" or "cool." But because there's just no turning away from the violence being visited on particular human bodies (e.g., Black and Indigenous), as well as nonhuman bodies, on a massive scale. What makes politics and justice pressing for education is that not everyone bears the same responsibility for climate change or telling the truth about colonialism.

Educators striving for multispecies justice know full well these struggles won't end in their lifetime, or likely the next few lifetimes. This is easy to imagine when it comes to the mass extinction(s) currently underway. Many species our ancestors once knew are gone or leaving. And they're not coming back. In any event, teachers often feel and share powerful forms of love and fidelity, such that their commitment to imagining a better world is inextricable from their commitment to students.[4] The calling these teachers feel has little to do with test scores or career readiness. It has to do with the desire to find modes of living that locate pleasure and value outside of profit, consumerism, and domination.

Much can be said about the tenacious global forces that seek to privatize public or common resources for the benefit of just a few people. Michael Hardt and Antonio Negri's concept of *Empire* describes this multifaceted global imperial power as the confluence of modernity's destructive and controlling forces – white supremacy, colonialism, and capitalism – that seek to exploit all social and biological life.[5] The goal of Empire is wealth and capital accumulation, but the labour it needs to feed itself is increasingly "immaterial." Creative products that can be exchanged digitally now drive global capitalist economies. The production of subjectivity is vital to maintain Empire's labour needs. In other words, the battle for hearts and minds has become even more central to global politics. Teachers face a serious dilemma when it comes to the purposes of schooling. Do our efforts simply carry out the wishes or strategies of Empire? Or are there aspects of our work with students that resist and/or escape these forces?

Empire is sustained by something called *biopower*, which can be seen as the power exerted by modern institutions, media, and corporations to harness and control the conduct of both humans and nonhumans. Add to this the fact that these forces are systemic and coordinated. Blaming one or many individuals isn't sufficient; the forces of Empire go beyond any one government or network of corporate influence – though focusing our attention on a government or corporation is a good place to start. Former US president Donald Trump is a case in point. To many on the political left the real problem was not Trump but rather rampant inequality, the decline of social programs and education, the long-standing assault on science and democratic institutions, and the maintenance of white supremacy as an integral part of daily life in the United States. In this way, Trump was essentially a conduit of ultra-nationalism, white supremacy, environmental destruction, and the erosion of basic institutions.

While political power and social control existed well before European colonization and capitalist economies, the ability of Empire to invade most aspects of social and ecological life relies on the controlling forces of modernity. These controlling forces include the ascendancy of private property as the basis of law and social organization, colonial expansion and dominance, and the uniform translation of species and nonliving parts of our shared world such as water and soil into commodities. The exploitation of the "natural" commons (forests, oceans, soils, etc.) is dependent on legal frameworks that incentivize their commodification, removal, destruction, and ownership. The right to own large amounts of property is basically the right to exclude others. This is the very same logic colonial systems used to dominate non-European peoples.[6] If there's any good news it's that Empire is historical and material. It therefore can be changed completely (think Stephen J. Gould). The possibility of refusal, and therefore an alternative, always exists. The exercising of biopower has profound implications for education and will continue to shape our discussion of ethics throughout part 1.

A glimmer of hope resides in the creative powers of modernity in the idea that it's always possible to (re)create and (re)think our current moment. No proposed order of things, earthly or divine, has the final say on anything.[7] The power of creativity is immanent here and now and is open to all. Nurturing multiplicity and shared common worlds is an act of resistance to biopower. Education is situated at the nexus of biopower relations because it both exercises and resists the forces of Empire. It's one of the main sites where the power to control conduct is exercised, but it's also a site where ethical resistance to this power can happen. The messy predicament for educators goes well beyond the daily challenges of teaching and learning, and yet these daily challenges are often involved with biopower, as students and teachers go about their daily lives in the communities in which they live and labour. A simple question like "Should we take action against unequal access to drinkable water?" is about systemic oppression, but also the daily acts of drinking, washing, cooking, and so on. Educators, like it or not, are always caught between forces of control and resistance.

No matter how you slice it being a teacher is intense. Not only do we contend with things like patriarchy and economic disparity on a daily basis (often unwittingly), we're also charged with how to respond to these political contexts with our students. It's therefore important for educators to explore how ethical ways of living are entangled with political contexts on a larger scale, and how the attachments and practices of everyday life and identity come to bear on questions of collective existence. This involves finding productive relations between ethics and politics. Philosopher Elizabeth Grosz relates ethics and politics together in this way: "The open-ended nature of the future, its capacity to deviate from the present and its forms of domination and normalization, necessarily link an ethics, how one is to live, with a politics, how collectives, and their constituents, are to live and act together and within what protective and limiting parameters."[8] Even though ethics is at the core of education, questions of collective existence form the terrain of possibility by which students and teachers forge ethical relations and ways of being. Any in-depth discussion about ethics and education would be deficient if it didn't in some way address systemic oppression and environmental destruction. Not just as an exercise in virtue, but because the subjects are unavoidable. It would actually be embarrassing today to speak of ethics without any reference to socio-political or ecological issues. Many religious communities are now finding their ethical relevance questioned in this regard, and many are in fact rising to the challenge.

For Amitav Ghosh, the fact that climate change and environmental collapse are still not at the centre of literature and popular culture is a great failure of imagination.[9] In many ways it's not so difficult to imagine the doom the planet faces. The number of post-apocalyptic movies keeps expanding. Series like *Snowpiercer* and *The Hunger Games* show that humans can vividly picture the "end-times."[10] Fredric Jameson notes that utopic dreams are steadily falling in number, while dystopic ones are on the rise.[11] It seems that it's easier for people to imagine widespread disaster than alternatives to economic disparity and environmental ruination. Media and popular culture have normalized the idea that higher taxes and alternative energy are not viable options for societies. But does that logic actually align with what our students think is desirable and reasonable? Why is it often so easy for young people to imagine something different? Dystopias have already been visited on Black and Indigenous peoples for centuries. The difference now is that a dystopic future awaits most people in the Global North. A job for educators involves cultivating a desire for building just futures that overrides the blind and immoral acceptance of environmental degradation and rampant inequality.

Although students and teachers may express a desire for more harmonious forms of living, in the end they may not actually want to act on this desire. This is because our imagination gets captured by interests that harness our desires, but these interests and desires are not the same thing. In other words, desire is more fundamental than the interests that capture it. For example, a teacher may have an interest in becoming a principal or superintendent to gain the admiration of their colleagues, make a higher salary, or feel successful. However, the desire to be loved or to love one's community exists at a much deeper level and is altogether different and much more important than these interests. The point here is not to "hate on" administrative work but to critically question the interests that are tacitly, or explicitly, presented to students and teachers. These interests might revolve around financial success, fame, beauty, achievement, or recognition. In other words, these interests may not actually be what we collectively desire at all.

Today, many of the things we're meant to be interested in are shaped by forces of Empire, or biopower, that attempt to harness or redirect our desire towards personal success and consumerism. Wanting to be successful while countless others die, in this generation or the next, is not a natural thing. Wanting a palatial home is an example of how desire is captured by interest in a commodity. In reality, this home is simply a hunk of cement, plaster, and wood invested with a wider socio-cultural meaning. In political economy, the social relationships that affect the economic value and meaning of something is known as commodity fetishism.[12] Much of what people buy today has mostly to do with what they believe a particular commodity represents in relation to themselves and the world. This explains why acquiring these commodities never leads to real pleasure or a realization of what people desire deep down. Rather, wanting such a thing is the result of coordinated forces of privatization and capitalism. Working against the grain of such interests, which are global in scope, is painstaking and perplexing. This is because the media and governing institutions typically work to de-emphasize community involvement and instead encourage individual investment only. Decoupling the interests of big business and short-sighted governments from what we collectively desire is always possible. So long as teachers and students exercise the freedom to look for ethical ways of living collectively.

The Inescapable and Uncanny Anthropocene

Educators need to engage urgent social and ecological contexts in ways that fundamentally question how we live and see ourselves. One way to begin is by asking very basic questions: for instance, Am I actually less racist than my parents? Is climate change real? What makes me think I'm a man or woman? No question is too simplistic. In fact, the more naive the question the more students are forced to examine their fundamental understandings of self and world. Giving students time to pursue issues they care about is vital. Eventually details emerge that give their concerns a life of their own. The details often point to a complexity that demands different viewpoints and ways of knowing – which ultimately lead to more engagement with the issue. It is often effective to plunge students into the middle of a controversial topic to have them experience its strangeness. My students in Ireland, whose education system is still unduly rigid, seemed to be the most disconcerted by this pedagogical move. When teachers plunge into controversial topics they encounter a form of shock. We are shocked when the world we thought we knew doesn't align with reality. This was the case for many white settler Canadians when the "news" of the atrocities of Indian residential schools hit the mainstream media. According to the conservative ethos of education, which is to reproduce the social world as it is, controversy does not belong in educational spaces. Real controversy, that is, as with those things that directly challenge long-standing mores and beliefs. And just when you think you've exhausted a topic there's always another angle to explore, for example, the lack of racial diversity in many environmental movements or the anthropocentrism of human rights.[13]

For the past few years I've found the Anthropocene to be a perplexing and thought-provoking concept for students. I cannot begin to describe the full significance of the Anthropocene in this chapter, but I can outline why it's a productive starting place for educators. The Anthropocene is a proposed geological epoch named after the species that has effectively changed Earth's geological and biological make-up for millions of years to come ("anthro," from the Greek, meaning human or human-like). The Anthropocene is a proposed geological epoch, one that has multidisciplinary supporters like Nobel Prize–winning atmospheric scientist Paul J. Crutzen, to succeed or replace the Holocene epoch.[14] The Anthropocene has also been picked up by artists, activists, and social scientists, and is arguably becoming part of the cultural imaginary. Whether the Anthropocene is ever officially accepted by scientific institutions, like the International Commission on Stratigraphy, remains to be seen.

The Anthropocene is not only mind-boggling, it's also a thoroughly ironic concept. The irony being that human exceptionality is exactly what's led to ecological precarity, and yet the Anthropocene is still named after our species. As if humans didn't get the message about being the centre of attention. There's also the problem of lumping all humans together under the Anthropocene, when some people bear more responsibility for both causing and addressing environmental collapse. The Anthropocene is a very attractive concept for the arts and environmental humanities precisely because of its magnitude and poetic promise.[15] It offers a compelling set of phenomena, simultaneously historical, geological, biological, spiritual, political, and cultural, that warrant a re-examination of literally everything.

According to Simon Lewis and Mark Maslin there are several markers that can be used to pinpoint the onset of the Anthropocene.[16] While there is still no scientific consensus around the "officiality" of these markers, it is true that there are multiple markers of irreversible human impact on the planet. Finding consensus on which singular marker and date should indicate the onset of the Anthropocene is beside the point. All of them are relevant. For Lewis and Maslin these are the markers precipitating the Anthropocene:

- colonization of Indigenous peoples and relocation of flora and fauna
- recent megafauna (large animal) extinctions
- spread of agriculture and the replacement of natural vegetation
- industrial revolution and the burning of fossil fuels
- post-1945 build-up of industrial chemicals such as microplastics
- large-scale testing of nuclear weapons

While Lewis and Maslin go into significant detail about these markers there's one very important thing to note about this list. The binary separating things that are natural from things that are cultural can now be viewed as a strange and destructive fiction. The colonial projects of Europe and North America, along with the racist ideas that fuelled them, are more than just socio-cultural manifestations of political events in human history. They are also geological and biological phenomena. Things as diverse as the Manhattan Project, monocrop agriculture, car companies, and Barbie dolls can no longer be siloed or put into little Mattel-sized boxes, each in its own corner of reality.

The Anthropocene is not just when things get serious, but when they get profoundly weird. It's what ecological philosopher Timothy Morton calls a *hyperobject*.[17] An object so large and multi-sided it's impossible to understand from one vantage point or location. Trying to understand the all-encompassing context of the Anthropocene requires going beyond the disciplines of the natural sciences. The ecological crisis is something that has to be engaged on a spiritual, cultural, and political level. Humans will have to gear their science towards environmental concerns, but they will also need to attune their sensitivity to the aesthetic changes caused by environmental degradation such as the disappearance of birdsong, drier summer days, and the collective melancholy these things bring, tasks for which Indigenous knowledges and epistemologies are indispensable.

The Anthropocene helps teachers and students see that maintaining rigid boundaries between things can lead to trouble. Modernity has created unnecessary dichotomies between science and story, nature and culture, and humans and nonhumans that keep us from the thoughtful relational work that needs to be done. The stories many people tell today exclude nonhumans or don't feature them or their livelihoods as vital to everyday existence. The forces of racism and colonialism that work to exclude people of colour from wider canons of literature are largely the same forces that push nonhuman beings to the margins of thought. These forces work to privatize experience, granting the right to exist – to be, to love, to relate – to some and not others. However, an ethics for the Anthropocene can't be about arriving at some uncontaminated present where everything is in perfect order. The planet has never been pure or free of disturbance; it has always been wonderfully strange and dynamic. As Alexis Shotwell argues, believing in a "naturally static" world means believing in a world that actually *resists* education. It would mean believing things could only be seen in one unchanging, and unrealistic, way.[18]

The difficulty educators and students experience in thinking beyond boundaries has partly to do with the power and control that disciplines exert. There are multiple meanings and contexts for educators to consider regarding the notion of (a) *discipline*. It can refer to a way of knowing the world, such as an area of study like chemistry or geography or Irish literature. It can also refer to a particular set of techniques or practices such as stained-glass work or stoicism. Discipline can also refer to something punitive or ways of limiting and controlling people for a variety of purposes. Realizing the ethical potential of education requires looking at the problematic, yet productive, relationship between education and discipline in a wider sense.

Discipline Is Always Double

The word "(un)disciplined" appears in the title of this chapter to emphasize two ideas. First, education always involves processes of "disciplining," ways of conducting our attention, thoughts, and practice. Second, education is a continuous struggle to find different ways of thinking and acting,[19] of subverting older discipline(s) and finding new ones. While education can veer towards disciplining or (un)disciplining it inevitably involves both relations to discipline. Considering this "double articulation" of discipline can help teachers and students see that, at every moment, there are inherited practices and ways of thinking that are valuable but there are also some that need to change. Seeing discipline as a dual concept also helps us recognize its ambiguous and ambivalent ethical status. In itself, discipline is not bad. While discipline involves exercising power and control over people, or the self, it can also be an enabling force. On the one hand, the academic disciplines of history and geography have developed specific methods of documentation and topographical analysis that are necessary to identify and attend to injustices. On the other hand, these disciplines have been used to create and justify systems of control to the detriment of workers, minorities, people of colour, colonized peoples, and nonhumans. In this sense, history and geography work in tandem with educational institutions to control, suppress, and nullify inconvenient truths, people, and other living things.

One of the most insidious examples of educational institutions acting as harsh systems of control is the Canadian Indian residential school system. The primary goal of these schools was to eradicate Indigenous languages, ways of living, community ties, sense of identity, and Indigenous peoples themselves.[20] The student death rate alone shows how schools and school subjects are easily incorporated into brutal systems of discipline and control. Besides demonstrating that colonialism is alive and well in Canada, residential school atrocities show that schooling itself is still viewed uncritically, as if it were a perfectly natural thing for children to leave their homes and spend much of their lives in large cement buildings learning state-sanctioned curricula.[21]

Perhaps one reason why many of us "assent" to this system is because it is easy to see how subject disciplines do extraordinary things in the world. Physics and world literature allow people to explore new dimensions and deepen everyday experience. In a very real sense people benefit from attuning or disciplining their conduct, practice, and attention. Yet, at the same time there are many dubious and destructive aspects of discipline(s) if we think about disciplinary techniques and systems of control. Education that takes its ethical calling seriously must somehow contend with the dual nature of discipline(s).

Discipline is integral to how biopower operates, not just in terms of controlling conduct, but also in constituting an individual's subjectivity. For better or worse, the various disciplines, and disciplinary techniques of institutions, all work to shape students' identities and what they can think and do, as well as the deep personal attachments that anchor them to these ways of being. Irish history and literature, for example, teach students about what it supposedly means to be Irish, why they should care about being Irish, and the different possibilities for life in Ireland. The tricky thing is determining the extent to which these aspects of identity are coercively imposed or freely chosen. Indeed, a sense of self emerges somewhere in between the two. The point here is that many aspects of self are not chosen but come from the larger social order. In this way, disciplinarity is essential for thinking about how ethical ways of being are both afforded and limited. Education effectively creates these affordances and limitations.

Discipline however gives shape to an ever-elusive "otherside." It attempts to limit what is possible, only to have these limits exceeded. An important philosopher who thought a lot about discipline is Michel Foucault. Foucault's early work outlined how various forms of discipline and governance worked to constitute a subject's innermost attachments.[22] It's too easy to view discipline, say, in the form of strict rules for behaviour, as something that simply masks a person's "real self." While this may be true to some extent, discipline also constitutes a person's (or subject's) sense of self and identity. In other words, there's a strong link between identity, who we think we are, and discipline, or who we've been "made to be." Though Foucault is most known for his work on modern governance and power, his later writings examine how one might work towards self-actualization and reflexivity. To do these analyses Foucault needed an altogether different archive of texts and knowledge, and thus turned to the Greco-Roman classical period.[23] Foucault was interested in how people cultivated an ethics of self-care and reflexivity before things like mass schooling, organized churches, nation states, and global capitalism emerged. Foucault's scholarly trajectory, from examining modern forms of governance to how a person might work on themselves as a form of ethical resistance, is also one of the overall trajectories of part 1. Educators need to understand not only how people come to conduct themselves and relate to the world, but also how they innovate and transform their conduct and relations. This potential for innovation forms part of the ethical terrain of education. And the need for realizing this potential has never been greater.

In the everyday lives of students and teachers the word "discipline" often refers to school subjects, like engineering, art and design, and languages. No matter what you teach or study – sailing, biochemistry, Chinese history, or creative writing – disciplines shape the relations one has to oneself, others, and the world. The relations established by disciplines distribute the effects of power by making some things possible and by restricting or occluding other possibilities. For example, the sciences often limit what constitutes a legitimate issue of concern based on a narrow set of sanctioned research activities and lab practices. Engaging the public and valuing other viewpoints as equally legitimate and worthy of attention are not approaches scientific disciplines typically encourage. Adapting a scientific investigation to accommodate these equally important community viewpoints is simply not part of the research training for the vast majority of scientists. So while the methods of science open doors to different ways of living and thinking, many of which are ethically desirable, they also foreclose others.[24] Any relevant science education today must recognize the importance of transdisciplinarity and the equal value of non-scientific knowledges in matters of care and concern. A useful exercise for a teacher can be to write down or map some of the relations a discipline establishes in order to identify how teaching and learning are tied to certain forms of disciplinarity. Depending on how each of us is educated and socialized, and recognizing that the same education can benefit some students and destroy others, these relations should look slightly different for each person.

A person's relation to discipline(s), along with the power exercised through their techniques and institutions, will work to constitute the person as a *subject* of this discipline. Here the word "subject" has an interesting triple meaning (much like the term "discipline").[25] It can refer to a school subject being studied, like business administration or linguistics. It can also refer to a person "subjected" to the prerogatives, culture, and imperatives of discipline(s), that is, a subject with specific outlooks, aspirations, and relationships formed by disciplines. A third meaning of subject lies in its verb form, *to subject* or bring under control. This meaning has often been associated with royalty, as in a kingdom and its subjects. The notion of a disciplined subject, in all its permutations and meanings, is something the discipline of education needs to grapple with in order to understand itself.

The various ways discipline, or biopower, subjects people is referred to as *subjectification* – the process of being made into a subject (e.g., a subject of science, Ireland, capitalism, gender norms). All of us are already constituted, or in the process of being constituted, as subjects of various forms of discipline and knowledge. These can be scientific, cultural, religious, or technical – anything that seems crucial for conducting ourselves in the world and that provides some kind of ethical orientation. If I study to become an engineer, I'll learn how humans (should) relate to material infrastructures and nonhumans – whether this is explicitly discussed or not. However, what makes this process so tricky is that students and teachers do not enter educational spaces as blank slates ready to be shaped into something desirable by schooling. They are always already in the process of "becoming" subjects of the social and material world around them. If education is about ethics first and foremost, then an understanding of how various disciplines bring people to recognize and embrace certain ways of being in the world is indispensable.

Power and Conduct

Power is an important concept for the field of education because it helps explain how the conduct of students and teachers (subjects) is the target of institutional interests. Power in a social or political sense, the kind exercised through discipline(s), is best conceived as a relation that is exercised bidirectionally. There is always the possibility that power can flow from the oppressed to the oppressors, from child to adult, from student to teacher – though it appears to flow in the other direction most often. The exercising of power unidirectionally, flowing only from the powerful to the powerless, is often in the interest of those in authority. While the exercising of power sounds negative, and the destruction created by exploitive biopower is most definitely heinous, there's nothing about the exercising of power that is inherently bad in itself. Sometimes, as is the case with COVID-19 government regulations, the exercising of power can be a good thing. The same can be said for disciplines. While some ways of exercising power can be beneficial, modern schooling has inherited a "power problem." For example, Canadian education, in many instances, focuses disproportionately on achievement for nationalist reasons. How is this nationalism a dangerous distortion, and to what extent? How much of this nationalism constitutes "reasonable" resistance to larger colonial powers like the United States and United Kingdom? The answer lies in how much the exercising of power enables various forms of life or how much it undermines these forms of life. This is one measure that can be used to evaluate any ethical way of being.

People are very often attracted to the different ways power is exercised because they seem productive and positive. In the *History of Sexuality, Volume 1*, Foucault provocatively challenges the widely held notion that power always represses people. Returning to the COVID-19 example, we can ask ourselves, if enforced distancing and mask-wearing were so awful why did large segments of the public embrace these strict regulations? In fact, it was often everyday people who demanded these regulations. Foucault's critique of the "repression hypothesis" was a mild rebuke of orthodox psychoanalysis and Marxism that prevailed in Europe in the 1960s and 1970s. For Foucault, power is neither good nor bad. Rather, power is productive. In this way, it is most helpful to look at what power does. For example, the disproportionate dropout and suspension rates of Indigenous and Black youth in North America and the violence exercised against queer youth in schools have the effect of benefiting particular students – white, middle-class, neurotypical, cisgendered, straight.[26] Power operates through enabling, coercing, and restricting the conduct of human and nonhuman life. It mostly operates indirectly to create the structural, emotional, aesthetic, and ideological conditions that promote specific conduct. Just look at the layout of most traditional school classrooms. Student conduct is very much "prescribed" before students even enter the building.

Close examination of power relations helps to shed light on how injustices related to economic disparity, white supremacy, colonialism, and environmental destruction persist – even when there are very strong moral and ethical reasons to put an end to them. The fact that power operates in distinct ways through schools means education is never politically neutral. This is because the current state of rampant inequality, for example, between the Global North and South, takes a lot of biopower and violence to maintain. Exercising biopower is partly how modern education systems fulfil their mandate of preserving the status quo, making it difficult to challenge the taken-for-granted ways students and teachers come to recognize ethical ways of thinking and being. The ethical responsibility of educators involves intervening at the level of conduct. Not just the day-to-day conduct of schooling itself, but the possibilities of different conduct in a variety of social and ecological contexts. This ethical responsibility includes setting the conditions by which different ethical ways of being can be realized or conceived. The intensive calling educators feel is inseparable from the work of ethical differentiation itself: a bold and conscientious challenge to a current, and problematic, state of being. In everyday language it might sound like this: "I want to help others find a better way. I may not know what that is exactly. But I can feel it."

Looking only at how major institutions shape education gives an incomplete picture of how power operates. For example, government departments use tax revenue to fund schools, establish curricula, or institute particular policies to achieve particular aims. These strategies of power can be thought of as "macro relations" of power. However, power is also exercised through "micro relations" at the level of individuals. Micro relations of power are perhaps the most significant because they relate directly to everyday conduct and therefore become a target for social control and resistance. The way certain people are addressed in an email can relay micropower relations. So can the way people take up space in a conversation, either by dictating what's to be discussed or taking up "airtime." The term "mansplaining" draws attention to the fact that, historically speaking, it's been men (mostly white, straight, cisgendered) who've "explained" things to everyone else. However, the conditions that allowed men to speak over others had to be created by the law and social norms, as well as the everyday relations of community, school, and family life. A Canadian flag situated at various points in a school brings together the idea of micro and macro relations. The symbol itself connotes a macro political context (the G7, colonialism, etc.), and at the same time the effect of seeing the flag in a prominent place, on a flagpole or classroom wall, repeatedly affirms a sense of national identity. Even geopolitical power is felt at the "capillary ends."

Schools are situated within both macro- and micropower relations. From the macro side of things they circulate official discourses and knowledges about the world (scientific, geopolitical, cultural, religious, etc.). They also provide the material infrastructure needed to organize and "sort" bodies, for example, by maintaining class and racial division through inequitable government investment and direct or indirect school segregation. From the micro side, disciplinary techniques such as attendance-taking, grading, and reward schemas that favour particular expressions of learning and the compartmentalization of classroom space all shape the conduct of students subjected to these techniques. In this way, and as alluded to above, individual students (and teachers) in school systems can also be viewed as "subjects." Foucault thought of institutions such as school systems as apparatuses of power (or *dispositifs* in the French). An apparatus brings together all the knowledges, techniques of control, material structures, and discourses that attempt to conduct the conduct of subjects. Another example of an apparatus of power would be a police force, like the Irish Garda Síochána. Strangely, it's the school system that serves as the best example of an apparatus of power. This is because many of the techniques and strategies of discipline in schools need to be made obvious to young people. Depending on the scale of analysis, education systems could also be seen as part of a larger government apparatus of power. Indian residential schools were arguably part of a larger government apparatus whose colonial aim was assimilation and genocide. An important point to note about scale, however, is that it can change easily. This is because scale is produced by the social/natural entities that comprise and surround it. In this way, it's not useful to focus on any micro scale (e.g., a classroom) or macro scale (e.g., government policy) too rigidly (a point that will come up in chapter 6 when we look at sociomaterial assemblages).

Schools work to constitute students as "subjects of knowledge" along with other institutions such as the family and religious organizations. Through the "conduct of conduct" students and teachers come to view their choices and purpose in life as more or less unproblematic. The effect power has on conduct therefore has profound implications for the ethics that guide people's daily lives. Throughout part 1 we will

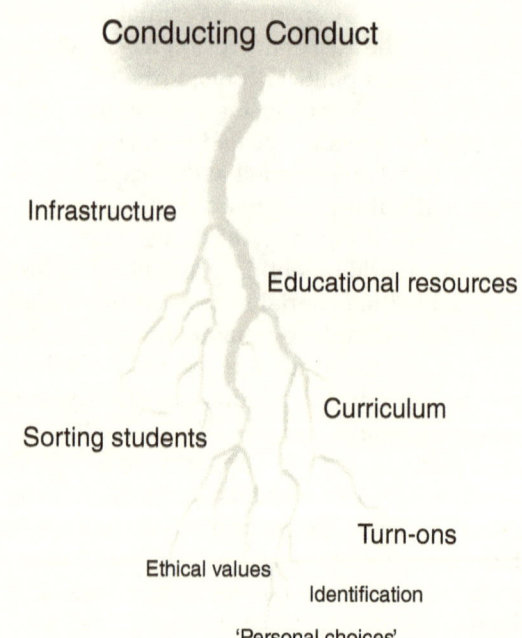

Figure 1.1. Conducting conduct through the apparatus of education.

continue to address critical questions of ethical subjectivity and how ethics involves establishing relations with self, others, and the world.

The effects of power become visible and are felt at the capillary ends – at the level of bodies and visceral experience, where people's conduct is directed and bodies are marked, nurtured, or punished. At the level of populations, the coordinated shaping of conduct, directly or indirectly, can be referred to as biopower. In some ways, Foucault's concept of biopower is somewhat analogous to electricity. Like electricity, power doesn't reside literally in someone's hands or position, it can only be viewed or felt through its effects or as it's exercised. It would be more accurate to say that power in the social world, just like electricity, can be harnessed by humans. Electricity requires a generator of some kind, and socio-political power some kind of institutional apparatus and/or social relations. Figure 1.1 uses the metaphor of a lightning strike to show how biopower might be exercised through an apparatus of power like education. Power in the socio-political sense is something that conducts conduct.

If we imagine power to be somewhat like electricity, we can see how it can be "discharged" at the capillary ends – at the level of conduct of living beings. Through the allocation of resources, the discourses of curriculum, the normalization of certain desires (e.g., heterosexual and consumerist), schools shape identities related to sexuality, ethnicity, and race, as well as constitute which ways of being, speaking, and thinking are acceptable and unacceptable.

It's more common to think of power as flowing from top to bottom (from macro to micro), from institutions and organizations such as a ministry of education down to the level of a primary school classroom. According to Foucault, however, "power comes from below."[27] That is to say, power in the social world is generated from below. Since power manifests at the level of bodies, where values, choices, desires, and ethical conduct are constituted, the power to do anything collective begins with(in) these bodies. For example, it is student learning that ostensibly legitimizes the existence of schools. If large groups of students are unable to learn or accept the conditions of learning, changes can be made at the level of staff, curriculum, or administration. It is the various modes of everyday life that ultimately give shape to, and invest authority in, the organizations that govern. Educators and students might then consider exactly how the exercising of power happens, what it does, and who it's for. A critical view of biopower helps educators better understand how teachers and students are brought to think about meaning, purpose, and enjoyment through schooling, as well as how they might collectively work "from below."

What's both complex and extremely personal is how student and teachers are completely entangled in the very systems they wish to change. Desire, ethical commitment, and a sense of self often cannot be fully disentangled from power. Sexual orientation is a good example of how educators and students are simultaneously attached to the very thing they're compelled to problematize. Many aspects of our relationships with others are normalized though institutions such as schools, as well as heterosexual ways of understanding things like gender and friendship. While many would happily change the heteronormative way our schools have traditionally functioned, people nonetheless have attachments to how they've come to know the world that are not just familiar but personally affirming. It is important to recognize such attachments as teachers and students rightly go about questioning and reformulating them. The same can be said when critiquing other markers of identity like nationality, ethnicity, and other aspects of self that are seen as authentic.

While educators may help students become critical of governments, corporations, and their apparatuses of control, attachments to national narratives and sentiments are nonetheless communicated through the symbols and curricula of schools. This means that while students need to be critical of these narratives they are also simultaneously attached to them. Young people are often wary of Canada's continued colonial dominance and apathy on climate change. Yet they're also expected to feel pride in their country and encouraged to continually explore what it means to be Canadian. To be critical of power is to be critical of something integral to how we've come to understand ourselves. Power will always be a recurring topic for educators because of its relation to freedom and mastery. If we master something through education are we not also limiting our freedom? Or does mastery provide a new kind of freedom? The answer to these questions is not so obvious because power is often ambiguous. It really depends on what students master, and on what grounds, and what or who it enables or disables.

One way power is exercised from below is through collective social and political movements that demand change from public institutions. Within the context of education there are many examples of courageous students, teachers, parents, and community members engaging in collective action to change things from the bottom up. Consider the following examples:

- *Quebec student protests:* In 2012 Quebec university students and their unions went on strike and took to the streets in opposition to proposed hikes in tuition costs (roughly 50 per cent over six years) and restrictions on their right to protest (under Bill 78).[28]
- *Testimony of Canadian Indian residential school survivors:* Many survivors of residential schools shared their stories of brutality between 2008 and 2014 with the Truth and Reconciliation Commission. This testimony led to the government-mandated Calls to Action for Aboriginal people and settlers in Canada.[29]
- *Youth Strike for Climate:* In 2019 thousands of students, community members, parents, administrators, and teachers in school districts around the world organized school strikes to protest global inaction on climate change. The conservative nature of schooling was made apparent when many schools failed to support the climate strikes.[30]

It is the daily interactions of living beings in their community that generate the ideas, infrastructures, revenues, and wealth needed to exercise biopower in the first place. Governments, institutions, and corporate networks exercise power and shape conduct; however, it's at the level of everyday conduct that our collective existence ultimately begins and ends. Conduct, how we act, is a vital part of the terrain of both ethics and education. This is true whether education is viewed as an apparatus to control conduct or as a site of resistance to control, and whether education is rule-bound or unruly.

Given the necessary tensions between ethics, politics, and education, where should our focus as educators be? On large institutions and social movements or on the way we go about everyday life? The obvious answer is both, but it's not so simple. Changing the world through education must involve transforming collective organizations and institutions. However social and ecological transformation also happens from below by changing the way we live and what we expect from institutions on a day-to-day level. Having a critical relationship to discipline and power means being open to new forms of ethical self-creation. And it is at this level, the level of self-creation, that educators are of the utmost importance.

Power Is Also the Personal

Students and teachers are not just blank slabs ready to be moulded. Rather, a person's very sense of self often is intimately attached to various forms of discipline and power. To illustrate this it may be useful to talk a bit about how discipline has been formative in my life. Maybe it will also explain why I'm very interested in these topics.

I was introduced to the idea of a "discipline" during my undergraduate years as a biology student, where I was brought to "master" a body of scientific knowledge. As alluded to above, the inclusion of non-scientific knowledges was generally not valued. In my everyday interactions, essentialist views of gender, sexuality, and identity were often in plain view.[31] Like the terms discipline and subject, "body of knowledge" also has more than one meaning. It usually refers to a totality of knowledge: all one could know about something. But the term also reveals that bodies and knowledges are tied together in that knowledge can literally inscribe itself onto bodies as cultural, political, and material forms.[32] To put it another way, while a student works to master a body of knowledge, that knowledge, in a way, also works to master a student's body. This happens, in part, through the internalization of a set of rules about what can be said or done, and what constitutes a potential "error" in view of the discipline. Ask yourself: would an Indigenous spiritual education and a master of business administration program come to act on bodies differently? How do some bodies understand themselves as racialized and gendered subjects of particular knowledges while others are oblivious? What complicates this is that the same body of knowledge, say American history from a Eurocentric perspective, can mark different bodies in different ways.

In my experience, being a student of the biological sciences sometimes involved giving special explanatory authority to scientific theories beyond the purview of science. This is because we were implicitly taught to give science epistemic authority when considering ethical or moral issues, because the scientific ways of knowing were superior. Being a "science person" (a term I'm borrowing from education professor Maria Wallace) has traditionally required fidelity to the way science views itself "from the inside." This includes the way the sciences have approached, or ignored, social, moral, ethical, and political problems.[33] Not once in my degree did we comprehensively tackle a problem like eugenics or debunked theories of race and academic performance. There was a tendency to believe that intelligence is innate, and that training scientists involved dividing geniuses from imbeciles. Again, nobody had to state this explicitly, nor were such understandings intentionally communicated. Still it is not all that surprising that the Nobel-winning scientist James Watson, who helped to work out the structure of DNA, also holds dangerous racist, sexist, and eugenic beliefs.[34] My education up until the age of 28, which includes my teacher education in Toronto, didn't help me to question mainstream views that were often sexist, racist, and materialistic. This education seemed to be supportive of, or blissfully oblivious to, the dominant ideologies of North American life such as (neo)liberalism, individualism, and colonialism that saw people, land, or nonhumans as relatively worthless or ripe for exploitation.

No matter how sophisticated science's methods might be they cannot, by themselves, account for science's own ethos or political underpinnings.[35] Many of our views about science actually come from outside science itself. According to historian Thomas Kuhn, scientific paradigms – accepted ways of thinking about the natural world – are kept in place by particular practices, methods, and social norms.[36] This doesn't mean science isn't anchored to evidence and empirical data. It simply means that what constitutes valid enquiry is partly determined by social, cultural, and political factors that can be identified if a historical or analytical view is taken. However, the relationship between the production of knowledge and the social world goes beyond mere political influence. In modern systems of governance there exists a long-standing relationship between objective knowledges and the exercising of biopower, and between the natural and human sciences and what governing authorities suggest, advise, or compel people to do.

This is because objective knowledges, especially those that operate as discourses of "truth," can legitimize the exercising of power.

The relationship between knowledge and power exists irrespective of whether a facet of knowledge is actually true. It need only be regarded as true.[37] This puts disciplines that purport to be objective, like chemistry or history, in a very intense position. The sciences are heavily funded by governments because they are valuable for governments. Governments often use objective knowledges to aid in the management of populations in terms of health and sanitation, but also to achieve military advantage and economic competitiveness. Scientific knowledges have and will always come to bear on questions of collective existence. But it's a mistake to think that just because science might avoid ethical issues it's devoid of ethics or doesn't orient people towards issues of ethical importance. Quite the contrary. There are always ethical systems operating in any community, whether we're consciously aware of them or not. Ethical relations are at work, for example, in the way video gamers treat each other in their online communications, whether gamers talk about them or not.

Power is also exercised through the ideologies of everyday life. For some, ideology is an outdated term that doesn't adequately explain complex social phenomena. Understanding things like class conflict and systemic racism means also understanding the material infrastructures (e.g., segregated cities), legal institutions (e.g., tax law), and daily practices (e.g., streaming of racialized students) that maintain racial inequality.[38] It's not just about how people have come to think about race and class. But ideology isn't just a way of thinking. Rather, ideology encompasses all the taken-for-granted ways we come to understand reality. Whether we're talking about romantic relationships, employment goals, or the needs of students, we always speak within ideology. Ideology is not the opposite of "true speech" as is commonly thought. It's more accurate to say that all thought, discourse, and even material structures exist within ideological frames. Much of what students and teachers come to understand about the world and their own histories is largely constructed by the wider social world. Yet these taken-for-granted understandings have great influence over our lives.

My religious upbringing sharpened my academic and professional interest in ideology and discipline and how students are brought to see themselves as ethical or moral beings in the world. I grew up attending the meetings of Jehovah's Witnesses with my mother and siblings from about age four to fourteen. One thing I'm grateful for is the time spent reading the Bible. More specifically the stories in the Bible. These stories are foundational to the mores and archetypal narratives of many cultures today. However, what I found interesting later in life were the explicit ways the organization constructed a particular sense of community and reality through their literature and daily practices. Jehovah's Witnesses do this by establishing particular

- styles of dress – e.g., dresses for girls and suits for boys
- literature forms – e.g., magazines on moral and doctrinal issues
- uses of language – e.g., terms like "in the truth" and "new system"
- ways of affirming belief – e.g., tracking proselytizing hours
- rules for socializing – e.g., preferably with Jehovah's Witnesses
- doctrines about what exists – e.g., demons controlling this world
- life goals – e.g., the promotion of technical over academic education

My aim here is to emphasize the efficacy and transferability of certain practices. Similar practices can be employed in organizations such as schools, clubs, or political groups. They are practices that both enabled and constrained possibilities in my childhood.

When I was 28 years old I taught for a year in the People's Republic of China. It was probably the most valuable experience of my life. My partner and I lived with her two siblings in a Beijing Hutong. Day-to-day living meant learning Chinese (Beijing Hua) and a completely different set of cultural references. One of the things I noticed in China was that the historical (and sometimes current) propaganda images from the Chinese Communist Party bore a striking similarity to the Jehovah's Witness magazines of my childhood. You'd think the images used by a millenarian Christian organization and a Communist propaganda bureau would seem very different. But to me they had an uncanny resemblance. This was likely because the intent of the images was similar: to portray a new world for the faithful that only a great power can bring about: one a new world order brought about by devotion to Communism, the other a new world order brought about by devotion to God. Images in both the *Awake!* magazines[39] of the Jehovah's Witnesses and in Chinese propaganda posters depict the joys of everyday labour and social interaction in a picturesque environment, albeit from different historical contexts.

It would be a mistake, however, to think that images circulated by the Chinese Communist Party and the Watch Tower Tract Society are more ideological than those of North Face advertisements, the evening news, or war memorials.[40] The ideological messages of television, social media, and schooling are arguably much more powerful precisely because people don't notice or remark on their ideological content. The advertising and marketing industries perhaps understand this best. Power and discipline are ubiquitous in modern life – and our relationship to discipline and power is specific but at the same time shared with others.

I believe growing up a "Witness-kid" and teaching in China made it a little easier for me to recognize, or be interested in, the subtle messages coming from mainstream media, schools, and other organizations that give "official" accounts of how the world works. When I became a graduate student I noticed that my ideological views really mattered to people, especially myself. Just like my childhood with the Witnesses there were "in group" people (e.g., people who worked with big grant holders), particular ways of talking (e.g., the use of prefixes like "post"), and social practices (e.g., conferencing) that disciplined the edges of our lives. The key point here is that how we see ourselves is highly contingent on education and socialization, and is the result of many repeated practices and techniques of discipline, power, ideology, and so on. However, "who we think we should be" is a highly open and variable question. And educators can take some comfort in that.

Fidelity and Infidelity

Most teachers in places like Canada, Ireland, and the United States are from relatively privileged groups. Meaning the majority are white, more or less middle-class, neurotypical, and settler (in the case of North America). Education systems, which are also systems of discipline and biopower, have generally worked well for them. However, discipline and power operate very differently when it comes to Indigenous peoples, people of colour, and sexual/gender minorities.[41] This is easily seen with the underfunding of Indigenous education in Canada, graduation rates for Black and Indigenous youth, and suicide rates of 2SLGBTQI+ youth. White supremacy functions through a system that dispossesses and marks black and brown bodies as well as those who do not submit to the dominant ideologies and structural arrangements that privilege whiteness.[42] In other words, social location and life history make a huge difference in how power and discipline operate. Subjects that seem impersonal and/or universal, like science and history, have traditionally privileged those who are white, male, and straight.[43] Since the teaching force in places like Canada, the United States, and Ireland tends to be largely white, straight, and middle-class, to redress that imbalance the content of education should rightly revolve around the experience of oppressed peoples (as well as nonhumans). The ethical responsibility to challenge disciplinary power lies most heavily with those educators that already benefit from the social order because of their social location alone.

In order to change the world we must believe it is and should always be in flux. That things change, that different things continually emerge biologically, socially, culturally, and ecologically, is a fundamental aspect of reality. Likewise, ethical ways of being in the world necessarily change. The challenge for teachers and students is to facilitate ethical ways of being in relation to this difference. As this book progresses the importance of difference to ethics and education will become clearer. This idea of a world in flux also applies to politics. Progressive politics entails a challenge to accepted boundaries, structures, and modes of thought in the name of the radical democratic principle of equality.[44] Who and what deserves equal consideration – ethically, legally, ecologically, and politically – is constantly expanding. A notable example of this expansion is the push to extend to bodies of water and land actual rights enshrined in law.[45]

Just because being part of social and ecological change may feel right doesn't mean the everyday experiences that go along with that won't be difficult and overwhelming. A straight white male teacher who refuses the power invested in him by the social order will face a number of difficult experiences in his career. But for those who are not white, straight, or middle-class, daily life is often much scarier and more difficult. Educators that work against the social order will find life more difficult, even arduous. But this doesn't mean that educators shouldn't work against the oppressive effects of biopower, or that good feelings are not involved at various points along the way. The choice of living a more difficult life is part of the ethical calling of an educator.

Philosopher Judith Butler points out that most people don't question who they are and how they should live for frivolous reasons. They do so because they realize life, the way they've been brought to live it, is untenable and unliveable. For Butler, going beyond the limits of how one comes to see oneself or how one lives in the world shouldn't feel like some heroic quest. Rather, it should feel like an unavoidable or necessary crisis. Butler puts it this way:

> One does not drive to the limits for a thrill experience, or because limits are dangerous and sexy, or because it brings us into a titillating proximity with evil. One asks about the limits of ways of knowing because one has already run up against a crisis within the epistemological field in which one lives.[46]

Consider that 2SLGBTQI+ youth are still facing marginalization, violence, and dehumanization on a daily basis. This is true despite advances made by gay-straight alliances in schools and queer activists on marriage equality and the acceptance of diverse families. It would be misleading to think that youth who nurture different loving relationships and forms of expression do so because they suddenly decide there's a more ethical way to live. Butler is suggesting that people challenge normative power relations when they cannot continue to exist with the way things are. This "impossibility of existence" extends to students living in poverty as well as to Black and Indigenous youth, and raises some key questions for educators: What is unliveable for many of our students in local and global contexts? What is no longer tolerable? What are the limits and constraints that must dissolve before a state of crisis ends? If educators don't try to face at least a small fraction of the dangers their students face, how can they maintain their roles as ethical guides?

These questions aren't just practical. They're intellectual. Yatta Kanu and Mark Glorr describe teachers as "amateur intellectuals ... who are sceptical of mainstream political and social trends and who raise moral issues at the heart of even the most technical and professional activity."[47] As intellectuals, educators should question their surroundings or social milieu. They should also question anything presented to them as commonsensical or complete. No matter how painstaking or futile this work may seem at times, the position of educator already comes with varying degrees of privilege and power. Educational settings do not exist outside of ideology and power. There is therefore no way to be sure that we're not transmitting dominant ideologies and the effects of power through our words and practices. This is a basic lesson of the structuralist school of thought.[48] Structuralism, which relates human activities to larger, overarching structures, offers partial solutions to the problem of ideology. For example, Roland Barthes's work focuses on the way right-wing ideological speech presents myth as taken-for-granted fact or history. The way to combat this form of violent speech is for educators to focus on actual historical and material details/circumstances in the world.[49] Therefore, another ethical challenge for educators is to align their pedagogies with the real historical and material circumstances of the local and global communities they serve.

"(Un)disciplined" was the original title of this book. It was meant to acknowledge how everyone, in some way or another, has already been disciplined. At the same time it also suggests people can work against or move beyond certain forms of discipline. Within all of us there exists the potential for both fidelity and infidelity to power and discipline. This dual potential strangely matches the age-old dual function of education for conservation and for transformation. On a practical level it means occasions will definitely arise where educators and students should *not* do what is expected of them. This might mean disregarding what is thought to be a "proper" ethical course of action.

Questions of fidelity become important when educators teach about things like climate change, which requires a collective global response rather than individual responses within a market system designed to grow capital for the rich. Unfortunately, the good feeling that comes from buying "green" dish soap and toilet paper is actually factored into the commodity price. Green consumerism essentially means paying corporations to take no action on environmental concerns. Should educators and students show fidelity to a capitalist entrepreneurial culture that offers only short-term comfort? Or do they show fidelity to the worlds we share with other living beings that are being poisoned and destroyed? It may seem obvious, but what makes this decision so complex is how intimately attached people are to the ways in which they've been brought up and come to see their lives. Changing the way we live is harder than it looks because of these deep attachments.

Philosopher Alain Badiou argues that fidelity has a crucial role in love and politics, both of which involve the creation of "new truths" and "new worlds."[50] Love and fidelity therefore play a key role in building just futures, and, like many things educators encounter in their role as ethical guides, they are intensive. Love and fidelity cannot be measured or quantified. Instead, they are known through their contrasting relations with other feelings and states: love to indifference and fidelity to infidelity. Education as an ethical calling will therefore involve moments of both love and indifference, fidelity and infidelity.

Locating ethics at the centre of education doesn't mean privileging an ethical code or way of being. It means recognizing the primary role of educators in setting the conditions for ethical engagement and transformation. It also means keeping the questions of ethics and imagination open-ended. Thus, educational theory and philosophy have never been more needed. Rather than providing a universal body of ethical knowledge that will answer all questions of ethics and being, like biologist E.O. Wilson once dreamt of,[51] we need to keep the ethical core of education fully open to questioning such that the search for the "right way of being" or the "right ethics" is beside the point. Education needs to dwell on the disturbing issues and mysterious phenomena of the day. It needs to provide students the chance to be "unfaithful" when it's necessary to do so. It also needs to give students the chance to be faithful when a different ethics or a more enabling way of being presents itself.

2 Multiplicity and the Commons

Being, after all, is just another way of saying what is ineluctably common, what refuses to be privatized or enclosed and remains constantly open to all. (There is no such thing as a private ontology.)
— Michael Hardt and Antonio Negri[1]

Politics in modern times doesn't just happen in big cities but is entangled with "life itself."[2] You might think: "life itself … but that could mean so many things." And you'd be correct. Today all forms of life – biological, social, educational, and so on – are within reach of the various apparatuses of biopower and governance. These apparatuses of power, school systems being a major one, conduct the conduct of subjects for a variety of purposes. The most damaging of these is the unfettered growth of capital at the expense of human life, more specifically black and brown bodies, as well as nonhuman life, as seen with the extinctions of the Anthropocene. Nurturing life in spite of these forces of control and dominance, or biopower, means engaging biopolitically. In this chapter I discuss the importance of responding to the various ways biopower exerts control over life in destructive and exploitative ways. Drawing from the work of Antonio Negri and Michael Hardt[3] I suggest that a collective response from educators and students should involve nurturing the commons: all the things we share in common, those things which in turn allow difference to emerge in the world.[4] Growing and preserving what we share in common also nurtures life in its multiple forms.

This chapter, like the others, encourages educators to think, create, and teach with vivid concepts. One reason why the commons is a valuable concept for educators is that it effectively ties the ethical and political together. Engaging politics is essential to carrying out our ethical roles as educators. The relationship between politics and education is infinite in scope, and it's always worth (re)approaching this relationship from different vantage points. This is especially true in our so-called post-truth society, where the realities of marginalized and oppressed people (and other species) have been distorted by conspiracy theories, fascist movements, right-wing revisionism, and the same-old colonial histories. As Derek Ford suggests, we are not "past" the truth today. Instead the truth has been brought into new relations with political forces that demand a better understanding of the politics of truth.[5] To be post-truth, if this is really a thing, is to be over the idea of truth without politics. This has major implications for the ethical calling of education. If education is about learning and speaking the truth, a politics of truth must be engaged alongside this truth. Ford describes the "post-truth" educational predicament in the following way:

> The post-truth, in other words, opens up a political project as well as a pedagogical one. The political project involves the power relations that compose truths, and the pedagogical project involves *how* we engage ourselves, each other, and the world in transformative processes as we formulate and realize these truths.[6]

The point here is that the political and the educational (pedagogical) are intimately linked. If ethics is the core of education, then for every political project there are always corresponding ethical-pedagogical projects that involve how we engage ourselves, others, and the world in transformative ways. What people should seek through education are moments of political creativity, connectivity, and mobility – as opposed to the immobilization that comes from viewing students as less creative or insightful than their teachers who "know better."

Delving Deeper into Biopower

It's probably a good idea to review some aspects of discipline and biopower discussed in chapter 1 before delving deeper into these concepts. The exercising of biopower is coordinated, directed, and made possible by what Foucault calls an apparatus or *dispositif*.[7] Schools and systems of education comprise these apparatuses of power and control. Biopower is exercised through educational institutions; the dissemination of official discourses occurs through curricula, disciplinary techniques like the awarding of grades, and the arrangement of bodies through streaming programs. However, the exercising of power has to do with more than just control. It involves conducting how people conduct (or want to conduct) their lives. Power involves not only coercion but also purposeful nurturing and attachment building. So, it's not an exaggeration to say the stakes of power today is life itself.

Chapter 1 also discussed how educators and students are situated at the capillary ends of power. Educators guide the conduct of students in accordance with power or in ways that resist it. Since power is first and foremost productive it's often difficult to know when and how to resist. This doesn't mean teachers and students should do nothing. "Staying neutral" is itself often a choice to maintain the status quo and all the violence needed to keep inequalities in place. Educators and students are faced with the ethical imperative of engaging power one way or another. Resisting power is usually the most difficult, because it's not always clear what people are actually struggling against. For example, fully relegating students with special needs to mainstream classrooms without the necessary supports may just be a way for governments to shirk their responsibility to these exceptional students. Foucault cautions that the targets of these struggles with/against power are not always obvious and are much more personal than people realize.

Struggles with biopower today involve things that make a difference in the lives of people on a day-to-day level. Same-sex marriage rights and for economic and social assistance programs are some basic examples. Whenever people struggle for new freedoms, institutional protections, and so on, they are often fighting against forms of biopower that largely determine how they relate themselves and others. As Foucault puts it:

> To sum up, the main objective of these struggles is to attack not so much such-or-such institutions of power, or group, or elite, or class but, rather, a technique, a form of power. This form of power that applies itself to everyday life categorizes the individual, marks him [sic] by his own individuality, attaches him to his own identity, imposes a law of truth on him that he must recognize and have others recognize in him. It is a form of power that makes individual subjects.[8]

For Foucault, it's the practices of subjectification – those practices that make us all subjects of knowledge and discipline – that are at the heart of all struggles with power. This helps explain why the (re)production of subjectivity has remained a crucial social and political question in the social sciences and humanities for the last sixty years or so.

Let's take the example of the widespread school climate strikes of 2019 mentioned in the last chapter. The involvement of teachers and students in Regina, Saskatchewan, was limited. It included making signs and marching to the provincial legislature building to demand action on climate change. However, it was a substantial act of resistance to government inaction considering that Regina Public Schools took the outdated position that their role was only to teach *about* issues and not get involved. However, some secondary school students at the march took to the microphone and told the crowd that their science teachers not only discouraged them from attending the climate march but failed to teach them basic facts about climate change. It's easy to imagine that the objective of the march was to influence the provincial government into making more environmentally sound policy. But another equally important act of resistance was to engage in a form of protest that wasn't sanctioned by their school or school boards. In other words, the major act of resistance was in their conduct and the subsequent recasting of ethical relationships with the planet and its beings. Transforming institutions is crucially important, but to do that it's also important to protest at the level of everyday conduct and ethical relationships. Since power comes "from below" it's possible for a collective to (re)formulate institutions. In this case, the conduct of students and teachers tried to change life-as-usual on the Canadian prairies. The kind of imagination needed in both primary schools and universities is one that expands the ethical and political possibilities for students and teachers. Chapter 3 addresses the need for this kind of imagination.

Another point from chapter 1 that bears restating is that biopower today is a coordinated series of forces that seeks to control and exploit life in the service of capital production. Hardt and Negri call these coordinated forces Empire. It's impossible to disentangle colonialism from capitalism, systems that emerged at a particular stage in European modernity. Contending with biopower requires a multifaceted response. Reforming social safety nets and social services must be accompanied by a detailed environmental agenda that addresses global economic precarity. Schools help outline the "vital" goals (e.g., employment) and attitudes (e.g., entrepreneurialism) needed to sustain Empire. There's a peculiar ambiguity at work in biopower as students are often brought to a particular ethics or way of being in the name of personal health, safety, economic interest, and so on. Even school subjects that don't seem relevant to everyday life still work to constitute a student's relationship with others, themselves, and the world. For example, science education frequently describes healthy activities for human beings, though the primary focus is often individual health and not the health of the entire community. This individualistic focus is curious in that the chief overall determinant of health and lifespan is socio-economic background. Change at the level of communities should logically be an ethical priority in classrooms.

Public health discourses, which includes science education, have historically been entwined with colonial categories of race and citizenship because they single out "who" is in need of intervention, for example colonized communities of colour, in relation to the goals of the state.[9] Today, initiatives to "include" marginalized groups in STEM programs, while well-meaning and entirely relevant, may overlook how racisms and colonial mentalities are still present in educational discourses. For example, education systems continue to outline "who" is deficient and/or in need of "civilization" through science education. Even the most benevolent of educational initiatives can still be entangled with biopower.

Since at least the seventeenth century the modern notion of a "population" has been key to how biopower operates. The concept of a population and its milieu (or environment), something that might seem commonsensical today, has also been integral to the development of the biological sciences, economics, and political science.[10] For the past four to five centuries, populations have increasingly become an object of analysis for both the sciences and the "art of governance." In Europe and elsewhere, sovereign rulers who exercised their authority through direct discipline of subjects, for example in public displays of brutality, gave way to bureaucratic governments that administered and attended to large groups of people in a variety of strategic ways. Populations have become objects of intense focus because they can be manipulated, nurtured, exploited, and monitored through census data, public housing, taxes, health care, standardized education, militarization, state welfare measures, food systems, waste management, infrastructure projects, colonial expansion, and so on. Historians of science have long studied the convergence of economic concerns, education, and the sciences.[11] Michele Murphy's historical work traces the link between research on insect populations and political governance, and how the discipline of population biology had a lasting effect on economics and political institutions.[12] Murphy claims that "there are many possible ways to trace the extensive history of the economization of life."[13] And as science education researcher Kathryn Kirchgasler notes, race has come to play an essential role in economizing global populations. Indeed, racial hierarchies can be maintained even while denying the existence of race or racism because economic potential, instead of "cultural" and "biological" markers, has now become a revamped site of racial violence. But governing populations takes more than just economics and the life sciences. This economization also involves disciplines, like the geological sciences, that focus on resource extraction and the subjugation of colonized lands.[14] Any objective knowledge that informs how people ought to live their lives, for better or for worse, has become fair game for modern governments and extractive industries.

Overall, it's more accurate to think of biopower as having two simultaneous targets: individuals and populations.[15] Schools, as apparatuses of power and governance that work in conjunction with other apparatuses like public health, attend to the creation of what are deemed to be productive and responsible subjects.[16] Biopower targets the conduct of populations and does so in ways that cultivate particular practices, conduct, and outlooks at the level of individuals. This means that teachers – arguably more than bureaucrats, police, lawyers, soldiers, and doctors – are necessary conduits for biopower. Yet teachers are also key to resisting this power. This is because they facilitate reflexivity at the level of conduct and ethical differentiation. They help students navigate the (intense) difference between the world as presented and the world as it should be. Teachers help students "be otherwise." What makes this ethical responsibility intense is the fact that education today is often co-opted by the forces of Empire. The family and mass media are probably the only institutions of influence that rival public education today.

As mentioned in chapter 1, biopower sounds like the stuff of dystopian science fiction. The extraction of vital forces from people as they walk around in a simulation, like in the *Matrix* film series, is not such a bad analogy. But that's far too simple. Biopower is also concerned with how populations grow and develop. Historically, this has involved strategies that determine who is allowed to let live and who to let die. Ann Stoler's work linking coloniality, desire, and race is particularly interesting because it shows how colonial domination relied on hierarchical notions of race and sexuality.[17] Some bodies (e.g., white, able-bodied, straight) were made to live while others (e.g., people of colour, non-gender-conforming) were left to die. A basic question educators need to face is how we're complicit in making sure some live and some die. For example, is it right that privileged students learn only about their own health when millions have no hope of living healthy lives? What's biopower got to do with it?

Chapter 1 briefly outlined two basic forces of modernity: control and creativity. These forces say something about how power works. Since power is always exercised within a relationship, resistance is always present. And if power comes from below, we can think of this resistance as coming first. Resistance precedes the exercising of power from above. The idea that power comes from below is behind Hardt and Negri's call for a renewal of its emancipatory and immanent forces.

Instead of dispensing with modernity altogether people can embrace their creative powers here and now.[18] A controversial but necessary part of Hardt and Negri's view of modernity involves challenging investments in a transcendent world. In other words, placing our hopes and dreams beyond the world here and now. Disruption of those transcendent ontologies that attempt to severely limit our thinking is one of the useful outcomes of modernity – the powers once attributed to the heavens descend to earth.[19] Christian institutions gradually lost some of their influence and authority. Hardt and Negri were inspired by the life and work of Baruch Spinoza. Spinoza's theological writings posited God as immanent to all creation, thus effectively abolishing the need for any transcendent dimension. However, immanent creative forces can become stymied and enclosed by controlling forces, forces that sometimes claim a transcendent authority. These forces seek to exploit creativity and what we share in common. For Hardt and Negri, harnessing these immanent creative forces means recasting modernity. Not in terms of an "anti-modernity" that will always be trapped in an antagonistic relationship with modernity. But by creating alternative forms of modernity, or *altermodernities*.

This may seem like a lot for teachers to digest. But politics, theory, and philosophy have long been part of education. And they all change together. No topic or curriculum should be above our grasp. Understanding that everyone has access to immanent powers of creation means there's always hope. At any moment of existential threat there's always the possibility of resistance. To be and do otherwise. The more pervasive biopower, the more pervasive the resistance. This resistance to biopower, the resistance which always (eventually) accompanies it, is what Hardt and Negri call *biopolitics*.[20] Biopolitics involves all the entanglements with biopower from below, whose stakes are the freedom to become different and conduct ourselves accordingly. Teachers face the dilemma of being a conduit of biopower, or being engaged biopolitically with the forces of biopower, simply because teachers and students are situated at the capillary ends of biopower. The good news is that the possibility of resistance is literally at our fingertips all the time. Resistance is immanent to the daily life and tasks of teachers and students. The work of educators enables the ethical reflexivity needed to forge different relations in the face of biopower.

Educators focused on real-world problems in their global and local communities create the conditions for students to consider different ethical ways of being. However, there's always some ambiguity to the work of ethical transformation through education. Does what we do just further the goals and strategies of biopower? If so, how do teachers know when this may be a good thing or a bad thing? Nurturing ethical reflexivity can't be separated from the biopolitical contexts that determine its value and meaning. Being aware of how biopower operates through schooling should give educators pause before they support or refuse certain interventions in the name of health, duty, or responsibility. As biopower is exercised through the discourses and structural arrangements of schooling, resistance happens at the pedagogical sites where teachers, students, and communities interact. It also happens at the level of school boards, parent groups, and policy making. Biopolitical resistance exists whenever there is some agonistic relation to biopower. However, there will also be lines of flight, ways of becoming different, that escape this agonistic relation, this eternal push and pull that characterizes biopower.

My doctoral dissertation involved a critical analysis of biology textbooks and how they worked to constitute different outlooks and subjectivities in students, and how they positioned students to make ethical choices in particular ways.[21] The discourses of the textbooks positioned students to engage with ethical issues from a Canadian government and a Global North perspective. Students were also limited to making decisions, or considering potential courses of action, from a relatively small subset of choices. These choices had to do with "lifestyle" changes, writing letters to government officials, and supporting legislative initiatives.[22] While there's nothing wrong with these types of actions, they often leave the social, ecological, and political dimensions of ethical issues more or less unexamined. A more socially and politically informed approach is needed, one that also takes into account the ways in which science is intimately concerned with how humans live their lives.[23] Through the apparatus of schooling, students implicitly and explicitly learn what constitutes a valid or important ethical issue as well as what can be thought or done about it. The way students are brought to different ethical ways of being is directly related to the shared world(s) we inhabit and create – because any time students think about what exists, as well as what could exist, they are considering something common to us all.

Difference and the Commons

So, how might educators respond to biopower without always thinking and acting on biopower's terms? Focusing on the multiplicities and relations of the commons, what we all share, is one way to respond to biopower on different terms. The commons can be thought of as a shared reality that, in the final analysis, can't ever really be privatized, though people will try to appropriate the commons for themselves. A fundamental aspect of reality is that the worlds we share are always, in some way, open to others. This shareable aspect of reality will come up again in chapter 8, which discusses solidarity with nonhuman beings.

To think of the commons is simply to think about anything that can be shared. Forests, oceans, libraries, and public schools are all, in their own way, a commons.[24] They are shared worlds and shared wealth to which we should all have access. We must recognize, of course, that access to the commons has been restricted or cut off for marginalized peoples and nonhuman beings due to colonialism, extinctions, and the pursuit of capital. Governments and corporations continue to enclose and exploit the commons for the benefit of a few. This is obvious if one looks at access to potable water for Indigenous communities in Canada.[25] The commons, its growth and shareability, can be viewed, alongside everyday conduct, as the stakes of political struggles. Education grows the commons by providing access to knowledge, exploring deeper ethical relations with nonhuman beings, and challenging hierarchies that enclose and abuse the commons.

The commons is co-extensive with difference in much the same way that ethics and politics are co-extensive. There's an essential connection between sharing things and the potential for diversity. Forests and libraries are examples of the commons that grow and regenerate through interaction and connection. The commons are made by a multitude of different beings. Forests are produced by many species of plants, animals, bacteria, and fungi. Libraries beget more libraries through the interactive practices of sharing the writing and knowledge of many different people and cultures. In turn, the commons, what is shared, sets the necessary conditions for the emergence of difference. Different animals or different books are made possible by the commons. The dissemination of free knowledge provides the grounds for students and teachers to become different, and experienced teachers know that students always innovate when given the opportunities and materials. In turn, only unrestricted and unexploited forests can support the appropriate species diversity for woodland biomes.

The important ontological relationship inherent in the commons is as follows: difference is made possible by the commons and, in turn, difference enriches and grows the commons. This relationship is true when it comes to biological life and public education systems. So, in order to share in vibrant forms of communal life, difference must be allowed to come forth. Imagine a school community where different ideas, desires, cultures, and creations are freely shared. The possibility of becoming different is made possible by these diverse forms of expression. The diversity or multiplicity of that community – the different viewpoints, ways of knowing, plant/animal species, ideas, cultures – simultaneously produce the shared (educational) commons. The same principle is at work in a forest biome. The more diverse and complex an ecological community is, the greater the capacity to provide/share different ecological niches, oxygen, ground water, food, shelter, medicines, and so on. The commons traverses the line between the social and the ecological by suggesting a direct relationship between sharing and difference.

The commons and its multiplicities can also be understood through the notion of intersectional identity. This is the idea that we all inherit, and sometimes choose, multiple dimensions of self, which are simultaneously political and personal, like race, sexual orientation, religion, class, gender, ethnicity, and so on. Power and politics come to bear on these dimensions of identity in ways that make it necessary for us to simultaneously consider multiple dimensions rather than just a few. Identity is always fragmented and performed. It's only through difference that forms of commonality emerge. Different bodies are multiplicities themselves, and taken together they form an unruly multitude that comprises the commons. This multitude is not a totalized whole, but multiplicities united by relationships, exchanges, dependencies, and solidarities that enlarge the commons. The commons provides the necessary substrate to live differently. In the case of biodiversity, healthy ecosystems are ones that enable more types of organisms to thrive. In evolutionary terms all unique phenotypic, physiological, and behavioural aspects of organisms arise from long-standing ecological relationships. The "availabilities" of ecosystems and the diversity of life cannot be separated because they're both entangled in contingency and possibility (again, think Stephen J. Gould).

The value of education as a form of the commons is dependent on its ability to enable multiplicities that, in turn, nurture and grow the commons. This conception of education as a commons is in sharp contrast to education as an apparatus of biopower whose purpose is to seek economic growth (e.g., as in "value-added" models of education). Assessing how a way of living nurtures or destroys the commons is one way to differentiate ethical and life-affirming pedagogies from those that are not. Educators can make sense of the many purposes of schooling by asking whether it enables our capacity to share and live differently or if it works to prevent sharing and/or the ability for all beings to live differently in the world. Teachers don't have to look far to find context for these questions. Schools, classrooms, and their extended communities are probably some of the best examples of the commons. Educators, parents, youth leaders, and community members spend much of their time protecting education from exploitation and privatization by fighting against things like corporate investment in schools, segregation through schooling, and inequitable funding models. The commons operates as an antidote to biopower because it disrupts the imposition of hierarchies and private ownership while having few limitations on how it might be imagined and evolve. The commons provides livelihoods for all beings. And since education is a form of the commons, educators will find their livelihoods growing and diminishing with(in) the relations of this commons.

I started teaching in higher education at the University of Massachusetts Dartmouth, which is on the South Coast near Fall River and New Bedford (think whaling and *Moby Dick*). I used the concept of the commons in my work with teachers. With a little searching it was possible to see how the commons took shape with the official and unofficial histories, land and ocean creatures, and the social and political realities of the region (Bristol County). The shorelines and forests of the Wampanoag homelands (e.g., Buzzard's Bay and Slocum River Reserve) were some the most fascinating and exhilarating learning environments I've ever seen. The commons as a problematic civic reality was also integral to understanding the state of Massachusetts. The very the idea of a commonwealth was part of the imaginary of Massachusetts. Boston Common is one of the first parks in the United States to be used as a common grazing area. However, the history of Boston Common raises the question of whether common spaces are necessarily free of control and exploitation. While Boston Common is still a public park it also serves as a symbol of colonial dispossession. Land acquisition was a major aim of the British colonies in North America, specifically the Massachusetts Bay Colony. Dividing shared land (commons) into private property for white Europeans, whether by individuals or by a state, remains a pressing issue in places with colonial histories. Central Park in New York City is another layered example of a commons built upon the erasure of Black and Indigenous communities (Seneca Village and the Lenape peoples of Manhattan).

There are two lessons of the commons that can be gleaned from these problematic examples. First, the commons have histories, which often entail destruction. Second, the commons constantly face multiple threats of enclosure and exploitation, whether it be from multinational corporations or colonial violence based on race, sexuality, geographic region, and so on. The result of exploitation and enclosure is, however, more or less the same: a few profit while most of human and nonhuman life suffers. Of course, sometimes a kind of enclosure is needed to preserve the commons. David Harvey argues that draconian measures will be needed to protect the Amazon rainforest from rapid destruction.[26]

Overall, nurturing the commons is an intense and pleasurable experience. The existence of the commons says something fundamental about reality on a basic ontological level: different worlds permeate each other and are therefore shared. A goose's world can be shared with the world of a water strider because the commons, and reality in general, is fundamentally open to all. Hardt and Negri state this in the epigraph to this chapter: "there is no such thing as a private ontology." Although people have tried to privatize knowledge, land, art, water, animals, people, and so on, ultimately nothing can totally control access to being or "how things are." Any form of being, relationship, materiality, expression, and ethics can always be shared. They are inherently "open access." Whether we're talking about marriage rights or giving back Indigenous land it's arguably the commons and the freedom to be different that are the stakes of modern biopolitics.

When thinking about the destruction of the commons it's easy to picture the loss of libraries and burning of the Amazon. But in addition to the loss of cultural and biological life there's also the risk of losing the ability to be different and be in relationship differently. Difference and relationship are two things education touches directly. The biggest danger for life today is the destruction and privatization of the commons by trading diversity and sharing for extinction and profits. It is easy to blame some stereotypical venture capitalist in a swanky mansion investing in overseas sweatshops. But blaming individuals does not get you far because people themselves do not actually possess power, though it can certainly look that way. If individuals held the power all it would take to nurture and grow the commons is a change of heart, like Scrooge's conversion in Charles Dickens's *A Christmas Carol*. That would be an educator's dream, and if only it were so easy. The threat to the commons is embedded in the social, political, legal, and ethical order. This threat exceeds the desires and daily decisions of individuals because, as far as humans are concerned, there has always been extensive technical, cultural, and social systems that manage the commons.[27]

Environmental historian Jason Moore argues that capitalism has a great capacity for ecological destruction because it has fully integrated itself into the natural commons (or nature). That it has, in a sense, *become* our nature.[28] Moore argues that the problem of capitalism runs deep, and that pointing out that the Nestlé corporation commodifies water around the world only addresses one symptom. And while economics never fully determines social, political, or ecological contexts it's absolutely necessary to consider the economic when trying to understand these contexts. This is because capitalism remains the over-determining backdrop by which people come to understand their lives and even life itself. For example, Sheila Jasonoff's work in science and technology studies demonstrates how modern systems of law generally do not value living organisms or environments unless they can be used for commerce.[29] If a field is fallow, or a space is "unused," it is often considered inert or dead, and is targeted to be "revived" through ownership and development. This logic is not limited to fields and forests. It also applies to the patenting of genes and genomes. For capital to continue growing, "resources" like land and DNA must "move" and "circulate." In other words, they must not sit still. In the United States the law gives entrepreneurs the right to own life. It stipulates how things can be removed from a natural environment and manipulated sufficiently to ensure ownership. Profitability of a living thing or environment strengthens a case for ownership. Educators therefore have an ethical responsibility to question the taken-for-granted social, political, and judicial order. If they don't, they risk complicity in the degradation of the commons.

What is sad and paradoxical is that exploitation of the commons eliminates those things we need and want and how they are produced in the first place. Exploitation of the knowledge commons is a very good example of this. In order for innovative ideas and practices to emerge in the sciences and humanities there must be exchanges between multiplicities (people, different literatures, nonhumans, etc.). However, as soon as knowledge is privatized and enclosed the very relationships that help produce this knowledge are cut off. This contradiction is actually encouraging for at least two reasons. First, at a fundamental level, it means that creativity in the sciences and literature is not dependent on any elite culture, taste, or genius. All that is required is a nurturing of exchanges and experiences that are shared in common.

Education that nurtures the commons restores it to the multitudes by dissolving the dividing line between the natural and social commons – because human knowledges, bogs, and oceans all inhabit overlapping shared worlds. To compartmentalize ecological issues as the exclusive terrain of science is to miss their cultural, spiritual, and social importance. Similarly, to compartmentalize human sociality to the arts, humanities, and social sciences misses the fact that human cultural activity is ecological and geological – as the Anthropocene extinctions and climate change clearly demonstrate. Education nurtures the commons by removing rigid hierarchies, instilling a sense of equality with other beings, and mobilizing students and teachers against enclosure of the commons through community actions. Education becomes a corrupted form of the commons when it maintains hierarchies and works to benefit some at the expense of the multiplicities that produce the commons in the first place.

It's now possible to see that the ethical potential of education exceeds a simple choice between conservation and change. Education becomes an ethical and political endeavour to nurture a shared reality in common. While it's important to acknowledge that educators nurture the commons just by doing their job every day, the context of an *uneven* Anthropocene, both in terms of culpability and vulnerability, requires a more purposeful and imaginative ethics. The following are some ways education can play a role in nurturing the commons:

1 *Make knowledge free!* Educators should freely circulate knowledge that is in the public interest even when it might infringe on copyright law. Digital technologies have made the free exchange of knowledge incredibly easy. Education must therefore provide access to this knowledge along with the critical tools to use it. Educators and students can also produce their own community-centred knowledges.
2 *Wreck hierarchies!* Education that nurtures the commons works to destroy structural inequities and flatten hierarchies, for example, by establishing equality between teachers and students.[30] Destroying hierarchies helps set the conditions for difference and imagination.
3 *Making more-than-human relations!* Education must create ethical relationships between species and abiotic entities that make life possible. Educators need to both (re)frame and innovate the multifaceted stories they tell.[31] These stories must feature nonhumans.
4 *Challenge (bio)power!* Educators must question those in authority who tell them there's no alternative but to exploit the commons. This is the violent message of both neoliberalism and right-wing populism. Populism puts things like nation, race, and creed in the service of depriving or starving neighbours (including nonhuman kin). Neoliberalism's mantra of self-investment and the dismantling of social programs ultimately grows capital for the rich.[32] Resistance to neoliberal culture and policy means putting community interests ahead of individual gain.[33]
5 *Expand inclusivity!* Education should privilege those that have first-hand experience of injustice because they are the ones who can expand "who" can be considered on equal terms (and on what grounds). For instance, environmental education professor Joshua Russell argues for queer eco-pedagogies that expand the boundaries of being and relationship.[34]

The commons has this uncanny way of escaping control precisely because it can never be privatized. One reason is that the commons produces forms of life that can't be predicted beforehand, as any ecosystem or school culture shows. All forms of social, ecological, intellectual, affective, cultural, and economic life are sustained by the commons. Whether one takes a dystopic, utopic, or practical standpoint the commons will remain at the heart of collective existence and desire. Education, and indeed life itself, would be more pleasurable if the desires of students and teachers were captured by interest in the commons and its diverse beings.

Education, Ethics, and Subjectivity

This chapter has attempted to bring two basic contexts for education together. One is dystopic: the exercising of biopower through the apparatus of education. The other is utopic: the collective growth of life and creativity through the commons. Since educators in modern Western societies are automatically conduits of biopower by virtue of their position in various institutions, they are responsible for setting the conditions for ethical reflexivity and becoming different. The onerous, but vital, responsibility educators bear points to the centrality of ethics to education. The constitution of subjectivities, and the everyday conduct that flows from them, are among the major ethical stakes for education. In everyday usage subjectivity usually refers to someone's personal outlook or worldview. However, it's perhaps best to view subjectivity as a set of relations of self: of self to self, self to others, and self to the world (see chapter 4). Education deals directly with how students are brought into these complex relations of self. Like the shaping of conduct, the shaping of (ethical) subjectivity happens through various disciplinary techniques and practices of schooling. Some of these techniques and practices are visible and obvious while others more subtle.

All areas of education, even those that seem relatively value-free, like science education, embody ethical questions that guide how students come to think of themselves and their world.[35] However, in places like the United States Big Tech and Big Pharma have their own ideas about how science education, and education in general, should proceed. Neoliberal reforms, which cut government spending for vital services in favour of entrepreneurial incentives and free market solutions, invest heavily in the (bio)value of students as forms of human capital and labour. Educational life has become a target of capital investment organized along the lines of race and class. The STEM movement, especially in its more corporate embodiments, is also a political project bent on producing human capital for corporations and competitive nation states more generally. Corporate education think tanks and lobby groups are not just promoting the infusion of industry-focused skills-training in school curricula, they often call for the restructuring of public schools to support their goals.[36] Under neoliberalism racialized populations in the United States are increasingly scrutinized according to how they respond to education reforms geared towards market logics and performance targets.[37] According to Clayton Pierce, school discipline has shifted from the strap or suspension to new categories of risk, neurological disorder, and entrepreneurial viability.

The constitution of subjectivity is essential to understanding education's ethical potential because education involves either a transformation or consolidation of various subjectivities. This sounds simple but it's anything but. What constitutes an ethics is infinitely variable. And what makes it even more perplexing is that the constitution of ethical subjectivity happens before we (as subjects) realize it. Teachers and students have to accept that their ethical outlooks and practices are always already being constituted through the discourses and repetitive practices of schooling, which constrain and enable particular ethical modes of being.

Besides being critical of educational discourses and practices what can we do? Judith Butler suggests that the practice of critique involves exploring our vulnerability to those things that "call us" to be certain kinds of people. That draw us to "who" we think we should be.[38] Butler follows Marxist philosopher Louis Althusser's expansive conception of "the law" to include the totality of the things that call us to be that person we think we should be.[39] The law in this sense entails all the different ways the dominant social order addresses us as subjects as well as how it simultaneously requires us to answer this address. Following Althusser's classic example of a policeman "hailing" someone with the authority of the law, this address generally sounds something like, "Hey, you there!" or "Hey, listen to me!" If we take "the law" as inclusive of all the official, authoritative, or indispensable ways we're addressed or hailed in the social order we can say that all of us are hailed constantly and differently depending on race, class, gender, age, ethnicity, religion, and so on.

Teachers and students can only *ask after* how they've come to be constituted as subjects of/to "the law" and be aware of their vulnerabilities and attachments as subjects. When teachers and students fundamentally question their vulnerability and subjection to the law or social order, how practices of subjectification have come to bear on them, they must also be prepared to be undone.[40] For example, learning the truth about the colonial legacy of the Canadian or British state can untether people to a major aspect of their identity. This untethering sets the conditions for new ethical relations but can also cause disorientation and discomfort. The same is true when people challenge their views of human superiority or how they've come to see their own sexuality.

So why buck those things that anchor us and provide a sense of strength, and an ethics that makes sense? Challenging how we've come to see ourselves – our relations of self – only happens when the social order produces conditions people can no longer live with. For example, the death of Coulton Boushie in southern Saskatchewan was a brutal reminder of the unlivable conditions Indigenous people face because of racism and colonialism.[41] For Butler, resistance to the practices and discourses that seek to dominate, normalize, and control is always possible. Here are four general ways this resistant can happen.

- *When the normative aims of biopower exceed their intended purpose.* For example, teacher training has historically conserved particular social structures and institutional arrangements. However, as teacher training became more academic to respond to the needs of states it developed a greater capacity to question the state's interests.
- *When subjectification practices combine to create different practices.* For example, the business logic of "accountability" when applied to community responsibility (public outreach) means that corporations now have new ethical responsibilities in the marketplace. Any social practice can have unexpected consequences when combined with other practices.
- *When the repetition of a subjectification practice is broken.* For example, attachment to certain kinds of masculine or feminine identities relies on repeated practices or performances of gender: certain vocabularies, clothing, and activities reaffirm gender identity on a daily (hourly) basis. Disrupting these sites of repetition opens up gender identity to new possibilities.
- *When something that should be recognized is instead misrecognized.* For example, students of science are increasingly coming to recognize that authentic science learning experiences must have community relevance. That is, students are increasingly misrecognizing disembodied and disconnected science learning as "real science" thereby forging new community-oriented practices of science and science learning.

In the end, educators should remember that the freedom to be otherwise exists prior to the exercising of power. Worlds are built by everyday humans and nonhumans no matter what conservative histories say about geniuses, heroes, and gentlemen.

While subjectivity remains a major focus for part 1 the next chapter leaves the topic subjectivity to briefly explore the importance of politics and imagination to education. It also addresses the problem of antiquation and theory – that is, to assume that new theoretical insights automatically make preceding lines of enquiry obsolete. Chapter 3 argues against rigidity in politics and educational philosophy, inviting educators to draw from different theoretical and political traditions. Concluding part 1, chapter 4 continues the discussion of subjectivity, resistance, and ethical reflexivity. Part 2 begins by exploring an "outside" to ethics based on human subjectivity, and gradually leads us to the terrain of education, ethics, materiality, and difference. But for now, let's turn our attention to politics and imagination.

3 Education Needs Politics and Imagination

It has seemed to me that something would be achieved if we began to realize how firmly we are locked into a present without a future and to get a sense of all the things that limit our imagination of the future.

– Fredric Jameson[1]

I wasn't sure about including this chapter. It's an appeal to educators to keep the horizon of politics and imagination open and a caution against theoretical rigidity and antiquation. At first, I thought it too polemical. It actually started as a bit of rant.[2] I wanted to address the occlusion of politics in education, because attending to social inequality and the environmental crisis requires a thoughtful and wide-ranging engagement with politics. Whatever that might entail. Politics is intimately intertwined with ethics as far as ethics addresses inequalities and exclusions based on race, class, sexuality, gender, dis/ability, and species. Progressive ethical codes for teachers require a commitment to equality, inclusion, and justice.[3] Any ethical response to injustice requires attention to politics because the collective imagination needs to be taken into account. In this chapter politics refers to something distinctly different than biopolitics or everyday uses of the term. Politics, according to philosopher Jacques Rancière, consists of acts of dissensus (versus consensus) that redraw what is sensible or possible in a community in the name of equality. Equality here should be thought of as a radical democratic principle. Not sameness.[4]

Though frequently esoteric, and sometimes annoying, the "post" schools of thought (poststructuralism, posthumanism, postqualitative enquiry) along with new/neo materialisms have been productive in forming new lines of critical thought in education. A postcritical stance recognizes that critique and the object of critique are co-extensive (which was always emphasized in the structural/poststructural school of critique I was trained in).[5] However, with the ascendency of these useful theoretical perspectives there also seems to be a reticence to engage collective politics in education. This occlusion of politics is frustrating because ethical engagement, reflexivity, and becoming are irrelevant to planetary survival if they don't engage overarching inequalities. A reticence to think about politics starves education of creative political concepts like emancipation, solidarity, and difference.

That Part of No Part

Education, as a field of research and practice, has actively avoided or restricted the discussion of social and political concerns in its literature until very recently. It was within the science education community that I became interested in politics – perhaps drawn to what was tacitly prohibited in papers and applications for research grants. The reality is that every field has a politics, just like it has an ethics. Locating it means paying attention to overarching exclusions, structural inequalities, deaths, or extinctions that have to do with what Rancière calls that "part of no part." The part of a community that's never counted as equal. Equal not meaning the same, or treating people the same, but difference coming to count the same. This is generally what is meant by equity today. Taking specific actions so that a previous unequal situation becomes more equal.

Making space for politics and imagination is part of the labour of building just futures through education. On a basic level, teachers, students, parents/guardians, and community leaders all have some insight into politics for the sheer fact that they labour. Labour, like art and experience, is a distinctly aesthetic experience. Although limited by space, time, and context, labour offers a horizon of creative experience where we *notice* that the world is acting on us and we act on it in return. Experiencing pleasure or emotion while labouring is part of this experience. Political engagement in education draws from the aesthetic experiences of teachers and students (as will be discussed in depth in chapter 7). And just as there are no set rules for what constitutes art, labour, and experience, there are no set rules for what constitutes politics and imagination. Art, experience, labour, and politics are open creative endeavours.

Addressing politics in imaginative ways can feel daunting to a teacher. Perhaps you're like me and feel you don't really have the ability to imagine anything. However, the burden of being imaginative and politically engaged falls to all of us, not educators alone. The primary ethical task of an educator, perhaps especially when it comes to politics and imagination, is to try and enable others. One of the things this book tries to do, perhaps the only thing it can do, is enable educators to think a little differently about the ethical work we do. Part of this ethical and political work involves bringing together what feminist philosopher Elizabeth Grosz calls a materiality and an ideality.[6] To get students thinking about the materiality of our shared common worlds (birds, paintings, novels, chloroplasts) as well as the virtual powers of creation and connective potential that pervades this materiality.

From a philosophical perspective, we might picture politics as co-extensive with all virtual and actual entities along immanent planes of thought, possibility, and materiality that are infinite. "Immanent plane" here simply means a virtual horizon where things exist in relation and possibility together. I borrow the concept from Gilles Deleuze and Félix Guattari, though I employ it here a little differently.[7] For instance, Deleuze and Guattari differentiate between the immanent planes of art, science, and philosophy while I think it makes more sense to conceive of one plane of immanent possibility and materiality (or one plane with an infinite number of "offshoot" planes).[8] However you might imagine this immanent plane or virtual horizon is totally sufficient. Politics is enacted along this plane through dissensus-making and the inclusion of those not counted equally – that part of no part. This isn't a prescription for politics but an infinitely open conception of it. What constitutes the material and virtual "content" of politics will always change. Figure 3.1 is a sketch of politics as dissensus – the inclusion of that part of no part along an immanent plane of possibility and connectivity.

Seeing politics as acts of dissensus that recast the visible community (what Rancière calls the domain of the sensible) by including that part of no part is a very specific way to approach politics. Politics in this sense is not representational democracy or the workings of a state apparatus. And while politics is reserved for those acts of dissensus that redraw who counts in a community (and on what grounds), every aspect of being is co-extensive with politics in that anything can become entangled with acts of dissensus. Viewing politics as dissensus in the name of equality spares us from platitudes like "Everything is political." It also helps educators to not confuse politics and ethics – even though they are fully entangled with each other.

The aim of Figure 3.1 is to show that politics, the inclusion of that part of no part, is a totally open question. It is immanent to the contexts where it unfolds. And, as mentioned in chapter 2, these contexts always have a macro- and a micropolitics.[9] The life and politics of a classroom exist at a different scale than the life and politics of the

64 Ethics and Subjectivity

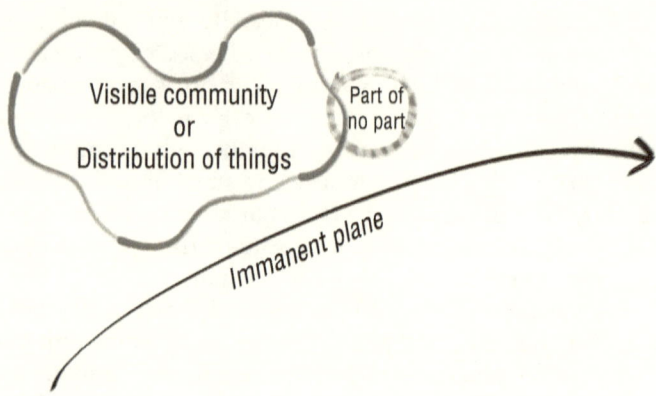

Figure 3.1. Representation of Jacques Rancière's politics of dissensus.

thousands of newcomers that pass through the state apparatuses of schooling in Canada, the United States, or Ireland. It's not really possible to consider a micro- or macropolitics alone. But it's important to remember that things like scales are social constructions that are tied to particular analytical perspectives. They change as perspective changes. Since politics has no a priori form it can never be founded on anything "proper" to a community itself. For example, in the United States politics doesn't reside in the Constitution, the White House, or state capital buildings. Instead, politics manifests as a challenge to the sensible or legitimate community in the name of equality.[10] Having an a priori for politics is like insisting that art must be about God, or that it doesn't include hip hop or country music. In a similar way Deleuze and Guattari argue there should be no a priori for theory, and that it's a mistake to assume that philosophy always pursues what is "good" or "true."[11]

The tentative nature of politics makes imagination essential to ecological and social justice. This is one reason why Derek Ford challenges educators on the left of the political spectrum to combine critique with "magical acts" of creation. Which is essentially a call for educators to dream.[12] To be sure, things like dreams and lines of flight are always unfinished and risky. For example, as a white male educator from Canada, I can't detach my imagination from settler-colonialism, patriarchy, heteronormativity, white supremacy, and capitalist relations.[13] To speak or think touches socio-historical wounds, contradictions, and oppressions. Yet, as a teacher, I realize it's better to take the risk anyway and perhaps help set the stage for acts of dissensus.

Calls to rebuild the political left and its forms of critique are emerging everywhere. However, a willingness to reimagine is a strength, not a weakness. Philosopher Jodi Dean argues that stagnation of the political left is the result of people losing sight of an expansive and infinite political horizon.[14] According to Dean, people are still imagining different forms of communism. Not the failed states of the twentieth century, but new and evolving forms of sharing and collective living. As Dean puts, "Communism is re-emerging as a magnet of political energy because it is and has been the alternative to capitalism. The communist horizon is not lost. It is Real."[15] Dean attributes the force and appeal of communism(s) today not to a definitive political philosophy or its twentieth-century experiments, but to a collective desire for more communal forms of life that elude people today. For Dean, "the absence of communism shapes our contemporary setting."[16] Desire for communal forms of living also haunts our present day in the form of lament and nostalgia.[17]

Acts of imagination are necessary to create collective forms of life, so it can be frustrating when the culture of education is uninterested in politics – especially when education is heavily embedded in strategies of power and is integral to emancipation and change. Without a commitment to politics, education has little capacity to help create just futures. Our task involves identifying the forces working to depoliticize and enclose curriculum and pedagogy.[18] Even disciplines as innocuous as science education are subject to neoliberal governance.[19] Sometimes objections to engaging politics in education can come from scientific realists who think scientific knowledge mirrors the world as it is. However, these same people also fail to understand that so-called neutrality is itself a political stance. It often requires a lot of violence to maintain the status quo. Resistance to politics in education can also come from "post" educators who are right to question what political engagement should look or feel like. However, in the process of questioning politics these educators may miss, or even prevent, possibilities for dissensus, resistance, and creativity.

In science education the occlusion of politics can be seen in the way the field approaches debates over the nature of science. These debates purport to be about epistemology, but they're also about the social, cultural, and political forces that inform how people think about science. The separation of politics from any academic or educational field is a testament to the prevalence of liberal ideology, which posits that some private rational core exists inside each of us tucked away from the world. According to this position, all human beings need to do to get some big logical picture of things is to jettison politics. However, since politics is about never-ending struggles for equality, the opposite is in fact true. To get a "big picture" of things educators need to engage with politics. To challenge the fairytale image of an inevitable and unproblematic global industrialized world, and reveal one that's historically contingent and held in place by exclusions and violence, educators need politics.

Working towards just futures means educators will have to be both faithful and rebellious to particular relationships, knowledges, people, and stories. This means making decisions involving fidelity and infidelity that can't be decided beforehand. This work involves simultaneously embracing and grappling with family, friends, students, community members, lovers, and colleagues who will both enable and impede a desire for political transformation. Fidelity and infidelity are risky – especially in their most intense forms of love-as-fidelity and love-as-transgression. Navigating these worlds requires educators to be more like artists who love, transgress, and facilitate new worlds in common.[20] Making room for politics is also an appeal to desire, create, love, and labour in the world.

The second half of this chapter is about affirming the practice of critique as a way of reading the world. The power of critique resides in the suggestion that another reading of any situation, text, or set of events is always possible. As we move forward in this book I feel it important to caution against prematurely antiquating older critical traditions, especially since this book draws from recent "post" schools of thought. Doing so can result in a loss of creativity, imagination, and ethical/political possibility. Indeed, many of the scholars educators draw from read across temporal and disciplinary boundaries quite freely. Both old and new approaches to theorizing materiality and criticality can help educators rethink our shared worlds in politically vibrant ways.

The Problem of Antiquation: Is Critique Passé?

There is no reading that works innocently beyond, before or beneath the theoretical, no reading that can put itself out of play.

– Ellen Rooney[21]

One potential problem with "post" scholarship and theoretical perspectives today is that they sometimes don't recognize the imaginative work of the past. As someone who draws from poststructuralism, posthumanism, and new/neo materialisms I've felt pressure to ignore older theoretical and political perspectives that don't fit neatly with what's considered *de rigueur*. For the purposes of this discussion there's no need to belabour what constitutes trendy theory today. I've used the label of "post" scholarship and theoretical perspectives, but that label likely isn't accurate enough and is more or less already antiquated itself. A "post" theoretical perspective is, in part, a perspective that's meant to succeed a previous one: posthumanism attempts to go beyond humanism; postmodernism beyond modernism; and poststructuralism beyond structuralism. Generally speaking, these perspectives are hopelessly entangled with the very thing they're trying to escape. Structuralism relates human understanding and social phenomena to overarching, often invisible, structures of thought, language, and governance. Yet, this is a major theme in poststructuralism. Humanism affirms human agency for the common good of people, while posthumanism simply carries some of the ethical traditions of humanism beyond anthropocentrism. Modernism, in its long history, has arguably given rise to every single idea in postmodern philosophy and culture. In some way, all postmodernism does is restore an immanent aspect to thought and creativity by questioning a priori categories and metanarratives. All post perspectives are limited in their attempt to move beyond the very thing they declare antiquated, outdated, or passé. Post perspectives, like all modes of thought, are at their most imaginative when they perform addition and multiplication operations. While it's possible to have revolutions in thinking, Deleuze suggests that thought is best viewed as a continual process of adding: We can think this ... and this ... and this ...[22]

Like many education scholars today I draw from posthumanisms, poststructuralisms, and new/neo materialisms because they're relevant to the environmental, socio-political, and ethical dilemmas at hand. These schools of thought offer new ethical vantage points to view the material-social world along with our nonhuman companions. Having said that, there are valid criticisms of these approaches, one of them being that they don't adequately or directly address politics.[23] Offering new ways of seeing and being in the world is important. But, while enabling new ways of being and dissensus in the name of equality, we must understand they are two different things. Just as it's important to recognize that theory and politics are two different things. Even overtly political art is not the same thing as the acts of dissensus arising from that art – which is not to say that art (or theory) isn't fully co-extensive with politics. Educators might ask to what extent their theoretical perspectives address, facilitate, or join acts of dissensus in the name of equality. These critical questions are similar to those asked of Marxism and psychoanalysis by thinkers who, like Michel Foucault, felt a critical reflexivity was missing from these inherited theoretical traditions.[24] In an age of right-wing populism, pandemics, and climate change, theory that helps enable politics and imagination is essential to education.

For literary scholar Fredric Jameson a transformation of consciousness comes from being shocked. In this way shock is a pedagogy.[25] White supremacy, mass extinction, and disposable populations are shocking when viewed against a material and historical backdrop. Using a backdrop with real material circumstances to make injustice visible is the core of Jameson's dialectical method. Shock happens when something that was previously unthinkable rears its head. In a dynamic and politically engaged classroom shock is wonder's twin. Wonder and shock invoke a similar aesthetic experience that says "I can't believe this!" The details of how millions have been dispossessed and killed by colonialism are shocking in themselves even without explanation. This is why reactionary responses to the behaviour of politicians can be misleading. What is shocking is not the racist and sexist comments of dictators, but the realization that white supremacy and patriarchy permeate all elements of contemporary life.

To take the thought of Jameson seriously means engaging with the creativity of older scholarly traditions. The Marxist theoretical tradition is often given the cold shoulder in education today, even though its concepts have been extremely useful since the nineteenth century. For example, the Marxist dialectical method is still important in contemporary thought. In its simplest form it states that the development of things should be thought of as a "back and forth" correspondence between the material world and the emergence of ideas and ethics. A materialist dialectical method may not seem very imaginative on the surface. It may seem obvious and easy to criticize. However, according to Jameson, a dialectical analysis comes with few a priori stipulations except attention to real historical events and multifaceted relationships.[26] Jameson's method of literary criticism involves determining what cannot be said in a particular context or moment, in order to elucidate the socio-political and historical forces that create these silences. A dialectical method can therefore reveal thinking that has not yet been stated openly – even though the material and discursive conditions for its emergence are present.

Another creative Marxist concept that's often used informally, but not given much credence, is *superstructure*. The basic idea is that the existence of all modern social phenomena can be traced back to overarching societal structures. The notion of superstructure embraces the major institutions, power networks, ideologies, and discourses of a "control society." Superstructure is also a productive political concept. Louis Althusser's work infuses the idea of superstructure with Baruch

Spinoza's theological notion of immanence, which leads to the supposition that both ideology (superstructure) *and* agency (freedom) are immanent in any context. Althusser's view of superstructure embodies Spinoza's notion that God – a God of substance not transcendence – is immanent and present in all of creation. "Believing" in some notion of superstructure, or at least overarching structure, means believing that fundamentally changing the nature of a structure also transforms social, material, and ecological relationships, and, in turn, believing that social, political, and ecological change also transforms who we think we are as well as the very air we breathe.

Recall our discussion of Foucault's notion of power in the previous chapters. Althusser's insight is part of the reason why Foucault, who was Althusser's student, was able to see that changes in a (super)structure itself are actually determined immanently "from below." Foucault's conception of power is arguably not a poststructural idea at all. It's an adaptation of a Marxist idea. With a more nuanced view of power and structure, the ethical and political problem of how people come to realize their powers of creation from below becomes more visible. It's likely that this structuralist/Marxist concept made it possible for Foucault to question how one might live life at the nexus of power relations. A poststructural perspective that dismisses structuralist concepts risks dismissing an important truth about the social world: that there are visible and invisible structures that are immanent in social life. This is not to say that educators need to look to Marxism, but that they shouldn't feel mired in theory that is new or old. Jameson looked to poststructuralist scholars like Deleuze to understand how the assembly of things in a piece of literature might work, as well as what the historical significance of this assembly might be. When educators disavow the creative power of different critical approaches, past, present, or future, they risk diminishing their own creative powers.

The "crisis of criticism" today is a reappraisal of critical authority or the idea that there's anything useful to gain from demystifying a text or practice.[27] It shouldn't come as a surprise that this crisis coincides with a crisis of the political left and a defunding of the humanities. The decline of the humanities, disciplines that deploy critical methods and theories, cannot be fully explained by the financialization and neoliberal control of universities. Ellen Rooney argues that the rise of STEM and blind faith in commercialized engineering has coincided with a suspicion of criticality and *symptomic analysis* (that is, reading the underlying assumptions of a text or phenomenon).[28] Antiquation, the action of declaring one thing obsolete or another thing newer and better, is a power(ful) move because it recharacterizes the present. Asking how some critical concepts in education become antiquated is important because what counts as creative thought in the present is at stake. While the antiquation of ideas in modern life is inevitable, and even desirable, the danger resides in leaving the political and ethical work connected to these ideas unfinished. Instead of dismissing a critical position as passé, Rooney suggests we celebrate the creative potential of critical practices to transform all entities involved in critique. Critique not only exposes another reading of something but the fact that a next reading is always possible. Reading the world is never innocent because it secretly works to create the next reading through the production of yet another form. This is what the epigraph to this chapter refers to. From a materialist perspective, a critical reading is not so much an act of a conscious subject but of material fields and their effects. It is something that undoes and is full of surprises. It affirms that *all is provisional*.

With Materialisms All Is Provisional

The main point is there will be no Adam – and no Jane – who gets to name all beings in the garden. The reason is simple: there is no garden and never has been.

– Donna Haraway[29]

It's no secret that materialisms have again become fashionable in theory and philosophy. What makes these "new" (or neo- or socio-) materialisms so attractive is that they provide critical educators and education researchers with "new weapons."[30] New materialisms attempt to recentre matter and materiality, as opposed to language and discourse, as the focus of critical analysis. They also seek to re-animate ontology, or how things exist, in order to rethink social, political, and cultural phenomena. How they do this is highly variable, and it's worth reading a range of seminal works to get sense of them (such as those of Rosi Braidotti, Jane Bennett, and Manuel Delanda). Indigenous views of how things are precede materialisms in their focus on relationships, nonhumans, and nonliving entities. Zoe Todd problematizes the recent turn to ontology and materialisms as yet another way Western philosophy colonizes and ignores the contributions of Indigenous peoples.[31] Todd's critique also highlights the role Western philosophy has played in colonization. I agree with Todd: Unless Western thought sheds its tendency to control, dominate, and trivialize different knowledge systems it will need to be more or less abandoned for the sake of ecological survival.

My aim here is not to have a general discussion about materialism and education but to caution against antiquation and philosophical rigidity. There's no good reason why educators can't draw from both older and newer forms of materialism. There are some basic similarities between older materialist thought (namely Marxism) and new materialisms. Both old and new materialisms cast doubt on theories of the modern rational subject as the origin of thought and social relations, and look to wider (socio)material fields for explanation. In this way, there's a general set of ontological, epistemological, and ethical-political questions that can be asked of materialisms. We now accept that there's no singular view of history – so why would a singular ontology explain social and material phenomena? The common-sense answer is that there should never be a singular theory of anything. Making room for politics and imagination means that a Marxist view of history or Donna Haraway's cyborgs are there to be used and reworked.[32]

The movement towards ontology and materialisms is one of the themes of this book, because they can help educators expand and nurture what we share in common. Philosopher Karen Barad points out that things that appear different in the world are "cut-together-apart." This means that even though differences are made in the world they're nonetheless entangled and co-emergent.[33] This difference could be between people, or it could be between a flowering plant and a moss. In the making of difference, or "cut," a space is opened for critical interpretation, perception, and an ethical response to this difference. Science cannot help but be important in a turn to materialism and ontology, as it contributes much to an understanding of matter and environmental problems. But there's no reason why science should always have the last word on reality.[34] No one discipline, along with its particular way of casting the world, offers a final explanation of our shared world. Any serious view of reality must also take the risk of being just one line of thought in relation to others.

The openness of the future is dependent on the creative powers of a multitude of both humans and nonhumans. It requires linking an ethics – how one might live (differently) – with a politics, with how a community is redrawn in the name of equality. A materialist ethics and politics must also engage the infinite planes of ideality because ideas are co-extensive with the material world and not separate.[35] The co-extensive nature of ideas and materials means that, as educators, we can feel confident in the creative intellectual labour we do. Engaging ideas means living and working in the real world. The imaginative labour teachers do is open, because all ontological concepts and ways of being are shared in common and are at play. There is no such thing as a private ontology.

Education always acts as a check against enclosure of what should be held in common, and a call to ethical modes of living that do not yet exist. The ethical task of increasing our creative powers is infinite in scope because difference always emerges as time moves forward. Education is therefore open to wild imagination and a collective desire for equality (politics) and being in relationship (ethics). It is in imagination and desire that we must ground ourselves, as counterintuitive as that might seem. The most pressing contexts for education – dying oceans, pandemics, truth and reconciliation – are difficult to face, let alone understand, without recourse to creativity, politics, and imagination.

4 Ethics and Subjectivity: The Vital Terrain of Education

It's hard to tell the difference between sea and sky, between voyager and sea. Between reality and the workings of the heart.

– Haruki Murakami[1]

I chose to open this chapter with a Haruki Murakami quote for a few reasons. First, Murakami's stories have become very important to me. They have given me comfort in times of upheaval or change. Second, his stories describe what it's like to be entangled in the social relations of late capitalism and a culture of hyper-individualism. Although this aspect resonates with me it's also a source of deep sadness and nostalgia. I encountered Murakami's fiction for the first time in Ukraine, where I was a middle school math and science teacher at Pechersk School International. About twice a year the school would host an international (mostly English) book fair, where the families of diplomats, foreign businesspeople, and teachers would purchase some bestsellers to get them through another six months abroad. The book fair represented an international canon – an alternative to the *New York Times* bestseller list and "Can-lit" favourites. The word "international" is misleading, however, because it masks how globalization has played out badly for billions of humans and nonhumans. As if nations, and the violence these imagined communities are founded on, was somehow natural.[2] It's more accurate to say that most people on the underside of international relations, are suffering the effects of global inequality, environmental degradation, poverty, and war.

Murakami's fiction endures because the question of whether one can forge a satisfying personal ethics amid global capitalism is a pressing question today. Characters in Murakami novels struggle with the alienation that characterizes modern life. This alienation is alleviated through a personal struggle for self-understanding, more specifically, the subject's quest for individuation, or the emergence of a self from experience and repeated forays into the subconscious.[3] Such a reckoning often involves a journey into primordial or magical worlds, the idea being that deep, meaningful relationships exist between worlds: the magical or uncanny, everyday reality, and that inner world just beyond conscious thought.

Murakami's fiction is problematic because the ethical response it provides to hyper-capitalism is an entirely personal one, meaning there is almost no space for politics or the notion of a collective (except for some nostalgia for the visionary politics of the 1960s in his early works). However, Murakami's work is a powerful reminder that the self remains a site of ethical becoming and resistance to injustice. To escape the loneliness of an individualistic society a person must cultivate the self. Murakami's fiction recognizes the apparent contradiction in this statement, and leaves the ethical content needed for self-creation to the reader. This is somewhat similar to the dilemma of the educator, who must help students find a better ethical path, but in doing so supply much of the ethical content and possibilities.

As mentioned in previous chapters modern education oscillates between two simultaneous functions: conserving the status quo and changing the status quo. Teachers are guides in navigating an older inherited ethics, one connected with authority, while trying to forge different ethical ways of thinking, acting, or living in the world. This chapter returns to a central problem of this book: how ethics is the core of education. Using concepts found in Foucault's later work it delves into questions of subjectivity, ethical reflexivity, and becoming. While part 1 ends here with the topic of ethical subjectivity, part 2 will begin by situating subjectivity within a larger material context or an "outside."

An Anthropological View of Ethics and Education

One of the main objectives of part 1 is to show how education is primarily concerned with ethics and ethical formation. Whether this education happens in a field, mosque, or school, the process of leading someone from one ethical position, mode of being, or subjective position to another is the foundation of the educative act. One major implication is that the purpose of a university or elementary school is first and foremost an ethical one. Another is that a pedagogical situation, where one person guides another, is absolutely necessary for ethical self-formation (and often it's a nonhuman entity doing the guiding). This context of ethical formation, which is at the heart of what we do as educators, does not require anything specific. The process is like some visceral connection through the "eyes of the other," as described by Emmanuel Levinas.[4] All that's needed is a guide who helps others "be" in the world – one who is in turn changed along with the person being guided.

Anthropologist James Faubion sees Michel Foucault's work as essential for ethnographic research into ethics. This is because Foucault draws attention to the long-standing existence of the "ethical guide" and how this figure remains relatively stable throughout history. As Faubion puts it:

> [Foucault] is at pains to point out that the ethical subject in training does not merely benefit from, but demands, "a master," a figure of already established ethical authority who is not merely worthy of emulation but also capable of serving at once as existential guide, psychological critical and practical advisor ... [Masters] very often preside at rites of passage, divulging secrets, offering support but also acting with great anthropological regularity as the violent midwives of social rebirth.[5]

Faubion affirms the social, ethical, and historical importance of educators as guides to social change. There is also a spiritual dimension to the ethical call to teach, manifested in its persistence and infinite possibilities. The realization that education is a site of ethical creativity is one of the most exhilarating experiences in being a teacher.

What has gone relatively unexamined in education, perhaps because it's in plain view, is the ethical fabric of everyday life. This is not to say that relationships have been ignored, or that ethical considerations haven't been a part of school life and curricula. It's to say that specific attention to the detailed ethical nature of these relationships has been ignored. In Canada, for instance, Indigenous ways of thinking draw attention to ethical relations. For Willie Ermine, ethics is a sacred and highly personal space that cannot really be known outside of a spiritual and community dimension.[6] As mentioned in chapter 1, Dwayne Donald views ethics as a vibrant and generative relation – something that happens actively with others.[7] Outside of Indigenous thought and formal philosophical writing, I've found relatively little that deals with ethics and education specifically. However, one educator that inspired me to think more deeply about ethics was David Blades and his "erotic" ethical encounters in science education. Through a visceral encounter with frogs that were about to be slaughtered Blades made ethics something tangible yet infinite.[8]

There are a few possible reasons why ethics isn't treated as a topic for multidisciplinary research in education. First, educational research is often expected to respond to the institutional interests of governments and school systems. While these interests have many ethical dimensions themselves, the tendency for research to produce measurable outcomes and recommendations leaves little room for thoughtful exploration of the ethical dimensions of education. In this way education, which is often accused of being too idealistic, actually suffers from being "too useful" to systems that wield power. Second, as pointed out earlier, education as a discipline has been mired in the social sciences for too long. Viewing education as exclusive territory of the social sciences puts arbitrary constraints on complex research topics like ethics. Only a transdisciplinary field like education can properly engage something as expansive as ethics.

This chapter outlines more concepts and methodological tools from Foucault's work that can be used to explore ethics in educational settings. The overall intent is to frame a critical approach to ethics, subjectivity, and ethical reflexivity in/through education. Going forward it's important to remember that subjectivity is an abstraction of how an individual has come to embody particular outlooks, purposes, relationships, and understandings in the world. There are many aspects of subjectivity that are ever-changing and unknowable. All educators can do is to try and outline the contours of subjectivity and the ethics embodied by relations of the self.

Chapters 1 and 2 discussed how education as an apparatus of power works to constitute subjectivities through discourses, material arrangements, and repeated practices. This chapter will focus specifically on ethics and subjectivity, how beings come to make themselves into ethical subjects. Recall how biopower works to constitute the subjectivities of individuals through the conduct of conduct. If ethics, at a very basic level, involves enquiry into how one should be (or what one should do), then it stands to reason that conduct and subjectivity would be targets for biopower. Again, using such a basic definition of ethics is necessary precisely because ethics is highly variable and complex.[9] Business has a particular ethics as do professional football, online dating, and hunting animals – and these ethical relations, codes, and ways of being vary greatly. A basic definition of ethics allows educators to imagine a diversity of ethics and therefore what ethics might be more desirable. Ethics of course is extremely intricate and context-specific – a simple description can never pin it down.

Yet I have reservations about the idea of ethics as the core of education. How is a turn towards the self an adequate response to things like the Anthropocene and white supremacy? Neoliberal education reforms would have students turn towards themselves, as entrepreneurs and sites of investment, instead of putting community interests first.[10] Neoliberal cultures have us see ourselves as projects of improvement and investment, which simply causes us to internalize the effects of exploitation.[11] Education that nurtures the commons needs to be placed in a larger biopolitical frame.

The Freedom to Speak Truth

Education as a space where students and teachers find better ways of being in the world, what could be called ethical self-formation, requires the freedom to be or think otherwise. As discussed in chapter 1, exercising power is coextensive with the freedom to resist, and this freedom always comes first. This point is key to understanding ethics as it relates to power and subjectivity. This is because *reflexivity*, the freedom to rethink or redouble critical attention on a practice, is integral to developing and refining an ethical practice or way of being. Put another way, without freedom ethics wouldn't exist as such. The nature and degree of this freedom give shape to what's possible. Anthropologist Cheryl Mattingly warns that giving too much credence to theories of social construction, enculturation, and ideology as determining factors for ethics may unnecessarily limit people's perception of their own freedom. However, not recognizing how the social world limits our freedom may also prevent people from understanding and exceeding these limitations.[12] However free we are (and some are more free than others), ethics involves the many ways this freedom to be otherwise is put into practice.[13]

Refusal is one of the best ways people can initially exercise freedom because it opens the door to another way of being. bell hooks, one of the most visionary theorists in education, pairs the freedom to resist with a responsibility to remake ourselves. hooks rightly notes that "in the vacant space after one has resisted there is still the necessity to become – to make oneself anew."[14] The delicate work that educators do often involves finding new freedoms and relationships within already established ethical canons. For example, this can be seen in the push by those who work within Catholic education to affirm the presence of God's grace for everyone, regardless of gender identity or sexuality. (Many Catholic educational institutions have resisted the Vatican's restrictive views on homosexuality and same-sex unions.) Indeed, there are educational settings where strict ethical codes are desirable, for example, in the training of doctors, lawyers, and clergy. Since freedom is always present, setting students on a path of continual self-creation is always possible. No matter how strict a system may be there's always some freedom to change what being ethical might entail.

Another aspect of ethics that needs more scholarly attention is relationality and relationships. For Dwayne Donald, relationality involves the qualities of sacredness and the inclusion of nonhumans (water, plants, birds, etc.) as equals. Opening up what it means to be "in relation" allows humans to expand their ethical-relational horizons. This expansion of ethics will be explored more in part 2. A turn towards Indigenous ethics is extremely relevant in a time of ecological crisis and a strong case could be made to abandon many modern Western ethical systems altogether. However, my view is that modern Western institutions, which are also colonial institutions, need to do the heavy work of understanding exactly how they are steeped in deeply problematic historical contingencies and have indeed been continually revising their fundamental values and concepts. Modern Western thought and institutions have the potential to help create better futures – but it's going to require decades of rethinking and revisioning. However, understanding ethics from a socio-historical perspective can help educators understand just how contingent ethical systems are. Even when it appears no ethical change has taken place for a long time, a close examination of the details reveals sharp differences concerning how and why people take up a particular ethical practice or way of being

Foucault's examination of ethics and sexuality in the Greco-Roman classical world shows how the cultivation of the self has come to be considered as essential to ethical self-creation.[15] In order to better understand how a subject might begin to develop practices of ethical self-creation, Foucault needed to choose a time period detached from the practices, knowledges, and techniques of the modern governing institutions and Christian traditions. These institutions and histories still wield a lot of influence over how modern Western peoples understand themselves today. In the absence of these large apparatuses of power, for example, before the age of mass schooling, how did people come to see themselves as ethical subjects? Foucault died shortly after publishing the second and third volumes of *History of Sexuality: The Use of Pleasure* and *The Care of the Self*, respectively), so it's largely been left to others to interpret these works. Volume 4 (*Confessions of the Flesh*) is not considered in this analysis though it may shed some light on how modern Western subjects come to understand how they tell the truth about themselves (their weaknesses, likenesses, characters, and even sexuality).

Foucault's analysis of Greco-Roman antiquity demonstrates that truth and justice were not always linked together in Western discourse.[16] Foucault argues that classical Greek philosophers grappled with this simple, but today rather odd, question: "How can one speak truth and justice at the same time"?[17] Great stories and heroic narratives were important in ancient Greek society, and these stories were told in particular ways. It was important to cast the social world in ways that expressed a particular established ethos and social order. According to Foucault, the historical relationship between narrative and truth began to conflict with an emerging ethos of "telling the truth." This is because the truth may not have been in accordance with the mores that the myths and traditional stories were trying to convey. To clarify this point we can look to different readings of the Old Testament. On the one hand, the stories of the Old Testament contain moral and poetic truths. The verses say something true about the authors, their relations to the world, and the ethos of Israelite/Canaanite societies, even when the historical-material reality surrounding the scriptures is revealed to be quite different. In some ways, looking for an ethical way forward through scripture involves taking the biblical narrative or story at face value: no further qualifications or historical details are needed. However, looking for an ethical way forward using the Old Testament as a record of scientific or historical truth puts truth and justice in tension. A more traditional reading of the Old Testament relies on a set narrative for its ethical basis, and a more modern reading appeals to historical evidence and the modern tendency to purposely look for new interpretations, or at least be open to them. Obviously, these ways of reading the Bible are not mutually exclusive – the point is just to show how truth-telling and justice are not necessarily linked together. It's possible to tell the story of the enslavement of the Israelites in Egypt and speak of justice – it need not have actually happened (like most foundational myths). However, if this story was somehow used to justify the policies of the modern state of Israel it would be extremely problematic.[18]

The tension between truth and justice, their convergence or separation, is similar to a fundamental tension between ethics and politics: how can people speak or follow an ethos in a political space of equality, where everybody's speech is valued equally and the majority rules? Foucault's work shows that this tension goes to the heart of democracy, and by extension democratic education. This can be seen in the ethical task of speaking truth to power, where it's assumed that there's something in power to be feared, and so it's ethical to speak truth in light of this fear. In the classical Greco-Roman world, speaking truth or communicating what one thought to be right, often carried a risk. This act of candid speech was known as *parrhesia*, which means to "speak everything."[19] There's an element of courage implied in parrhesia or speaking truth when risk is involved. Telling the truth in political settings, where everyone's voice is purportedly equal, also involves risk.[20] This is because a "less virtuous" ethics (or one that is "less true") can mix (equally) with a "more virtuous" one (or one that is "more true"). Since a political arena is a space where power manifests, speakers incur a risk by speaking truth – as when one speaks the truth about colonialism in Canada. Since classrooms are spaces where students come together ostensibly as equals, they too are places where speaking an ethos of the "good and the true" incurs a risk. That is, what should be done, said, or thought *despite* power. The difficulty in speaking out about Indian residential schools, for instance, demonstrates this power dynamic. Punishment and violence have kept all forms of dissent – naming the harmful and racist practices of these institutions – suppressed in schools and other spaces of political dialogue. Parrhesia is a useful concept for ethics, because the self, the truth, and an (alternative) ethos are all put into problematic relation. Understanding the difference between ethical systems may only happen when varying amounts of risk are involved.

What's an educator supposed to do with all this talk of freedom, ethics, and risk? If an educator is free to do and say what they think is best, but doing so incurs a risk, what should they do? Let's put this in the context of biopower. If the capillary ends of biopower are classrooms and schools, then putting a different ethics into play is potentially dangerous for students and educators if they speak against biopower. One of Foucault's points is that there is no easy solution when it comes to speaking truth or an ethics when risk is involved. Systems of deliberation and democracy, for all the good they do, will always face the problem of ethical differentiation: how are people supposed to tell good ways of being from bad when everyone's voice matters equally? A majority can never guarantee either truth or virtue. And this is also true for classrooms. But this doesn't mean that a space shouldn't be created for parrhesia – speaking truth and justice. If classrooms are indeed places of equality educators can put diverse ethical ways of being in dialogue with each other. It's impossible to divorce the risk (and freedom) of speaking truth and justice from the ethical calling of education.

Ethics as Relations of Self

In Greco-Roman antiquity, especially before Christianity, ethics had more to do with the relations of self. Foucault's work roughly formulates these relations as the self's relationship with self, with others, and with the world. As Dwayne Donald insists, ethics is relational. Using

Foucault to understand these relations is just one way to go about thinking of ethics as a relation.

A self's relation to self, perhaps the most important ethical relation, can be viewed as a self turned or folded towards itself. Teachers and students are constantly asked to turn their attention back on themselves. How do students and teachers make sense of their innermost thoughts, beliefs, and character traits? How does this understanding of self influence how one lives? Relations of self to others refers to relationships with other people but also with nonhumans and nonliving entities. If we treated insects and grasses as kin instead of as pests and weeds, for instance, how would that affect the long-term survival of an ecosystem and indeed humankind? Relations of self to the world has more to do with how we are brought to think of "worlds" and our place in these worlds. How might we ethically draw a community? What should I do, think, and see when I look beyond myself? What aspects of these worlds am I responsible for?

What constitutes these relationships of self to self, others, and world is infinite. Since these relations are completely co-extensive and entangled with each other it's best to think of them as intersecting relational dimensions for an individual or ethical subject. Figure 4.1. sketches these intersecting relations of self on three axes.

Let's take a minute to look at how the relations of self to self, self to others, and self to the world can vary greatly. For example, there's a big difference in simply acknowledging membership in a community and devoting one's life to the service of that community. Different relational positions can embody very different ethical relations of self. How one is brought to see oneself in relation to the plants, animals, and land that make up a community dramatically alters how one relates to others. What is perhaps most interesting about these relations of self is that they partly explain how a single ethical act, say planting trees, can be done with completely different sets of ethical relations. Planting trees could stem from a desire to look good in the eyes of others (what's known as greenwashing in the case of corporations). People might plant trees because they value participation in community initiatives. But they could also do it as an act of solidarity with nonhumans. All involve a specific set of ethical relations of self that are not mutually exclusive. Planting trees could easily involve all, or none, of these relations of self. Being attentive to these relations, for example by sometimes making them explicit, allows educators and students a greater degree of ethical reflexivity in coming to a preferred course of action, attitude or outlook, or way of being.

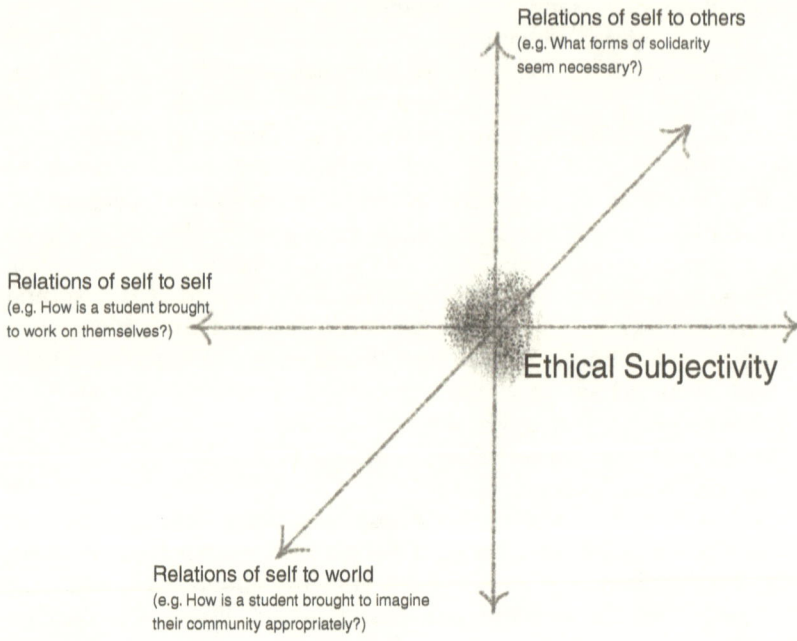

Figure 4.1. Dimensions of relations of self.

Ethical Reflexivity and Self-creation

For educators and educational researchers, thinking about ethics as a series of relations may seem a little ambiguous. For one, relations of self, others, and the world are simultaneous and coextensive, and so it may seem pointless to think about them separately. In addition to shedding light on relations of self, Foucault's exploration of Greco-Roman society elucidates four reflexive ethical concepts that might help outline an ethics or way of being.[21] Like relations of self, these four concepts – ethical substance, aspirational teleology, practices of subjectification, and techniques of self-creation – provide the beginnings of a methodology for exploring ethical subjectivity and ethical self-creation. These concepts fit well with the topics of discipline, power, and subjectivity discussed in the first two chapters. Here's a short description of each:

Ethical substance. What we perceive as the most vital part of ourselves, whether it be a soul or cosmic connectedness, concerned with conduct. Ethical substance today seems to increasingly have to do relationality and multiplicity (e.g., "I exist in relation"; "I am multiple"). How do teachers appeal to the most vital parts of ourselves?

Aspirational teleology. Refers to the ultimate purpose of a life, or where we hope to "arrive," for example, to achieve financial success or make it to heaven. Thinking about purpose compels students and teachers to consider the ontology that exists behind an ethics, as well as how it connects to hopes and dreams.

Practices of subjectification. The practices by which people are brought to recognize themselves as ethical beings. Through education, students are taught how to become responsible citizens, hard workers, good friends, etc. Biopower gives shape to these practices; however, resistance and alternative practices always exist. How is ethics intimately tied to tacit attachments and expectations?

Techniques of self-creation. Those techniques that students and teachers employ to become ethically different. Dialoguing, volunteering, or keeping a reflective journal are all techniques of ethical self-creation. Techniques of self-creation and modes of subjectification are different: modes of subjectification are those things one implicitly understands as needing to be done or embodied, while techniques of self-creation are tied more to the reflexive practices that bring about a different kind of ethical being. Accounting for these techniques, and making them visible to students, are useful exercises for teachers.

Educational research makes use of Foucault's rich concepts. Foucault subtly invites us to consider that ethical self-creation might operate as a mode of resistance and freedom in modern capitalist societies. One of the underappreciated points of the *History of Sexuality* series is how a seemingly obvious moral-ethical tenet, like a sexual practice or prohibition, is entangled in a web of social, political, and cultural relations. Foucault's examination of moral-ethical injunctions concerning same-sex relationships demonstrated how these injunctions often involved very different relations of self. That is, even when certain sexual practices seem more or less stable over time, their social, cultural, and ethical meaning can change drastically. Before Christianity, advising against same- sex relationships for men, as can be found in the writings of Socrates, involved promoting a more active position in relationships, as opposed to a passive one. This essentially meant advising men to remain on the dominant side of power relationships in terms of social standing, commerce, family relations, friendships, and sex. Once Christianity spread through the Greco-Roman world, a significantly different stance towards same-sex relationships was established. Although there were still injunctions against these relationships, these injunctions existed within a completely different aspirational teleology of divine salvation, punishment, and truth-telling practices like confession. Again, one of Foucault's overall aims was to show how ethical practices and relations change more rapidly than clunky moral-ethical precepts and rules, which tend to change slowly over time. Today, the difficulty of providing adequate protections for diverse expressions of gender/sex and sexuality, for example passing laws guaranteeing marriage rights, demonstrates that everyday sexual practices change much faster than any codified ethics.

Foucault asks not that people emulate European antiquity, but that they reinvigorate an ethical practice of freedom known as *ascesis*, which Foucault interprets as "the work one performs on oneself in order to transform oneself or make the self appear, which, happily, one never attains."[22] Foucault saw the stakes of gay rights, as well as prisoners' rights, as not just the attainment of rights themselves, but the freedom to construct different kinds of relationships and friendships.[23] For instance, Foucault anticipated that gay relationships would have a positive impact on heterosexual relationships, which are highly codified through practices of straight courtship, body policing, and patriarchy. In this way, Foucault hoped ethics as new relations of self might again serve as a mode of resistance,

> since most of us no longer believe that ethics is founded in religion, nor do we want a legal system to intervene in our moral, personal, private life. Recent liberation movements suffer from the fact that they cannot find any principle on which to base the elaboration of a new ethics. They need an ethics, but they cannot find any other ethics than an ethics founded on so-called scientific knowledge of what the self is, what desire is, what the unconscious is, and so on. I am struck by this similarity of problems.[24]

Foucault suggests that political movements, just like individuals, will always need a nuanced and fulfilling ethics to accompany them. However, this ethics is not something that can be easily captured by a political platform document or protest sign. Developing a new ethics is therefore something that can be easily overlooked by those seeking to resist biopower.

How might educators help students recreate themselves in relation to things like wealth inequality and climate change? Foucault's work illustrates the long-standing tension between rigid ethical codes and ethical self-creation. Anthropologist James Laidlaw describes this tension by describing the antagonism between a "morality of reproduction" and a "morality of freedom." This tension bears a striking resemblance to the antagonism between the two opposing purposes of education, conservation and transformation, mentioned at the beginning of the book. As we move into part 2, we see that the tension between rigidity and fluidity will continue to be a major theme in regard to thinking about an ethics of becoming different.

Ethical self-creation involves people working on themselves almost as they would a work of art. Foucault maintains that the art of ethical self-creation has been somewhat lost in modernity. However, it may be more accurate to say that this ethical self-creation is now directed by the strategies and techniques of large modern institutions or apparatuses of biopower. How do teachers and students engage in ethical self-creation when biopower already outlines the techniques people should use to work on themselves selves (e.g., getting good grades, building transferable skills, or having a gym routine)? The good news is that there's always some freedom to reinvent oneself in the face of biopower. Educators and students might veer towards those ethical courses of action or ways of being that are different than those offered by governing institutions and corporations Taking ethics to another level of deliberation and discussion means asking how an ethical way of being outlines who students wish to be.

As discussed in chapter 2, ethics involves the call to a subject's sense of agency and purpose.[25] Just like a subject's sensitivity to the law (in an abstract sense), ethical self-creation, resistance, and transformation all exist at the level of the call to be ethical. Like Althusser's notion of interpellation, susceptibility to this ethical call is active *prior* to a subject's realization of this call. What educators and students can do is question how the call to be ethical is made, what kind of conduct is called for, who or what is asking the question, and where the freedom to be otherwise lies. This is not to say that whatever calls us to be ethical is wrong, it's to say that a space for reflexivity is needed when answering this call to be ethical – a call to which we're all susceptible to.

Since subjects are constituted differently in the social order, ethical calls to action have different effects on different people. For example, the ethical call to make a sacrifice for the nation of Canada may motivate those who already feel validated by the nation (e.g., white, middle-class students) to act in ways that preserve a nation that validates them. Students of colour and Indigenous students may more easily misrecognize this call owing to the influences of colonialism, and therefore manifest a completely different ethical response, one that questions who such a sacrifice is really for and why. This is another reason why it's important for educators to begin teaching with the social contexts students bring to the classroom, as these will largely determine the possibilities for ethical reflexivity and self-creation.

Ethics or Politics? Yes, Please!

Several years ago, students in a Grade 8 eco-justice program made a trip to downtown Saskatoon in order to support an Indigenous protest against the Dakota Access Pipeline.[26] The local Catholic school board was concerned with the conduct of these students and their teachers, and took disciplinary action by cautioning these teachers and the community about "balance" and "critical thinking." But the Saskatoon students were very deliberate in their act of solidarity with Indigenous peoples and the nonhumans living along the Missouri watershed, as well as in their stance against expanding fossil fuel use. The response from the Saskatoon Catholic School Board clearly demonstrates that even when students and teachers speak and act ethically within the frame of school mission statements, which claim to want to protect the environment and make ethical commitments to communities, they take a risk. It's important to recognize that what seems ethical is often determined by power.

Italian sociologist Maurizio Lazzarato relates the tension between ethics and politics with a failure to deal with neoliberalism. Understanding the complex history of neoliberal restructuring and its weakening of public education globally is crucial.[27] Neoliberalism is not just a policy, ideology, or strategy to strip the state of its responsibilities and dump them on everyday people. Neoliberalism also presents itself as an ethical remedy: through investment in the self an individual is encouraged to find independence from state control in tumultuous economic times. What ethical alternatives can compete with the ethics of neoliberalism today?

Nurturing ethical self-reflexivity in modern capitalist societies means recognizing that what may appear as an ethical choice is highly constrained by the socio-political order. This means contextualizing choices presented under the prevailing ideology of (neo)liberalism. The choices provided to students always have to be contextualized because choices always have elements of non-choice. Take the example of career choices that are often presented to K-12 students. Career choice is often used to justify the knowledges, skills, and attitudes learned in school. However, what is often left out of such a discussion is the fact that white, middle-class students have countless visible and invisible advantages when it comes to their choice of career.[28] For students living in poverty, as well as Black and Indigenous students, career choices are often non-existent or withheld. A career choice most often does not involve a mode of being that forgoes personal gain for the benefit of the wider community. Even the decision to become a teacher does not, in itself, forgo personal gain. Assuming everyone gets to have a career reifies the ideological belief that an autonomous, unfettered individual simply chooses their vocation – rather than the other way around. Slavoj Žižek points out that choices are never just choices. Under the surface of all choices are meta-choices, that is, choices about the modality by which choice is constructed.[29] This is an important point when it comes to ethics because ethical choices are often presented as straightforward exercises in deliberation. In reality the context by which students and teachers are brought to be ethical is much more complex and constrained.

Jacques Rancière criticizes what he perceives as a turn towards ethics in the twenty-first century because it seems to have coincided with a turn away from emancipatory politics.[30] As mentioned in chapter 3, liberals in the United States became obsessed with former president Donald Trump's daily ethical violations, such as lying, harassment, and coercion, as well as his buffoonery and narcissism. While Donald Trump's conduct was egregious, what was most significant was the political battle over how everyday life was to be lived in the United States. For example, how would people come to view their changing relationship with North American ecosystems under the Trump administration? For Rancière, asking ethical questions outside of their political context reduces them to mere technocratic questions: Should we eat genetically modified foods? Is it okay to edit human genomes to make designer babies? Should we drive electric cars? Without taking into account the socio-political backdrop by which the ethical choice is given, the ethical importance of the question is diminished. Educators and students are left with ethical choices that, while somewhat relevant, don't really have any influence on the dominant social and political realities framing the choice. In short, the socially and historically constructed world becomes impervious to change when the context for the ethical choice is left unexamined. Despite what people might think, "scientifically literate" individuals are not automatically more or less ethical if they don't understand the urgency or stakes of their ethics.

From a biopolitical perspective, educational institutions engage those ethical issues directly important for governance. Schools are often free to engage issues that don't directly undermine biopower. This means educators need to find ways to directly address

- which issues are actually important to their communities regardless of what governments or corporations say;
- what kinds of ethical actors are needed to engage these issues, and explore with students how these identities are desirable (or not);
- a wide range of ethical conduct or actions available to students as well as what techniques may enable or develop these modes of being;
- the socio-political contexts giving shape to ethical modes of conduct, such as climate change, colonialism, economic disparity, extinctions, and white supremacy.

Addressing socio-political contexts, and the meta-choices (or non-choices) surrounding them, raises intense ethical questions around the destruction of nonhuman life and the growing gap between rich and poor cast along racialized colonial geographies. On the one hand, these contexts are not so hard for educators to conceive today. On the other, there's a great deal of under-the-surface violence that keeps these ethical-political contexts out of classrooms or depoliticizes them by making them technocratic and context-free.

To better understand the depoliticization of ethics we can look to the NBC comedy *The Good Place*, written by Michael Schur.[31] In the show a series of "afterlife experiments" are conducted by a comedic, and well-dressed, supernatural agent (played by Ted Danson) who tries to determine whether humans are essentially "good." Based on their decisions in life, humans go to either a good, bad, or neutral place for eternity. The protagonists demonstrate that being good *is* possible with the help of friends and honest efforts. The show exposes viewers to the following ideas: a) that moral philosophy is helpful but limited as ethics unfolds in real situations with real people; b) that being good is difficult because the world is complex, and choices have unforeseen consequences; c) that love is necessary to be good; and d) it is somewhat ridiculous to think that a higher power tabulates how good individual humans have been. Overall, *The Good Place* is endearing and educational. However, the show depoliticizes its treatment of ethics the way most TV shows do by not recognizing the political and ideological realities of its own content. While *The Good Place* recognizes that personal contexts enable ethical choices, it fails to address the larger social contexts that enable these same choices. The strength of the show is that it reveals an appetite for ethics, and yet it demonstrates how shielded from big ethical choices (meta-choices) people really are.

Concluding Part 1

Part 1 has explored how ethics is central to the practice and discipline of education, as well as how ethics is always in productive tension with politics today. Education, at its core, involves the production and transformation of subjectivity. However, it's problematic to restrict our discussion of ethics to considerations of human subjectivity alone. It's time to expand the discussion, and part 2 does this by considering ethics as something that goes beyond human-human interactions.

PART TWO

Ethics as Ontological Exploration

Our relation to the world is thus divided into two directions, one technical, the other religious, one oriented to a practical life and the other to a reflective and collective life, one projected outward and the other inward.

– Elizabeth Grosz[1]

5 Outside the Subject of Ethics

The most general formula of the relations to oneself is the affect of self by self, or folded force. Subjectivation is created by folding.

– Gilles Deleuze[1]

Subjectivity as a Fold of the Outside

This chapter moves away from centring ethics within a human subject by exploring an "outside" of subjectivity – which means exploring aspects of ethics that aren't really about humans. The Anthropocene has forced humans – mostly non-Indigenous modern Western humans – to face the reality that we're one species among many and that our worlds, ethical systems, and histories are more insignificant, incomplete, and threatening than ever imagined. Drawing from the work of Gilles Deleuze and Félix Guattari, this chapter builds on the discussion of the materialisms and posthumanisms in chapter 3. At the outset of part 2, let me restate that it's not necessary to use philosophy to explore ethics, and it's probably even counter-productive sometimes. Taking a theoretical approach, one that is more or less Western and specific, is just one of many ways educators might begin to think differently in precarious times. It is best to use the arguments and concepts of this book as jumping-off points into murkier, more interesting, waters.

The metaphor I will use to problematize subjectivity involves *(un)folding* it. This (un)folding makes it possible to imagine an "outside" to subjectivity: *how a subject and its ethics are simply part of a wider material world*. Relating ethics to more expansive nonhuman worlds is an important task for educators at a time when human exceptionality, the idea that humans are somehow superior to other life forms, is becoming increasingly difficult to defend. This exceptionality is related to racist, sexist, heterosexist, and xenophobic oppressions that are prevalent and undeniable today. While subjectivity remains a very important concept for ethics and education, considerations of (human) subjectivity are not enough to form an ethics of ecological survival and collective life in the Anthropocene. However, this doesn't mean a focus on subjectivity is somehow simplistic or unimportant. The intricacies and content of subjectivity will likely remain both mysterious and useful for seeking ethical ways of being in the world.

Transitioning from the thinking of Foucault to that of Deleuze and Guattari is not so difficult because Deleuze also wrote about subjectivity and ethics in his book *Foucault*, which was written a few years after Foucault's death as a celebration of his work.[2] The primary goal of this chapter is to follow Deleuze and Guattari in opening up the concepts of subjectivity, relations of self, and ethics along a horizon of virtual possibility. To think along these lines we need to continue to trouble the assumption that education is naturally a discipline of the social sciences, even though it's usually considered a social science by funding bodies and university administrators. We need to remain open to what the humanities, arts, and wider world outside of modern Western disciplines have to say about our ethical work as educators. This means suspending the idea that scholarship in education must always be focused on schools, students, teachers, institutions, and so forth. This chapter also attempts to deepen the relations between freedom, resistance, and control discussed in part 1, relations which are important for finding new ways of becoming different.

Admittedly, any attempt to unravel the concept of a subject also in a way preserves it. This is because it calls attention to the fact that any view of a world outside of subjectivity is itself a subjective projection of some "outside" world. In other words, any view of reality outside of human subjectivity is inextricable from subjectivity itself. Even the term "outside" implies an inside: so in a sense we are mired from the get-go. But even if it's impossible to get outside of human subjective experience, it's still incumbent on educators to try to consider ethics outside of the limited dimensions of human affairs and consciousness, considering that this sort of anthropocentrism has led to ecological catastrophe.

The question of how individuals are brought to see themselves as ethical beings – which is a foundational question for education – is the initial starting point for this exploration into subjectivity. This chapter's overall goal is to consider subjectivity in a kind of double articulation of interiority and exteriority, or, to put it another way, structure and freedom. To help illustrate I've included some diagrams illustrating this folding and unfolding of subjectivity.

Let's start with "Diagram of Foucault's thought" or "Diagram of the fold" from Deleuze's book on Foucault (Figure 5.1). Deleuze's ideas serve as a bridge between part 1 and 2 as the major concepts of part 1 are cast through more a materialist lens. In this original diagram Deleuze tries to synthesize some interrelated aspects of subjectivity and its relation to the world. The diagram is just a rough sketch, a drawing that tries to capture a subject's relation to an "outside." It requires some elaboration, so I'll begin with a brief overview of the diagram and its four parts. The four parts may seem confusing at first, but they're related to several of the concepts already discussed in part 1.

Figure 5.1 shows a relation between interiority and exteriority – an inside and an outside – or the fold of subjectivity. Zone 4 represents this fold. This is where the forces of the world constitute a new being with an inner subjective life. In this sense a subject is fully constituted by the outside. It owes its entire existence to forces other than itself (social, material, political, ideological, molecular, etc.). Around this subject is the *strata* (zone 3). The strata consists of codified knowledges, social structures and institutions, and material infrastructures that give shape to the subject and the "making" of subjects. Zone 3 would include all aspects needed to exercise control over bodies and conduct, such as official discourses, ideologies, institutions, codified ways of relating, as well as human infrastructures such as schools, housing, and roads. Strata is simply a descriptive material concept Deleuze uses to imagine how all these things that structure, control, and direct might exist, feel, or cohere together. If we take a broad approach to this concept we can view biological codes like DNA as something that stratifies or gives shape to human life. The strata doesn't just control bodies and conduct, it also provides coherence and affordances to a subject. Schools work to constitute how students come to see themselves in relation to various aspects of identity such as race, ethnicity, national, gender, cultural, religious, and class, which can be life-affirming, violent, or something in between. However, the threads of new affordances (new genders, new nations, different cultures, etc.) can also be found among the strata as well as outside of it. These affordances, how much subjects might innovate, are based on the amount of freedom a subject has. And there's always at least a modicum of freedom to resist. It's important to recognize that we're talking about subjectivity on two interrelated levels simultaneously: the individual subject and the wider social material world where the constitution of subjectivity takes place. It's impossible to discuss ethics and subjectivity without both.

96 Ethics as Ontological Exploration

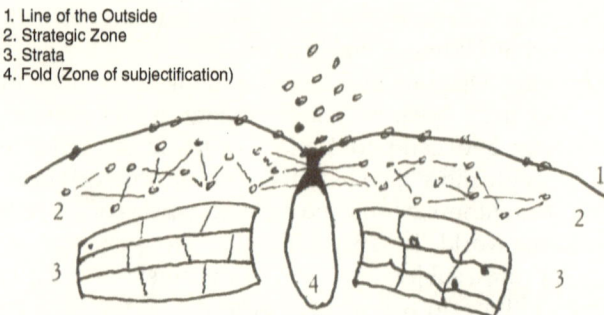

Figure 5.1. Gilles Deleuze's "diagram of Foucault" or "diagram of the fold" relating aspects of being and subjectivity.

Deleuze calls the space of affordance, negotiation, resistance, or agency the "strategic zone" – zone 2 in figure 5.1. In this zone, things are more "unstuck," possible, and connectable. The strategic zone represents the space where the subject experiences the interplay of elements both inside and outside the strata. Depending on how someone comes to view themselves these experiences can be highly variable. Things that exist outside the strata may be visible but not highly codified, controlled, or organized. Different ethical ways of being in the world are possible precisely because of the interplay between strata, subject, and those things that fall outside codified knowledge, experience, and structure, that is, those things that fall outside the strata (zone 3) and sometimes even outside the strategic zone (zone 2). This "outside" (zone 1) is marked by the "line of the outside" (labelled 1 in the diagram) and might be thought of as those things that cannot yet be synthesized, realized, or incorporated by the strata or the subject's being or conception of itself. These are things that seem to reside just beyond reality but can be glimpsed in some way.

The purpose of the diagram is to simply to help us think. It helps us picture the predicament of an ethical subject. The subject is represented by the fold of an exterior outside – represented in the diagram as the line of the outside (1) – that creates an interior (zone 4). One of the things Deleuze is suggesting through Foucault is that subjectivity is basically just the outside social and material world turning in on itself. In the process a relatively self-aware subject or internal system is constituted, and it's not so far off to imagine that living cells and social groups exist in a similar way. In other words, subjectivity – the hopes, attachments, outlooks, attitudes, and identities of individuals – is a product of the sociomaterial world. At least it finds its origin there. This means there's no transcendent aspect to a self. A subject is given shape; it is structured how "to be" by strata, organized knowledges, infrastructures, and various aspects of the social order that codify and organize a subject's reality. A self, or subject, is fully contingent with the trees, soil, water, and social forces surrounding them – which is not to say that people aren't unique. In one sense, the strata is separate from the subject itself, yet in other sense the strata makes up (the fold of) the subject. It helps form the subject itself – which is why the strata is readily accessible, knowable, and apparent to the subject.

A subject forms various *relations of exteriority* in the strategic zone with the strata that structure being and reality, as well as those things that escape codification in the strategic zone. Sometimes those relations of exteriority might extend beyond the line of the outside – new thoughts, objects, feelings, relationships that haven't taken shape yet. The strata, subject, and strategic relations are coextensive with each other. They reside on the same plane of existence. Deleuze's diagram (figure 5.1) affirms that a subject is an entity of the wider social and material world. The subject has some freedom to engage in strategic relations – because the strata can never totalize control. Ethical reflexivity is inherent to the predicament of a subject. This was a major point in part 1, but something slightly different is manifesting here in part 2: the introduction of a "material outside" to being and ethics. In this way, our exploration of ethics begins to escape the confines of human subjectivity. There's always the possibility to be otherwise.

Sketching Subjectivity with a Purple Crayon

Let's go through these aspects of subjectivity again in a bit more detail. One way to do this is by sketching the fold ourselves. Diagramming makes me a feel a bit like Harold in the book *Harold and the Purple Crayon*. The story features a small child named Harold who uses the blank pages of the book and a purple crayon to explore the limits of fear and find well-being.[3] Harold makes the reader question the relationship between the real and imaginary. In many ways they're the same thing. As Harold's purple drawings start appearing on the blank pages the reader is forced to (re)consider who (or what) might be moving that crayon and for what purposes. Drawing is a very simple gesture that affirms our immanent powers of creation. And this is arguably one of the overall lessons of Harold's journey. Imagination and creativity are dependent on a degree of openness (or in this case open drawing space). This is another reason why the humanities and arts are so important to educators. They invite us into this immanent creative space. Harold teaches us that it's always possible to draw something else!

As the epigraph to this chapter suggests, the making of a subject (or subjectivation), consists of a process of folding. A fold of the outside in towards itself. Describing subjectification as a fold means that subjectivity is constructed, socially and materially, from the worlds outside. Subjectivity is co-extensive with material reality. This may seem obvious, but the modern Western worldview has long maintained these as separate realms. But while we tend to think of subjectivity and our inner lives as sacred and separate the opposite premise makes just as much sense. The inner world of a subject is completely co-extensive with the outer world that created it. This also implies there's nothing transcendent about a human subject – nothing that places it on a different order than buzzards, foxes, and seaweed.

Viewing subjectivity as a fold helps to explain how the subjectivities and experiences of marginalized people are especially informative and relevant to social, political, and environmental issues. The fold of the inside for white, straight, able-bodied subjects is arguably constituted by different relations of exteriority, for example to the strata working to conduct conduct. This is one reason why epigenetics makes sense – trauma gets internalized from the very outset. However, the relationship between a subject and the outside is never a closed system and always continues to change. Subjectivity is therefore a kind of derivative of wider existence – the result of biological forces, socialization, and power relations folding in on itself. This folding, the emergence of subjectivity, is a manifestation of the biological and the social world and its many potential relations. Figure 5.2 is a simplification of these social and material forces folded inward to create the fold of subjectification or subjectivity.

The fold illustrates how subjectivity, while authentic in some ways, is also an effect of the outside. The hope, fears, desires, and sense of identity that a subject embraces largely originate elsewhere. Almost everything a subject values, reveres, and loves deeply comes from this outside. Even, perhaps especially, those things that a subject identifies as core aspects of itself, such as gender or cultural identity.

While this inside fold consists of the things that make up the world – biological structures, social forces, ideologies, environmental infrastructure – it is simultaneously the space of self-creation where the forces that create the subject in the first place are turned back on themselves through practices of ethical self-creation. As Sara Ahmed points out in her book *Willful Subjects*, the subject is also a place where the "will" is put into relation with a moral order. Historically speaking, it is

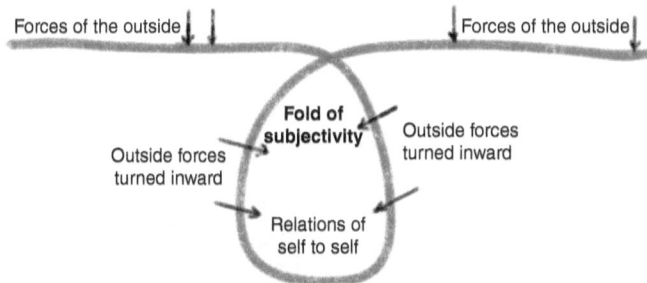

Figure 5.2. The fold of subjectivity as forces of the social and material outside turned/folded inward.

the social and moral-ethical positioning of this "will" that aligns some subjects with virtue and others with vice in the eyes of others.[4]

Let's dwell a bit on what this means about a subject's relation to biopower. At the ends of power, where power conducts conduct, there is an inherent resistance already at work in the self's relations to self. See how the forces of the outside are directed inward in figure 5.2. When the forces of the outside turn in on each other to "make" a subject, new ethical possibilities and practices arise that affirm or subvert this power. If, according to Judith Butler, the making of subjects (subjectification) happens through the repetition of practices, discourses, and performances circulating in the wider social and material world, it is the subject's capacity to relate all these things together differently that disrupts subjectification. The fold of subjectification is constituted by an outside; however, this folding also sets the conditions for different relations, including self to self, but also self to others and the world. The folding diagrams help explain why there's an inherent resistance when power is exercised. Somewhere in the fold of subjectification, the making of a subject, an independent relation of forces, a relation to oneself, is "hollowed out" and set up. These relations of self are nurtured through the various techniques a subject uses to create an ethical self.

Since the subject and the "outside world" are completely coextensive, relations of self end up affecting the outside world simply because subjects are made up of the exact same "stuff." Somewhat paradoxically, this is because a partly "free space of a subject," a set of external relations turned inward, has been established. This subject is made up of the outside, but is no longer entirely dependent on the codes, incitements, and material circumstances that have constituted it. Deleuze sums it up this way: "Foucault's fundamental idea is that of a dimension of subjectivity derived from power and knowledge without being dependent on them."⁵ Relations of self do not remain isolated from the social and material world; they are continually reintegrated. In this sense, when we talk about subjectivity, we are still talking about one immanent material world. The fold of the subject will, at various times, be virtually unfolded or unravelled when subjects come to realize they are capable of different relations and of becoming different.

Within the strata, practices of self-making look more like subjection: rule-following, conformity, normalization, categorization, and rigidity are all strategies of the strata. The very thing that ethical self-creation must work within and against.⁶ Ethical self-creation and the constitution of subjectivity from an outside are co-extensive. In this sense, giving an accounting of oneself without reference to the material, environmental, and political world is incomplete. But it's also misleading to discount the relations of self as irrelevant to the broader world, because human subjects are literally this broader world folded inward.⁷ It's also possible to think of subjectivity as a series of subfolds, thereby making what constitutes "an outside" more obscure and less certain. In other words, a subject that's folded multiple times indefinitely – the subfolds being the material body, relations of self, and other seemingly indispensable aspects of identity. It all depends on the specific consistency or terrain of an "outside."

In this wider material sense, subjectivity is even more infinite than the deep chasm of "inner" life that people usually picture. The many relations involved in ethics, including connections to the social and historical, take on a vivid ontological dimension through Deleuze and Foucault. While the relevance to education may not seem so direct, might not teachers at least dispense with uncritical attitudes towards the teacher-subjects and students-subjects that are so often the detached objects of educational research and practice? With a more materialist view of subjectivity it's possible to think about different ecologies, objects, and subjects circulating in educational spaces together.

Through an exploration of subjectivity itself it's possible to shift our perspective of ethics and education outside the confines of human subjectivity by showing how subjectivity (an inner life) is a fold of the outside world. But, if you think about it, isn't it inevitable that any ethics in the Anthropocene would eventually wiggle free of its anthropocentric shackles?

Language and Light – Knowledge and Materiality

So how might we think about this outside to subjectivity? Is it death? The ineffable? The "true" presence of others? A strange dark world?

Since the Enlightenment, especially under the influence Immanuel Kant, Western philosophy has been sceptical of the notion of direct access to, or knowledge of, the material world beyond human perception. That is, direct access to things in themselves. Most modern thought today, including in science, is based on the idea that whatever can be known of this outside world is entirely entangled in perception, subjectivity, bias, human cognition, and so on. This is, according to modern "progressive" epistemologies today, quite true. Humans can only know the world through the senses, ideological constructs, collecting empirical data, and so on, in other words, in the correlation between actual things and how they are accessed or perceived. This has been a productive philosophical standpoint because it means that disciplines like the sciences cannot equate data about reality with the absolute nature of reality. However, the fact that humans cannot directly access reality outside subjectivity – only through the senses, scientific measurement, and ideological constructs – does not mean that speculative thought cannot grasp this outside reality or "things in themselves." It also does not mean humans are the only entities who experience a gap between reality and appearances. (This particularly anthropocentric problem will be considered in more detail in chapter 8.)

For Deleuze, an ethics must somehow address this outside world beyond human consciousness and human-human relations. The question of possibility for an ethical subject has to do with asking what is possible here and now. What are our "foldings"? Folding is a good metaphor for subjectivity because the fold is always contingent on the outside that constitutes the fold. This is why it's often only possible to talk about subjectivity in stratified or "ossified" identities after the fact. Attending to relations of self helps to break up these ossified identities by focusing on what happens when those relations of the outside are turned inward to the self and then outward again. Indeed, subjects have unknown and unpredictable material and social powers. This realization is important as people seek an ethics that understands our intimate relations (or kinships) with nonhuman beings and entities.

The fold of subjectivity is also an example of how difference emerges in the world. Ethics, freedom, resistance, and self-creation are directly tied to the emergence of difference. The struggle for ethical self-creation can be seen as a struggle to become different. Not making room for the emergence of difference is to directly and intentionally stifle ethical reflexivity and creativity. One of the primary ethical responsibilities of teachers is to set the conditions for becoming different. Giving students the chance to explore new attachments, identities, relationships, and ways of living fulfils the deep ethical calling of education. It's not just about showing students how to be but about giving them room to experiment.

Envisioning ethics as *becoming different* is one of the major departure points of part 2. While part 1 emphasized how education is primarily about bringing someone from one ethical subject position to a better one, part 2 positions education as a way to enable different ways of being in the world. In a sense, we're leaving a more Euclidean world of ethics and entering one with messier contours and topologies. Again, this is not due to some realized virtue, but because the realities of our shared ecological crisis and rising social inequality make it necessary.

There's one more critical ontological point to emphasize with the folding diagrams: the differentiation of the strata, how both the material and the discursive structure reality for subjects. On the one hand, knowledge and language codify and set limits; on the other, materiality orders and structures existence. Deleuze refers to these different aspects of strata, different aspects of our reality, as *language and light*. What can be said or expressed and what can be seen or sensed. Taking schools as an example of strata, the buildings, distribution of human and nonhuman bodies, as well as the land where learning happens are material aspects of this strata (*light*). The discourses that both constrain and enable thought and action in schools, like curriculum, instructional discourse, student voices, and policy, take part in processes of expression and overcoding (*language*). Both of these aspects of strata mediate and give shape to the strategic relations subjects have with the world. Both give some sort of shape to ethical modes of living. The challenge for ethics is to move beyond the strata, codes of conduct, and human-human relationships and engage a wider relational material world. Rock formations, emails, flowering plants, and roadway signs all come to bear on ethical being. Animal and plant communication is inextricable from the ethics of food production and distribution that have enabled human societies.

Subjectivity, seen as a fold of the wider material and social world turned inward on itself, is a sociomaterial problem. How do educators and students see the current material predicament for living beings in relation to the expressive elements, both language and light, around us? What's the range of our powers? How might we facilitate new relations and ways of being even if they can't quite be actualized yet? Where's our strategic zone?

Thinking itself is vitally important here because it happens between what can be sensed and what can be spoken – between language and light, content and expression, materiality and discourse. Thinking relates all these together in unexpected ways. Deleuze makes a comparison between the fold of subjectivity and the pineal gland in the brain, that internal organ responsible for sensing the change in sleep cycles and seasons beyond the body.[8] The pinial gland (which, incidentally, looks like a fold) is where the reality of an extreme "outside" – the movement of the sun and the earth – is in direct relation with the enfolded gland or body "inside." The diagram of the fold is also a lesson about thought as an integral relation between inside and outside, language and light, subjectivity and objectivity, and the breakdown of these dualisms. To think is to engage in acts of (un)folding, where relations of a folded inside, created by the outside, in turn change the outside. To think is to break free of what one already thinks and let difference emerge in the world. We rethink the past in the present moment in order to think otherwise in the future. We rethink the outside by constituting an inside so that the outside might be changed for the better. So thinking is a material process through and through. Most importantly, thinking about subjectivity as a fold of the wider material and social world allows us to begin to locate ethics outside of human subjectivity.

A Short Note on Spinoza's Ethics

It was only after finishing the second draft of this book that I realized just how much the writings of Baruch Spinoza influenced the work of Deleuze and Guattari. After reading Deleuze's book *Spinoza: Practical Philosophy* during a rainy autumn in Westmeath I felt compelled to add this short section on Spinoza's ethics.[9] In short, a discussion of Deleuze's ethics would be lacking something without some mention of Spinoza. Every time Deleuze's work veers towards ethics Spinoza is in the background. If I had begun this book during that very wet fall of 2020 I probably would have started with the "whirlwind" of Spinoza (as Deleuze thinks of it). But better late than never.

Spinoza was a seventeenth-century philosopher who wrote as a "twice exiled" Jew in the Netherlands. Twice exiled because Jews were generally in a state of exile in Europe at this time, and on top of this Spinoza was an outcast in his own Jewish community. This peripheral position, in part, arguably led to his belief that virtue doesn't reside in the merits or demerits of society. This system of reward and punishment simply compels one to obey. Spinoza sought an ethics beyond this demerit/merit system, in other words, beyond human and divine judgment. He sought a life-affirming ethics that increases one's powers and cautions against those things that diminish these powers. In Deleuze's work we see similar flights away from structure and strata in order to enable one's powers and the powers of others. Ethics is about being in the world, not about prohibitions and pronouncements.[10]

Spinoza's ethics of affirmation and life focuses on the body and its limitless potential.[11] Deleuze paraphrases the limitless potential of a body in Spinoza's ethics with the statement: "We don't yet know what a body can do."[12] We can see Spinoza's thought at work in Deleuze's materialist concepts such as "lines of flight" and "bodies-without-organs" (discussed below and in chapter 6). There's no good or evil in Spinoza's ethics, just those things that allow our powers to grow or diminish. This means there's no need for an external transcendent judge to decide what's good and evil. Rather, the "good" is determined at a material-bodily level. Good and evil for Spinoza retain a critical distance to any system of signs, meanings, and power (or strata). There's no extra dimension to ethics. It is something immanent – to be determined here and now in terms of how the powers of living bodies grow or diminish.[13] In this way, Spinoza's ethics not only touches the material but the geological, biographical, biological, and political.

This expanded view for ethics is important when including nonhuman entities into ethical ways of being in the world, which will be discussed in the next chapter using the concept of assemblages. Mapping the material world as an assemblage of material and discursive entities positions ethics as a test of "enablement" or "disablement." The simple questions educators and students can ask at any moment are: Are my/our powers increasing or decreasing? Which powers might these be? How do they work? At odds with this view of ethics is the imposition of a grand morality – which for Spinoza is always reactionary and joyless.

We can understand Spinoza, and by extension Deleuze and Guattari, as driven by an "ethics of life" that stands against those destructive, and often transcendent, forces turned against life such as capitalism, racialized hierarchies, heteronormativity, and judgmental moralities. Instead, people must turn to an ethics of joy – towards increasing their powers. That is, increasing their embodied power of life beyond good and evil. An ethics of life seeks to grow our powers beyond the mishaps and certain death that await us all.[14]

Spinoza's project, according to Deleuze, is a plan of *composition*, not organization. An ethics of joyful life is one we compose, not as the product of strata or something that must organized to some grand ideology. And don't educators always find themselves caught between spaces of composition and organization? Don't both come to bear, in their own ways, on ethics and the many ways we all work to create and affirm ourselves? In a sense, part 1 of this book worked with this tension between organization (the state of things) and the need to compose a new way forward, that is, a way to maximize the life-giving powers we have to affect and be affected for the good along with all the intensity this might bring. The art that my children, Luca and Joseph, create is pure composition. Joe draws things like colour bands – lines of colour with just the slightest semblance of order and organization. Luca makes familiar faces with crazy noses or hairstyles. Both Joseph and Luca (age 14 and 16 respectively) make intensive compositions. Due to their autism, they are not preoccupied with organization when it comes to drawing. The strata has little effect on them.

Hopefully, a bit of Spinoza's ethics will shine through the rest of this book. Let's resume our journey by delving into a few more concepts from Deleuze and Guattari.

Rhizomes, Lines of Flight, and Becoming Different

Do you really believe that the sciences would ever have originated and grown if the way had not been prepared by magicians, alchemists, astrologers, and witches whose promises and pretensions first had to create a thirst, a hunger, a taste for hidden and forbidden powers?

– Friedrich Nietzsche[15]

Sketching an "outside" to subjectivity enhances our ability to think that ethics involves something more than human subjects. On the surface, and in times of ecological crisis, the idea that ethics involves lakes, grasses, and insects actually makes a lot of sense. Finding a different way of being in the world is possible at any time, and these different ways of being all originate from various *lines of flight*. A line of flight is a concept from Deleuze and Guattari's *A Thousand Plateaus*, the second of the two volume work *Capitalism and Schizophrenia*.[16] In its simplest form a line of flight is any action, thought, or way of being that escapes what confines, controls, or overcodes. It is a movement away from what presents itself as apparent, actual, inevitable, or commonsensical, and so on. In this way, a line of flight is a movement towards the *virtual*, and therefore towards different actualities that maximize the dimensions and possibilities available to a being (human or nonhuman). It's impossible to tell where a line of flight might lead, and this is what is exciting about the concept. Recall from part 1 that a first point of resistance is refusal. When a student or teacher refuses what they've been instructed to do they stand on the threshold of unrealized virtual possibilities. The virtual is real. It just has yet to come into actuality. Ethical self-creation can be thought of as a "flight away" from those modes of being deemed necessary by controlling forces.

A line of flight is immanent to a context, meaning it's virtually possible to take a line of flight anytime. In other words, something unexpected can happen. Teachers know it's always possible for one student to take the class in an unexpected direction. As soon as students utter their unique thoughts, or veer off course from the intended curriculum, the dimensions of the classroom virtually increase for everyone. This doesn't mean all lines of flight are desirable or that they always embody an ethics worth keeping. The ethical value of a line of flight, how lines of flight might be ethically differentiated, has to do with their enabling power. If a line of flight, or an ethical way of being, enables nothing, and/or only works to destroy, its ethical value or potential diminishes. Teachers should also be looking for ways to enable students' ideas. This is an important ethical practice because there is no a priori form for what a line of flight might look like. Where lines of flight come from, or what they might do, is always an open question. Just like a text is more about what it does, or what it enables, rather than what significance has bestowed on it from the outside.

Lines of flight can therefore be seen as ethical acts of resistance or pleasure that move towards a different, more desirable, way of being. Exploring what it might mean to live as another species through stories is one way to take a line of flight that just might foster better relations with our nonhuman kin. Lines of flight move beyond the way reality has already been socio-politically, biologically, morally, or ethically structured. And they don't just have to do with human affairs. A developing seed or embryo takes multiple lines of flight as it adds dimensions of possibility through the transcription of its DNA, cell division, and interactive changes with its environment. The environment also gains dimensions of possibility through its interaction with the organism. It's easy to see how enabling lines of flight might be ethically necessary during times of environmental collapse (which can also mean returning to the past in new ways). For teachers and students, lines of flight are always possible no matter how dire the situation might seem. Our conversation about ethics and education has now shifted towards ontological considerations, that is, thinking about how things are or might be.

The concept from Deleuze and Guattari my education students like the most, perhaps because it comes from fungi and plant worlds, is the *rhizome*. The best way to conceive of a rhizome is to picture the wide-ranging, and sometimes multispecies, plant stems existing below forest floors that allow trees to communicate. A rhizome in a philosophical sense is a system with no fixed centre – a flat, non-hierarchal assemblage of pathways (or possibilities) that arise in the interplay between structures and lines of flight.[17] In this way rhizomes and lines of flight co-constitute and enable each other. As more lines of flights are taken, more non-hierarchal, horizontal pathways become possible. The more that non-hierarchal, horizontal pathways are made available, the more likely a line of flight will occur.

Rhizomes consist of multiplicities that defy set structures and categories. They also vary in form. For example, fungal rhizomes and knowledge networks are quite different. One establishes flat connectivity through organic connective tissue, the other through fibre-optic cables and other wireless technologies. Something that is qualitatively "rhizomatic" under certain conditions may cease to be so when conditions change. The same might be said for an ethics: at times it may be relational, reflexive, and exploratory, and then suddenly become rigid and cease to be non-hierarchical and open.

I think the concept of the rhizome has been a hit with the students I teach because it allows them to explore their interests in new ways. One of the things Deleuze and Guattari were trying to think through is how knowledge and being might escape already-known structures. Deleuze and Guattari symbolize this already-known structure as a tree. In a tree there are always roots, stems, branches, and leaves in a given order, and there is always a top and bottom. Schools and modern Western knowledge systems have historically been modelled on the metaphor of the tree. The crest and motto of the University of Toronto is a good example. Underneath the crest of an oak tree the motto reads "Velut arbor aevo," which means something like "may it [the learning or learned student] grow like a tree through the ages."[18] Deleuze and Guattari describe rigidly structured aspects of material and social reality as *arborescent*. The concept of the rhizome challenges a rigid structural view of knowledge – an unquestioned view of history and of hardened identities – because all directions are theoretically equal in a rhizome. Just like an actual fungal or plant rhizome that grows under the earth as a tangled root system, rhizomes are horizontal pathways of thinking or being that subvert the idea of structure itself. Horizontal here simply means things don't follow a set hierarchical structure but rather grow in an adventitious way. Figure 5.3 is a basic representation of a rhizome and rhizomatic system by curriculum theorists Noel Gough and Warren Sellers (Warren Sellers being the visual artist).[19]

As Figure 5.3 shows, rhizomes are non-hierarchical, and do not necessarily progress in any one direction. This adventitious aspect of rhizomes means that any patterns or set structures that may appear are

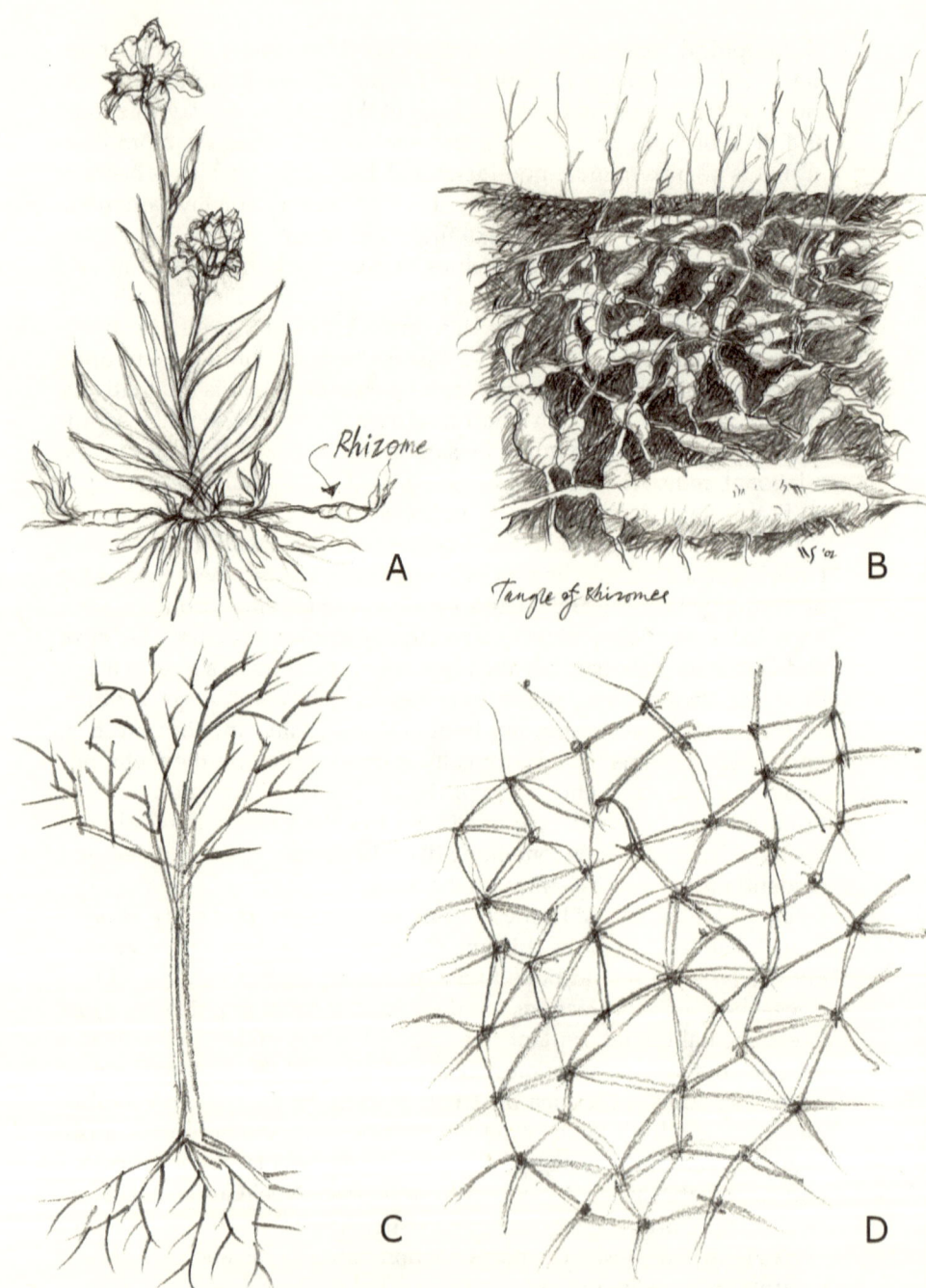

Figure 5.3. (A) Rhizome in relation to root-stem-flower. (B) A tangle of rhizomes. (C) Closed "arboreal" system. (D) Open rhizomatic system.
* Gough and Sellers, Changing Planes, 96–100.

only jumping off points. Each strand in a rhizome is potentially connected to all other parts. The World Wide Web is rhizomatic because every site can touch any other instantaneously (though parts of the internet are structured and made arborescent). While modern Western knowledges are quite arborescent and tightly structured, the way they grow and differentiate is often rhizomatic. As rhizomes grow through connection they give rise to new structures. Plant/fungal rhizomes give rise to new stems, flowers, leaves, roots, and so on, which are not rhizomatic themselves but arborescent or tree-like. The rhizomatic and the arborescent exist together, though in European modernity the rhizomatic has arguably been subordinated to the arborescent. This is also true of ethics in general. Although rhizomatic thinking and being enable the conditions for lines of flight and finding new ethical ways of being (and vice versa), it doesn't mean more rigid ethical codes or ways of being cease to exist. There is nothing inherently better about the rhizomatic, as compared to the arborescent, on an ontological level. The point is that modern knowledges and institutions have structured their worlds in ways that have allowed oppressive hierarchies and systemic violence. Think of the many ways the rigidity and hierarchy of modern schooling have had disastrous results.

What people seem to be slowly learning in Anthropocene times is that there is no pre-set form for things like politics or even a commons. Rhizomes function by multiplying rather than negating. They affirm multiplicities by saying continually, "Yes, yes, and there's also this and this!" Things become rhizomatic when they're connected to multiple points or entities simultaneously, when they become part of an array of multiplicities with no apparent beginning or end. Flat, horizontal classroom communities that work against hierarchies are rhizomatic in this way. Where the interests of students and the community intermingle it's often impossible to tell where one starts and another begins.

Rhizomes increase and decrease according to their dimensions of possibility – the more students are allowed to connect with others the greater the potential for new shoots and beginnings. Brains and minds are rhizomatic in this way. Stifling them, reducing the dimensions of possibility, is always difficult as thoughts and memories can instantaneously be connected together. Just as there's always freedom to resist power at its capillary ends, there's always the possibility to connect and increase one's dimensions (another ethical lesson from Spinoza).

Chapter 2 mentioned two general responses to biopower and the controlling aspects of modernity such as capitalism, colonialism, and white supremacy. One response is to engage biopower on its own terms, while another involves trying to escape these agonistic relations, that is to resist, but not on biopower's terms, and move towards (becoming) something different. This is perhaps the most essential aspect of a line of flight, and what rhizomatic thought and being enable. A movement away from what is presented as the *only way* or *the only relation*. A stultifying image of reality that Deleuze refers to as the "dogmatic image of thought"– thought without any awareness of its many presuppositions.[20] In some ways, the history of modern Western philosophy is one of the most stifling examples of a dogmatic image of thought. While there's nothing wrong with a history of thought in itself, this image of thought becomes violent when it passes for thought or thinking itself – when it prevents deviations from its singular image.

Educators open up this dogmatic image when they set the conditions for becoming different and thinking differently. When they resist stultifying students with some predestined image of thought. Enabling difference is a self-less task – yet it involves maximizing our collective powers and possibilities (all the folds) and shedding those rigid identities that limit instead of enable. It means maximizing our dimensions of possibility by subtracting that identarian dimension that prevents (our) becoming in the first place. This is what Deleuze and Guattari refer to as *n-1* dimensions, where n is the total dimensions of possibility minus that 1 dimension that prevents our becoming different.[21]

Shedding those rigid aspects of our identity doesn't mean that other aspects don't enable or empower. Minority identities are often flights away from dominating or imposed identities (such as nationalist, gendered, or imposed cultural identities). Contending with things like pandemics means letting go of things like exclusionary national identities, because vaccine hording and health care inequality aren't solutions in an increasingly connected world. Showing solidarity with 2SLGBTQI+ communities ultimately means shedding strict gender binaries of male and female and a heteronormative understanding of intimate relationships, (including friendships). So, this *n-1* formulation applies to dominant identities of the strata, ones that restrict, overcode, extract, limit, control, and so on. To become ethically different means dropping that part of ourselves that limits and binds us to narratives of domination, stultification, and/or impossibility.

The dropping of stultifying aspects of our identities is an essential part of processes of becoming. It's understandable that many people don't want to become different. Sometimes there are very good reasons for this. However, even religious conservatives have deep attachments to processes of becoming. Becoming Christian, for example, often involves dropping a former identity to take up a new reality and new ethical commitments. This was the case with the Apostle Paul, who arguably paved the way for dropping Jew/gentile and man/woman distinctions before God. A line of flight, a move to become different, can be seen as the outer limit of the rhizomatic. It is an increasing of dimensions at those outer limits such that everything changes, where a brain thinks different thoughts or when a new collective emerges from a multiplicity or assemblage. Lines of flight exceed what is actual, what is presented to us, by adding virtual dimensions that are just as real but not actualized yet. To refuse aspects of life under modern capitalism or neocolonialism is to take a line of flight. The move succeeds if it increases the possibilities for responding ethically and politically.

Insightful critiques of Deleuze and Guattari's concepts, along with some other poststructural concepts, have been voiced, particularly from Indigenous scholars like Sandy Grande, Eve Tuck, and Glen Coulthard. There are good reasons for rejecting or leaving aside poststructural or sociomaterial ontological concepts like fluidity and becoming. Sandy Grande argues that making things like identity too fluid has been used (directly and indirectly) as a rationale for assimilation and the "dismantling of tribal life."[22] When employing concepts like becoming and fluidity one should ask how these concepts may work to further colonization and Western hegemony. While it's important to problematize identity as defined by blood, DNA, or distinct codes of culture, it's also important to recognize how colonial institutions have systematically worked to destroy and dissolve the self-determination of Indigenous peoples globally. Eve Tuck makes this point in her essay "Breaking Up with Deleuze: Desiring and Valuing the Irreconcilable."[23] One of Tuck's main reasons for "breaking up" with Deleuze, and by extension other poststructural theorists, has to do with the relationship between desire and "a self." My reading of Tuck's argument goes something like this: If things like desire and becoming are largely guided by forces outside ourselves, how is it possible to nurture a self-guided desire fitting of an activist, lover, or community member? While this question doesn't capture the power and detail of Tuck's critique, it highlights a productive tension for ethics found in this book. Is ethics relevant as a reflexive, creative, and self-directed human domain? Or is it something that escapes human intention, cognition, and desire? In a similar vein, Glen Coulthard's book *Red Skin, White Masks* questions how notions of fluidity would actually work for the struggles of Indigenous peoples whose cultural expressions may not conform to such notions of being. Such concepts may have no way of interceding in the "non-fluid" neocolonial institutions needing transformation.[24] If the concepts put forward by Deleuze and Guattari don't work, if they are counterproductive or disabling, they should be left alone or rejected. It is very likely that Deleuze and Guattari would have agreed with that sentiment.

Concepts like rhizomes and lines of flight are useful because they free ethics from a rigid or binary logic where one action, response, or context prescribes another. For Deleuze and Guattari, the rhizome and, by extension, ethics thrive off multiplicity. If we apply these concepts to the curriculum we can see their productive power. Indigenous educators often point to the Earth itself as the long-standing and all-important holistic curriculum for millennia.[25] Is curriculum something that arises out of multiplicities, connections, and free relationships – or is it defined content, with set outcomes, that is arranged beforehand for predetermined students? A rhizomatic approach to curriculum and pedagogy celebrates and nurtures the multiplicities that comprise our shared commons, while recognizing that these multiplicities have relationships and give rise to various structures, traditions, and moralities in the world. There will be structures in the world, but the chance to break free of these structures is immanent to each moment.

Becoming different requires subtracting those aspects of identity or structure that tie us to a particular way of being. In terms of the fold of subjectivity, this is because majoritarian identities are largely constituted from the outside, the result of an outside fold turned inward. To a significant extent a subject is an effect of biopower and its techniques and institutions of control. While minoritarian identities maintain necessary community ties and resist white supremacy, colonialism, and imperialism, majoritarian identities are largely antithetical to the ethical lines of flight needed in Anthropocene times. Deleuze and Guattari's "algebra of becoming" ($n\text{-}1$ dimensions) is a subtraction of those hardened aspects of identity that prevent becoming.[26] The tricky part for teachers and students is to differentiate those aspects of identity that have ethical purpose and give meaning from those that prevent us from becoming different. It's impossible to say beforehand what these identarian aspects might be, but students and teachers might start by examining those aspects that have become unthoughtful, closed, and destructive. There's always some ambiguity in deciding whether to cling to arborescent or rhizomatic forms of being. Educators must consider in detail the state of the world and their ethical calling of leading students to better futures. However, education in the early twenty-first century almost always begins in arborescent institutions. There's always a strong ethical imperative to take an ethical line of flight from the rigidity that surrounds modern Western education. There's always a strong ethical imperative to create a rhizome.

For educators thinking in terms of rhizomes, lines of flight, and other related concepts is a question of method. Rhizomatic space is analogous to an interactive and ever-changing *topological map* with infinite possibilities for expansion and change. In contrast, arborescent space resembles a *tracing*. Something hardened and petrified. An educator must consider how both lead to a different ethics, an ethics based in "how things are." While rhizomatic space is about becoming different, arborescent space is about remaining unchanged. While hardened arborescent tracings can always be put on a dynamic map, the same dynamic map can't be integrated into a static, unchanging tracing. There's an ethical and methodological asymmetry here: a dynamic, rhizomatic, ever-changing map can produce an arborescent tracing – but not the other way around. For Deleuze and Guattari problems arise when we think the world should exist in one set way. Though stable structures exist and are necessary, the world is always changing at different levels of scale and speed in ways that are co-extensive.

An obvious ethical problem for educators and students resides in determining when a line of flight should be taken towards becoming different. Since lines of flight do not follow any a priori structure, asking what constitutes a line of flight, or whether it's "right" to pursue one, is an unanswerable ethical question. And for good reason. Very often it's desirable to hold close to the teachings of elders, heed what government has to say during a pandemic, and celebrate a canon of literature, keeping in mind that wise teachings, evidence-based pandemic guidance, and works of literature are also the products of multiple lines of flight. It's therefore important to ask what ethical horizon is created by a line of flight. What results from increasing our dimensions of possibility? What are the "molecular" lines of possibility and connection? How are things like body hair, tampons, and farm equipment essential parts of an interconnected and intersectional feminist ethics and politics? How does the simple provision of feminine hygiene products in schools work to revision the purpose of schools? How are these micro-revisionings mappable in dynamic relation with other working parts?

A rhizomatic ethics is relevant for teachers and students wanting to connect ethics to the wider material world and ways of becoming. And this becoming, for Deleuze and Guattari, always involves processes of "becoming minor" – again shedding a majoritarian identity that overcodes one's way of being.[27] Majority ways of being aren't wrong in themselves. They become problematic when they're used to mask multiplicities and possibilities for being. Differentiating oneself ethically often involves breaking away from what is deemed commonsensical and "good."

114 Ethics as Ontological Exploration

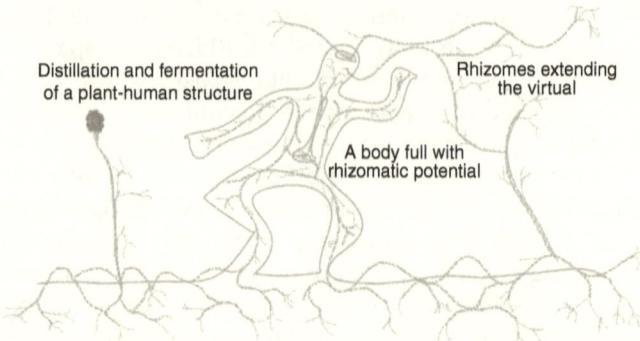

Figure 5.4. Rhizomes giving rise to virtual and actual becoming(s). (Diagram based on work by Marc Ngui.)

Artist Marc Ngui's visual depictions of Deleuze and Guattari's *A Thousand Plateaus* captures how rhizomatic ways of being, with their lines of flight, virtually innervate all structural/actual bodies.[28] Figure 5.4 shows how the rhizomatic pervades both actual and virtual realities and gives rise to other arborescent structures.

Rhizomatic elements always exist, either virtually or actually, in any social, biological, ecological, ethical, or political milieu alongside structural bodies of all kinds. Deleuze and Guattari refer to bodies "shot through" with rhizomatic potential and possible lines of flight as "bodies-without-organs." In such a body, multiple forms and potentials are manifesting, but only virtually. And while it may be ethically desirable for the virtual to manifest actually, virtual lines of possibility are not fully bound by actual forms. So somewhere between structure and a line of flight there's always the possibility to reach out and form a new rhizomatic connection. Figure 5.4 contains a flower labelled "distillation" and "fermentation," both processes of food production. This flower is depicted in Ngui's original drawing and is meant to illustrate multiple connections between plants and humans that enable countless lines of flight. It would be a useful exercise for educators to map the many relationships between rhizomatic potential and arborescent structures, between the virtual and actual, in their educational milieu.

Deleuze and Guattari's major lesson for ethics and education involves recognizing the ethical possibilities that exist virtually just beyond actualization. What is presented as important is often, at best, just a jumping-off point. While majority identities and understandings will be evident, we should continually seek a minority path of becoming (different). There will always too be a majority politics – the kind that has everything to do with biopower. Accompanying majority politics today are majority ethical systems like neoliberalism – those that praise individualism over community investment. Through Deleuze and Guattari we have left the large island of human subjectivity and are paddling towards a less anthropocentric and more materialist ethics (understanding that this ethics will still have anthropomorphic aspects to it; we are humans after all). Ethics needs to become a more-than-human consideration precisely because modern Western humans have separated their ethics from the world(s) in which they live. And while (some) humans have grossly overstated their own importance, in an uncanny kind of way, the importance of human action today cannot be overstated.

This chapter has taken ethics and subjectivity and placed them in a kind of ontological fold using the thought of Gilles Deleuze. In doing so, it has slowly introduced the idea of a material, nonhuman, and 'outside' to human ethical subjectivity. Concepts like rhizomes, folds, outsides, strata, lines of flight, and bodies-without-organs are more about creating movement than reifying some actual image of themselves in the world. This chapter's main goal was to try and open up ethical possibility and imagination. Such imagination would be able to connect ethics to oceans, forests, and mammals, but also seemingly unimportant material things like sidewalks, video games, and midge flies.

Ethics in part 2 is perhaps best thought of as an intensive endeavour, rather than something conscious or reflexive. Intensity here doesn't just have to do with human emotions. It refers to states of being connected through difference. The next chapter will explore this intensive ethics through the sociomaterial concept of assemblages.

6 Assemblages and the Emergence of Difference

Every hundred feet the world changes.

– Roberto Bolaño[1]

So far this book has argued that ethics is central to education in a variety of ways. Chapter 5 developed the idea that the human subject is just one entity (or fold) in a larger ecological, social, and material reality that needs to be considered when finding new ethical ways of being in the world. No matter how important it is for humans to understand their own ethical relations to self, others, and the world, a much larger ecological, material, and social space constitutes the stakes of human ethics today. Ethics today must engage the nonhuman material world,[2] not as globs of inertness or inferior species but as equal entities and with equal consideration. An ethics based solely on human-human relations, or the inner workings of a human subject, is arguably a massive malfunction of human societies today, some societies (e.g., modern Western) more than others (e.g., Indigenous). It's evident that this general malfunctioning of *Homo sapiens* has led to an environmental crisis. It's crucial to remember that until recently in Earth's history humans have only been a small part of global ecological space.

There are probably an infinite number of ways of expanding ethics to include nonhumans and materiality. In Saskatchewan, Canada, expanding ethics to include nonhumans often involves engaging local Indigenous knowledges, spiritualities, ceremonies, and ways of relating to nonhuman kin.[3] At best, it might be said that modern science and Western philosophy are beginning to catch up with Indigenous ways of knowing by affirming that humans are not above other life forms, that they're not the pinnacle of creation. I try to guide new teachers as best I can towards Indigenous ways of knowing and living, by appealing to a shared sense of purpose. I always expect to fumble a bit, like I do with most things. Whatever my personal shortcomings, by engaging Indigenous ways of knowing and living in the world, it becomes clear that modern Western thinking needs to radically change for the sake of planetary survival. And if modern Western thought can't change, or doesn't lead to just futures or better ways of being, then it should be largely abandoned.

This chapter explores a sociomaterial context for ethics and education using Deleuze and Guattari's concept of *assemblages*. Ethics here becomes an emergent phenomenon of material, human, nonhuman, and discursive entities. Although I take a particular theoretical pathway in this chapter, I do my best to avoid a dogmatic ontology. Thinking about how things are, or how things might be, should not lead educators into an "onto-theology" or rigid metaphysics.

Thinking outside anthropocentrism requires thinking about how reality might work – even if this thinking seems counterintuitive at times. Science shows us that reality is often counterintuitive. As someone involved in teaching future science educators, I understand how science is very good at elucidating "how things are." However, one problem with science today is that it has gradually pushed out other disciplines like art, education, theology, and philosophy that can tell us much about our shared reality. On the one hand, science is highly relevant to ethics, which was immediately obvious in the early stages of the COVID-19 pandemic. On the other hand, the capabilities of science increasingly extend beyond the reach of any ethics that might curtail them. We see this with resource extraction, with the genetic engineering of humans and other life forms, and with military spending to enhance nuclear arsenals. Our ecological crisis requires thinking about our shared interconnected world in ways that move with and beyond the modern sciences. If education, which includes the sciences, is going to work towards better futures, it must draw from many different ways of knowing. Using philosophy and theory to think about the material world, in this case as assemblages, doesn't negate science. It simply takes the bold step of thinking about reality in ways we may not be accustomed to. The label "sociomaterial" means that social well-being and justice drive this view of material reality. Let's move forward by developing the concept of an assemblage using the thought of Deleuze and Guattari, as well as that of Manuel Delanda.

Viewing the World as Assemblages

It is absurd to think that complex self-organizing structures need a "brain" to generate them.[4]

– Manuel Delanda

The term "assemblage," as Deleuze and Guattari employ it, essentially refers to a self-organizing system of parts. Self-organizing here is meant very broadly and includes human intention, as human activity is not fundamentally different than insect or plant activity. The various parts of an assemblage exhibit emergent properties that depend on the capacities and relationships of these parts. Cells, neighbourhoods, and food webs are all examples of assemblages. They are systems of cooperating parts that have unique properties depending on the capacities of their heterogeneous parts. According to Manuel Delanda, the world consists of an infinite array of assemblages at different levels of scale (micro- and macro-levels) that exist relative to each other.[5]

Assemblages are greater than the sum of their parts, as the saying goes. But they're also less than the sum of their parts. What does this mean exactly? It means that assemblages cannot be reduced to the sum of their parts, because properties emerge at each level of scale that cannot be fully attributed to the parts themselves. For example, throwing together a bunch of students, tons of money, dormitory buildings, and some newly hired professors would not constitute a thriving public university system on its own. The ethos, culture, and ideas of a university system must emerge as the diverse parts of the university and public interact and nurture each other over time. Having said this, the parts of an assemblage also cannot be fully determined by the whole, because parts have their own capacities that can function independently to some degree. So, for example, no matter how good the university system is in a place like Massachusetts, the culture and academic programs of these schools do not determine the actions, capacities, thoughts, and relationships of its educators and students. We must recognize, of course, that the whole of an assemblage does exert an influence on its parts, and the interplay of its individual parts can ultimately make or break an emergent property or integrity of the whole assemblage. Thinking about the world as assemblages means not reducing parts and wholes to each other. This sounds simple enough. It also resonates with Deleuze and Guattari's ontology concerning transcendence. Wholes are not transcendent: they emerge from parts. Assemblages are immanent to the interactions of their constituent parts, which means that phenomena in the world can be examined without recourse to anything beyond the here and now (even if some things are inaccessible somehow). This also means that an ethics derived from any assemblage or system is also not transcendent.

Another aspect of assemblages is that they display *morphogenetic* capacities.[6] This means that complex phenomena can be generated without human intention, intelligence, or a supernatural power. This aspect might be appealing to those who like science. Whether we're talking about the evolution of mammalian sociality or global weather systems it's readily apparent that the world generates complex assemblages. Therefore, we can think of complex systems emerging materially, biologically, ecologically, socially, and historically without the need of a conscious designer (although sometimes there are conscious designers!). To see our shared world as a series of assemblages is not an argument for atheism, rather it's a call to an ontology and forms of analyses that take symbiosis, cooperation, and collectivity seriously. No one discipline – sociology, the natural sciences, art, philosophy – can sufficiently describe assemblages or what emerges from them. Thinking with assemblages requires a transdisciplinary approach. As the epigraph for this chapter suggests, every hundred feet the world is assembled differently. And with differing assemblies comes the potential for a different ethics. Through the concept of assemblages it's possible to move a little farther from an anthropocentric ethics.

One thing assemblages help educators do is to question the reified generalities that mistakenly present themselves as detailed systems or individual entities that one can point to. An example is the use of the term "state." A state is a dynamic interplay of people, materials, institutions, nonhumans, relations, and discourses. To say that one could point to something called "a state" would be, according to Delanda, misleading. But more to the point it would be analytically unhelpful. This is because reified generalities often operate as idealisms that mask detailed material and discursive relationships, parts, and circumstances, such as the real causes of poverty and environmental racisms. Literary theorist Roland Barthes eloquently demonstrated how right-wing rhetorical strategies relied on the mythologizing of history, everyday objects, and cultural values to hide real material circumstances and relations.[7] If one cannot literally point to or describe an entity it will not easily lend itself to assemblage thinking. This is because a generality cannot effectively act as a part of an assemblage and can obscure how different assemblages, as well as parts of assemblages, at varying levels of scale relate to each other (remembering again that scales are relative to an analytical context or perspective). Things that can be effectively outlined or identified, such as the food web for elk and aspen trees, bacteria cells, the departmental structure of a faculty of education, and the local economy of Mullingar, Ireland, lend themselves best to assemblage thinking. The point here is not to dispense with generalities – we use them all the time in speech – but to be aware that generalities cannot take the place of real entities or parts of an assemblage. Remember too that entities can be both virtual (e.g., future plans) and actual (e.g., windmill turbines).

Thinking with assemblages makes the ethical landscape feel much more expansive and detailed in that tracing an ethics also involves non-human entities. Ethics becomes an ecological-ontological exploration. Thinking about the world as a series of assemblages requires working with parts that have histories and specific details, even if these details are virtual. Dogs can be incorporated as part of an assemblage because they're both a biological species and a historical entity that can be traced by processes of speciation and domestication. They're also capable of exiting the world through extinction. Traceability is important because the different parts of assemblages need to be as interfaceable or real as possible – like Dubliners or prairie grasses. Ideas, too, can be part of an assemblage because they have detailed content, histories, and relationships. In summary, we can view the parts of any assemblage as immanent. Not transcendent but traceable here and now. Plant cells, political parties, plankton, scientific theories, and geological formations can be parts of assemblages and assemblages themselves because they have specific histories, capacities, properties, and details that allow them to interface with other parts.

A label that can safely be applied to the sociomaterialist ontology of assemblages is *realist*, because assemblages affirm the actual and virtual reality of entities. Yet, the approach is also speculative and exploratory. In virtual terms we might think of assemblages and their parts as emerging along *ontological planes* at varying flows of time and space (the same infinite plane or horizon that was introduced in chapter 3). These ontological planes form an open horizon where the emergence of different entities, such as new species, events, or ideas, exist in immanent relation with each other. These relations can be temporal, material, ideological, or virtual. Imagining connected ontological planes, where different entities cross over and connect is, in my view, a little different from the more abstract and singular planes Deleuze and Guattari envisioned around one set of concepts or one discipline (e.g., philosophy, science, art). On an open ontological plane, diverse entities from the past, present, and future flow together. Of course, these interactions are limited by the virtual, actual, and temporal realities surrounding these ontological planes.[8] The aim of imagining these ontological planes is to help bring the material and social together, even if just virtually. It's also useful to have some sense of how time operates ontologically, because it is through the temporal that difference emerges in the world. Imagining how different entities constantly emerge in the world through time can help educators realize the ontological-ethical importance of difference.

History itself involves the temporal emergence of entities along planes of emergence and connection – where entities such as biological species or events exist together in relation rather than in a teleological structure.[9] Figure 6.1 illustrates two hypothetical and interrelated ontological planes of emergence. One follows historical events and phenomena in human evolution and the other the current ecological crisis of the Anthropocene. Both planes include events that are social, cultural, geological, and biological.

The two ontological planes in figure 6.1 aren't drawn to any extensive historical scale, because the point is to show that these phenomena (both actual and virtual) exist together in an intensive relational present that includes the past and future.

There's also an ethical implication to these ontological planes of emergence. To exist on a plane of emergence and connectivity implies that some mode of existence (one that exceeds the human) is at stake. There isn't any real beginning to an immanent plane of emergence. *One always lands in the middle of things.*[10] It's always possible to put entities on a relational ontological horizon. From this perspective there's also no place for transcendent entities. Even spiritual entities might be best thought of as immanent to the world here and now, just like imagination, emotions, dark matter,

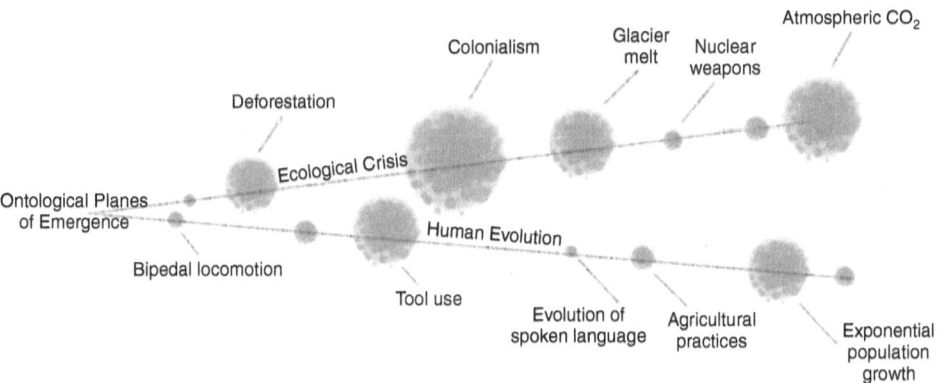

Figure 6.1. Two hypothetical and interrelated plains of emergence: ecological crisis and human evolution.

and heavenly bodies. In this way, there are no concepts, events, or material entities that can remain isolated from others forever. This has other ethical implications. For instance, it means that transdisciplinarity is more useful than individual disciplines for studying the world.

The historical emergence of assemblages happens on scales that have some independence from each other. In this way, assemblages and their parts are interfaceable and interchangeable, and have relations of exteriority that depend on the properties and capacities of their parts. Again, no assemblage, or part of an assemblage, is overdetermined by the whole or underdetermined by its parts. Since the parts of an assemblage have detailed immanent histories and capacities, and are relational and interfaceable, educators and students can begin to use the concept of assemblages to ask questions about how things work as well as how things might be different. One way to do this is by diagramming assemblages to see where possibilities for connection and change might reside.

Anything that can be easily connected with the parts of an assemblage can be said to be immanent to that assemblage. Entities that cannot be easily connected, like reified generalities and transcendent identities, should be avoided. Approaching the world as a series of assemblages means avoiding those things that cannot be cast as part of an assemblage or an assemblage itself. In other words, it means avoiding things that cannot be assembled and connected with other parts and other assemblages. Another crucial aspect of assemblages is that no level of scale is more complex than another. For example, it would be a mistake to think of a federal government assemblage as automatically more complex than the regional government assemblages that help comprise it. Again, assemblage theory refutes the idea that assemblages are totally determined by their parts or vice versa. This is because new capacities emerge at every scale. They occur both at the level of the whole assemblage as well as at the level of parts, which is why parts always retain some autonomy from the whole even when they are reliant on the whole for their existence. The concept of an assemblage is perhaps most useful for educators and students to help them understand how their own communities are put together through material-historical processes. For example, diagramming how schools and education systems function in particular locations, how ecosystems rely on complex relationships, or how social and political change is tied to interconnected material parts and discourses, can help educators and students see where possibilities for ethical engagement and social action might exist. Mapping assemblages can also lead to the creative expression of student ideas, along with exploration of the details that go along with these ideas. Another useful thing about "assemblage theory" (as Delanda calls it) is that its realist philosophy is fully compatible with scientific, social, and artistic ways of thinking.

Whether assemblage theory is appealing or not, we've begun to consider the relevance of nonhuman entities in relation to ethics. If an assemblage is a whole whose properties emerge from the capacities and relations of parts, we might then consider that an ethics emerges from how the parts of an assemblage *consonate* with each other or operate in sympathy together. This means that an ethics is never derived from a universal system, context, or set of axioms – no matter how unchanging some ethical practices may seem to be. It also implies that ethics has some autonomy from humans. Of course, the nature and extent of this autonomy is debatable. The most obvious objection being that without humans an ethics simply can't exist. However, this sounds eerily similar to the idea that without God there can be no ethics or morality! Let's think at a more fundamental level: a multispecies world like Earth has continually enabled different ways of being to emerge. Nonhuman animals have ethical-moral systems of their own based on things like reciprocity, survival, kinship, and learned behaviour. This does not diminish the importance of humans. They still have the ethical challenge of coexistence to work through. And that ethical challenge seems to be emerging within a specific material and multispecies context. The question of "what might we become" now becomes even more expansive and indeterminant.[11] There is no transcendent ethics to rule them all. And thank goodness for that.

Philosopher Karen Barad troubles the belief that differences between entities are pre-given outside of the phenomena from which they emerge. Barad maintains that differences, which includes differing ethical ways of being, are enacted and materialize in assembly with other diverse entities.[12] In this way ethics emerges as an entanglement with/in phenomena and their corresponding entities.[13] Each entanglement (or assemblage) enables specific *response-abilities*. That is, ways of responding to different entities and/or "allowing" other entities to respond and emerge. In this way, ethics becomes a situated and emergent doing, enabling, and responding. Relating Barad's thought to assemblages means viewing an ethics as dependent on how the parts of an assemblage emerge and connect: in Barad's terms, how they are "cut" in relation with each other. Barad coins the term *intra-action*, which essentially refers to how the nature of identities/entities are produced as they emerge together. Rather than viewing the world as separate pre-existing entities that merely interact Barad casts ethical agency and difference-making, in part, as processes of cutting-together-apart.[14] While understanding the full import of things like intra-actions necessitates some engagement with both physics and poststructuralism, Barad's work drives home the

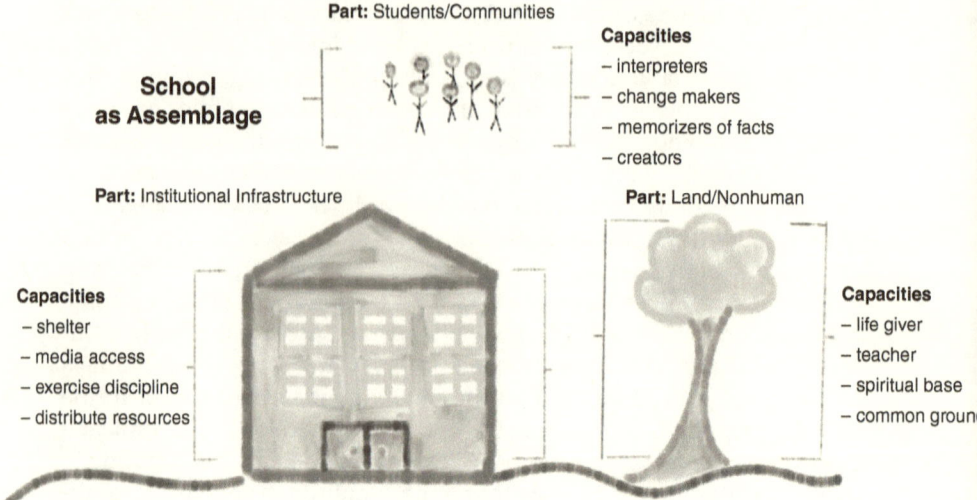

Figure 6.2. School as assemblage with its different parts and varying capacities.

idea that ethical theories are moving away from human-centred representational theories to more non-representational theories. That is, where ethics resides in local encounters beyond "the human."[15]

Now that we've laid out some of the ontological foundations for assemblages let's take a look at what a basic assemblage might look like, using a school as an example. Figure 6.2 is a diagram of some basic parts of a school assemblage with its parts and their varying capacities. A key aspect of assemblages is that they can radically change depending on how its parts interface with other parts.

Each part in the school assemblage has multiple capacities. The capacity of a part is what the part actually does and/or what the part virtually could do (its potential lines of flight). The capacities of each part depend not only on the part's constitution, but also on how each part is related and connected to other parts, which depend on their relations of exteriority (represented by the square brackets surrounding each part). While the properties of a part, for example what a school building is made of or how high it is, may affect its capacities and relations of exteriority, for example if the building can shelter large numbers of people or accommodate animals, the properties of a part do not directly determine a part's capacities or relations of exteriority.[16] The relations of exteriority are contingent on how the part is "plugged into" other parts, which again can affect or alter its capacities. Both the capacities of parts and their exterior relations to other parts are open to change depending on context.

While these details may seem methodological or philosophical only, they nonetheless point to the situated-material possibilities for ethics. Ethics here has to do with the interplay of a wide range of parts and wholes. Through assemblages educators and students might trace an ethics that takes into account a material and social world that's not assumed beforehand. Taking notice of the many assembled parts of our shared world(s), their degree of openness, relations, and varying capacities, can be a fascinating exercise. Realizing this variability and multiplicity is how the world changes every hundred feet.

Mapping Assemblages and the Emergence of Difference

Mapping assemblages can be done in much the same way as the mapping discussed in chapter 5. Mapping assemblages is a task of ethical evaluation and deliberation. This kind of mapping doesn't trace static things but allows educators and students to think about both material and discursive entities in dynamic ways that enable humans and nonhumans to grow. This is because assemblages map ethical potential. No longer is ethics just a human subjective consideration but one that exceeds human relations and considers part-to-part relations – human to nonhuman and nonhuman to nonhuman, and human to human. Ethics emerges in the unique materiality and relationality of an assemblage.

At this point it might seem like this book is offering some kind of progressive timeline to the study of ethics and education where: 1) humans develop ethical codes and practices to guide and govern conduct; 2) ethical conduct becomes an object of enquiry, refinement, and political intervention; 3) ecological and social crises prompt humans to develop ethical ways of living, being, and becoming that escape anthropocentrism. While there may be some historical relevance to such a progression in modern Western societies, it would be misleading, and somewhat dangerous, to see ethics as not constituting all these aspects simultaneously on the same immanent plane of emergence or consistency, as shown in Figure 6.1. It's more enabling to think of a multiplicity of ethics, ethical forms, and ethical relations because ethics involves increasing and enabling the powers of both living and nonliving systems together. At least, this is what an ethics of multispecies flourishing involves. Elizabeth Grosz puts ethics in this wider material context in the following way: "Ethics is thus irretrievably bound up with the movement of events, with how events may be 'lived' by both a living being and a nonliving milieu, with the corporeal and incorporeal forces they bear."[17]

Let's go back to our example of the school as assemblage. As a student, you probably noticed that some schools, or some aspects of schooling, are very rigid and tight, where a body cannot do anything outside of the expected norms for conduct. However, some schools may look completely different. These are schools where learning takes place in contexts with very high degrees of freedom in terms of what's learned and how. Both kinds of schools are examples of assemblages. According to Deleuze and Guattari one is just more *reterritorializing* (the former) and the other more *deterritorializing* (the latter).[18] A school that's stricter and more normative can also be said to be substantially *overcoded* with linguistic or symbolic components, such as narrow canons of literature, imposed curricula, strict dress codes, inflexible rules, or unrelenting ideologies. Conversely, schools with more degrees of freedom enable more lines of flight and possibility. These schools tend to set the conditions for more rhizomatic growth and interconnected transdisciplinary learning (see chapter 5 for the discussion on rhizomes).

Yet, even in a highly controlled school, things will happen that escape expectations and rigid structure. Students might organize a climate strike or a gay pride parade that purposely defies the discipline and rigid order of that tight highly controlled school assemblage. Tight assemblages, however, will try to *reterritorialize* anything – any line of flight – that breaks away from the assemblage by bringing it back into the strict confines of that assemblage. For example, a very conservative school may "forgive" students who join gay rights demonstrations and celebrations, but in doing so they are confirming these ethical actions are a mistake or sin. The administration, culture, ethical code, and mentoring practices of that school, all of which are parts of an assemblage, can potentially work together to make these students understand that, while their intentions are good, their actions are not welcome. In this way, the school (re)absorbs the defiant ethical action into its rules for conduct, social-relational structure, and dogmatic worldviews. Those same actions in a school with more freedom, a less overcoded and loose assemblage, would manifest quite differently. These schools would not have to adhere to a rigid ethical code or curriculum, or restrict certain forms of behaviour and speech. Students could more easily deterritorialize from this school as an assemblage, for example, by partaking in forms of expression and protest they feel are important. With more freedom to suspend and disrupt what they think they "should" be doing, students would engage in thinking and action that look more like lines of flight than with what traditionally passes for education.[19]

For Deleuze and Guattari, things emerge in the world within a kind of double articulation: material and expression, language and light, structure and line of flight. Assemblages are also doubly articulated: first, in

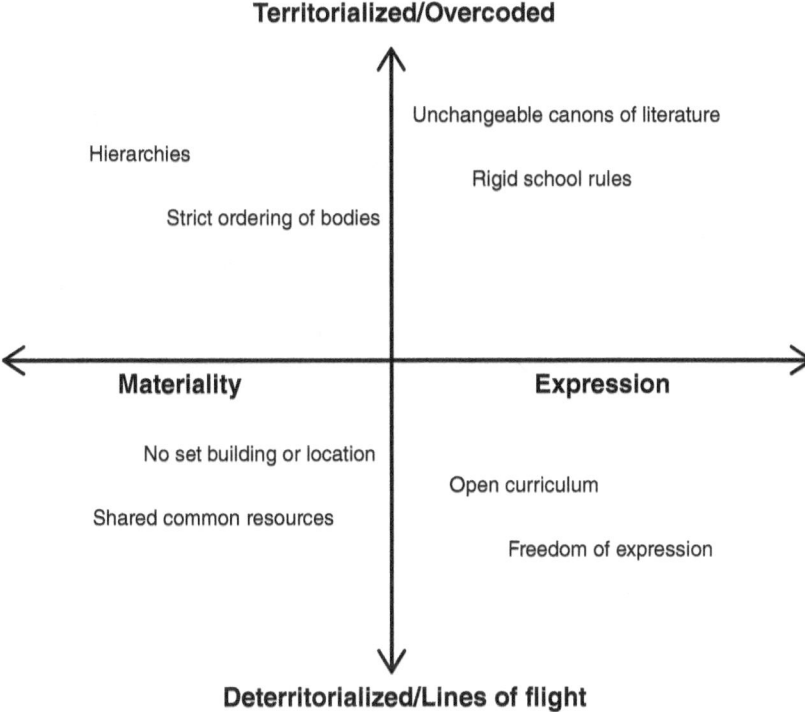

Figure 6.3. Assemblages can be overcoded or free-flowing in their materiality and expression.

their materiality in terms of their parts and connections and, second, in how they're overcoded by forms of expression such as genes, speech, computer codes, and patterns of sociality. Imagining the components of an assemblage in terms of their degrees of freedom and rigidity entails mapping them. We can virtually imagine and diagram assemblages – from beehives to street protests – on two intersecting ontological planes of consistency, what could be called a *tetravalent* plane. When we map assemblages, we map their material and expressive components along with their degree of structure or fluidity. Figure 6.3 maps where parts of a school assemblage might fall along these two axes.

Some parts of the school assemblage can be more rigid or free-flowing than others. Parts can also change in unpredictable ways, thereby changing the entire assemblage. Furthermore, schools can be integrated with larger or smaller assemblages that may themselves be more or less rigid. In fact, assemblages only exist, and are only real(ized), insofar as they integrate with different levels of scale (e.g., organism-family-school-county-polity).

The Deleuzian concept that characterizes rigid highly overcoded assemblages is *strata*. Strata, seen in a wider ecological sense, can consist of things like soil layers as well as human social organization. The strata keeps things in place, yet it can also stifle the heterogeneity of an assemblage – and restricting heterogeneity may lead to restricting symbiosis and the growth of life. A thick, palpable stratum in the human social world might be an authoritarian religious cult that punishes members for open communication with outsiders. In the plant world the xylem (or woody parts of trees) act like a stratum. Strata in themselves are not necessarily bad. But when new forms of life/living need to emerge (and can't) the various strata become an urgent ethical problem of being. A basic question emerges: What forms of assembly allow difference to come forth today? This question is especially relevant in neoliberal consumer societies, societies which promote individualism over community interests. While neoliberal institutions, governments, and corporations support some kinds of difference and freedom, this support is directly tied to the goals of capital accumulation and economic dominance. An ethics of difference that works against neoliberalism would nurture flourishing assemblages of human and nonhuman life. In every assemblage the question of ethical differentiation exists. In other words, some ways of being, assembling, functioning, expressing, and creating are more enabling than others.

Viewing the world as interacting assemblages at different scales jettisons a hierarchical view of reality. It's not just social fields like education that need a rethink. The biological scales of species, genus, and kingdom are trapped by an outdated nomenclature that offers little to no opportunity to imagine much interaction between these scales. Indeed, general biology education is also in need of a massive overhaul.[20] What gets left out is the way ecological life emerges through interfacing assemblages and their diverse parts and capacities across different scales. Biologists are recognizing this interconnectedness more and more. For any given assemblage there's a relative *macro* and *micro* scale not reducible to the other. Just like an entire watershed is not reducible to the river ecosystems that comprise it. Just like the friendships that exist in a school don't necessarily determine the long-term goals of that school. Teachers cannot really explain what happens in schools using the policy and initiatives produced in government offices, but neither can they explain what is happening at a national or international level in education though the daily practices of one school or classroom.

Assemblages help trace the relationships between parts, wholes, and strata. They make ethical possibilities more visible and help identify those parts and strata, material or discursive, that might stand in the way. Taking an assemblage approach means accepting that the scale of one individual student is just as complex and fascinating as that of an entire school system. Anything else would be a hierarchical ontology. This perhaps explains why older materialisms like Marxism are sometimes unpalatable to critical educators – larger economic realities are seen to always take precedence over matters of intimate personal concern. And while the level of an individual may not seem as important for creating just and sustainable futures, it is largely on this scale that students and teachers conduct their daily lives. The point is not to argue for the inclusion of the individual into systemic analysis, it is to argue for a non-hierarchical ontology. Ecological awareness and survival depend on such ontologies. The way students come to see themselves on a very personal ethical level is completely co-extensive – insidiously or benevolently – with larger governing apparatuses of control. Again, educators and students can map these interrelated assemblages/parts that function together in order to see where opportunities for becoming ethical or becoming different might reside.

An Ethics of Becoming (Minor)

One of the big takeaways of part 2 is that there's ethical potential in free-flowing rhizomatic educational spaces. Ethics goes beyond the question of what we should do to encompass questions of becoming and the enabling of our collective powers. What can make this tricky is that the world is full of many kinds of assemblages. There are times when a rigid plant cell is enabling and a free-flowing aqueous chemical solution is not. Although they did not approach assemblages as an overtly political concept, Deleuze and Guattari drew from Marxist notions of labour and capital flows, and the way they overcode social and ecological life, when creating their concepts. In modern societies of control and domination, the ethical potential of schools as enabling free-flowing assemblages is not difficult to see.[21] The intention of Deleuze and Guattari is to offer a vibrant ontology that shows how difference inevitably and wonderfully emerges in the world. Difference is vital to ethics, and educators pursue an ethics of difference when they create spaces for students to become different.

In this context, difference does not refer to how entities are separate. Conversely, it draws on the connections and relations between entities. The differences between a car and its driver, a host and its symbiont, and a pollinator and a flower all rely on their respective relations. Difference is a foundational concept that nurtures relationships, which doesn't mean there can't be distinctions.[22] Differences for Deleuze are not transcendent. There are no fixed or eternal differences between entities. Rather, differences are immanent here and now in relationships. They do not pre-exist entities but emerge alongside them. The ontological planes in figure 6.1 illustrate differences emerging in ways that emphasize the *intensive relationships* between them. In this way difference is productive and infinite. But what is even more fascinating about difference is that it continually emerges in the world regardless of whether it is desired or intended. Geology, art, technology, and evolution all demonstrate this continual emergence of difference.

Differences, as defined by their intensive relationships, are important because they drive natural/social processes.[23] For example, intensive differences in pressure and temperature drive weather, and differences in personality and desire drive friendships and erotic relationships. Without difference there would be a blank uniformity. A kind of death. Drawing from Henry Bergson's notion of time, Deleuze suggests that difference is *the* fundamental ontological aspect of our world. Difference emerges in the present moment such that the emergence of each thing and each moment is in some kind of relation to all past moments and things coming before. The relation between different moments and things changes in intensity as different moments unfold and different things emerge in an ever-changing present. Difference is therefore *repeated* in every given moment. It is the one thing that can always be counted on. It could be said, then, that all beings are in processes of becoming-in-relation, but on varying time scales and relational planes of emergence.

The implication of this view of difference for ethics is profound. Ethics, as a form of being, becomes something that's always emerging and differing. Ethics can never be universalized. Rather, it is something that emerges in relation to particular sociomaterial circumstances and histories, acknowledging that it's possible for some ethical forms to endure the life of a species or even a geological age. This means that trying to discern an overall "best" ethical way of being is futile. Let's again take the Old Testament Bible as an example. Even if we hold that its messages are eternal and universal, throughout the scriptures we see the intensive relations to Mosaic law change. The advent of Islam and Christianity is a good example, whereby different relationships to the Old Testament emerge. Beyond this, monotheistic morality itself has changed throughout the centuries. For example, some liberal Catholic institutions and doctrines would be virtually unthinkable two hundred years ago. Of course, ethical ways of being from the past are still relevant to present circumstances. The point is simply that ethics is intimately tied to the fact that difference continually emerges in the world. The ethics needed in education today involves enabling different forms of life through experimentation and creativity. Not because change is ontologically superior, but because difference is simply the ecological state of affairs. It enables, not for its own sake but as a nurturing of our collective powers beyond the human.

One of the primary goals of part 2 is to demonstrate how ethics is entangled with how things exist and to confront the idea of absolute ethical progress as well as multiply ethical possibilities to meet the dire challenges of the Anthropocene. A silver lining to the ecological crisis is that it has made ethical entanglement more visible to modern humans. A more rhizomatic ethics, one that seeks to connect, would enable different forms of symbiosis and a multiplicity of beings, things, ideas, and feelings to come forth in nurturing ways. Ethics must bring together various forms of the commons that enable difference to come forth temporally, materially, expressively, spiritually, bodily, ideologically, and so on. This kind of ethics might also be called an ethics of *becoming*.

Since ethics, just like any assemblage, doesn't exist outside of emergent historical and material contexts it perhaps should be seen as something that "works" – or not. Ethics is in the doing. This might seem bewildering because it would mean that ethics is both highly context-specific and extremely broad in that it could emerge differently from an infinite number of assemblages. This point about the specificity and breadth of ethics was made in part 1, except now we've thrown nonhuman material entities into the mix. Add to this a sense of ambiguity that arises from the continual co-articulation of rigid and free-flowing assemblages. The world is a strange place where tight, arborescent structures give rise to rhizomatic becomings, and where these becomings often establish structures that overcode and govern (through genetic code, language, and other material strata).[24] The only arbiter that can tell us the value of an ethics is how these assemblages enable or disable multiple forms of social and biological life.

Dwayne Donald reminds us to bring difference to the foreground as an "addition" process. Instead of introducing chasms, difference demonstrates "how our futures as peoples in the world are tied together."[25] According to Donald, there is nothing outside the context of ethical relations historically, socially, biologically, materially, or conceptually. If this is true it's incumbent on educators to keep expanding the boundaries of ethics and relationality. An ethics of becoming seeks to *become minor*. For Deleuze and Guattari, becoming doesn't involve being "folded" into the majority "as majority." Majority identities and ethics are part of the stratified material and expressive components that control and codify. To become minor requires dropping a majoritarian identity. The following are just a few aspects of what an ethics of becoming might entail.

Lose the Self! (at Least One Part of It)

As discussed in chapter 5, taking a line of flight to become different involves maximizing the immanent possibilities that exist here and now. Since there's no transcendental dimension, all possibilities are only realizable through the connections and capacities of assemblages, including the affective and virtual. The mathematical expression Deleuze and Guattari employ for this is $n-1$, where n is all immanent possibilities/dimensions and the -1 is the unique what or who that something or someone has been already subtracted from these possibilities. Subtracting what overcodes, what something or someone has been, or the very idea of the unique, is the only way to get from one to a multiplicity. Becoming means that something of the former or majority identity gets lost. An ethics of becoming would allow students and teachers to question the ossified identities, ethics, and ways of understanding ourselves that are no longer tolerable.

Deleuze and Guattari's use the orchid and the wasp as classic examples of hybridity and becoming, where we see the wasp-as-pollinator and the orchid-as-wasp-mimic. The assemblage created by the orchid and wasp is a symbiotic becoming space where both orchid and wasp increase each other's valence of possibility and become other. This example demonstrates the double articulation of deterritorialization and territorialization and their strange inseparability. The orchid and the wasp are an assemblage of heterogeneous parts, coded by DNA, bee communications, and the chemical signals of flowers.[26] The plant gains new vectors of life (new lines of flight and becomings) through the pollinating wasps. The wasps engage in eusocial behaviour, thanks to the orchid, that helps them to establish new relations with their environment (lines of flight and becomings). The wasp and the flower become together symbiotically: each entity increases the valence, powers, and possibilities of the other resulting in new hymenopteran communities and angiosperm gene flow. For educational communities, becoming different means shedding the identity of the dominant majority and engaging in mutual becomings. A first step is to shed that one dimension ($n-1$) that holds a destructive identity defined by a majority. A next step is to map lines of flight and movements of deterritorialization and reterritorialization as assemblages.

Make Maps!

Find ethical potentials. Take those *n-1* dimensions. Draw them. Diagram them. What are the material-discursive parts and capacities immanent in a particular assemblage? How bound up are they? What are the possibilities for flight and deterritorialization? How do discourse and language code the assemblage? As students and teachers become involved with social and ecological matters of concern, they can map how various parts fit together and see where ethico-political possibility lies. These maps are dynamic because they refuse to let a topic, issue, community, or question be put to rest. They extend the boundaries and elucidate (potential) relationships. Of course these maps will change as relationships change and different parts and capacities are introduced on micro and macro scales. These maps are inclusive because rigid structures and tracings, "old maps" that are unchangeable, can also be placed as points on a dynamic assemblage map. The goal is to add, relate, revise, and connect, to discover where ethical potential might reside, how beings might be enabled, as well as how ethics emerges alongside phenomena.

Figure 6.4 is an example of an assemblage of the politics of HIV transmission and is meant to show how an ethics might begin to emerge around a material assemblage.[27]

The parts of this assemblage consist of bodies that are categorized as sick/disposable, healthy/safe, queer/deviant, or straight/normalized. Add to this the chemical compounds and pharmaceuticals that interact with cell mechanisms, bodily fluids, and strains of the human immunodeficiency retrovirus. The parts also include the contact zones, neighbourhoods, and nations where bodies, both oppressed and oppressors, are entangled. How does the production of capital actively work to put some bodies at risk and make others well? Drawing out potential ethical engagements means taking all these entities into consideration without asserting an a priori to ethics around HIV transmission. How is an ethics of health and safety linked to the constitution of safe and risky bodies? What would an "ethics of protection" look like, and how might this look different, depending on how the social and ecological entities are assembled? The COVID-19 pandemic has made these particular ethical and political questions around viruses, humans, and protection pressing even for "safe" and protected bodies (e.g., white, middle-class, straight).

134 Ethics as Ontological Exploration

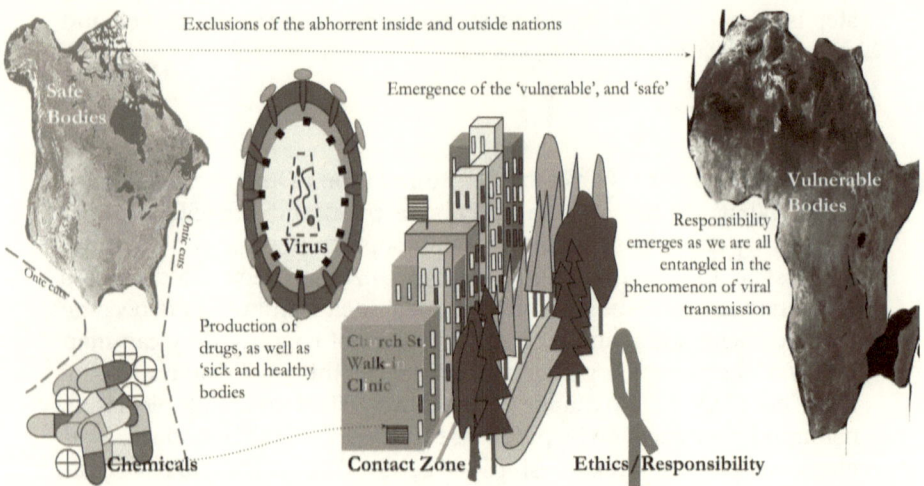

Figure 6.4. Politics of HIV transmission as assemblage.

Look for Intensities and Their Gradients!

Perhaps the best part about intensity as an ethical concept is that it very easily exceeds the confines of anthropocentrism. As suggested above in relation to difference, intensities have to do with the conditions of potential change. They can involve love, climate systems, and revolutions. They arise when there are large gradient differences which create *zones of intensity*. The intensive borders to these zones are different than the *extensive* borders that contain entities. This is similar to the way physics differentiates intensive and extensive properties. Intensive properties are indivisible. For example, density is an intensive property. If you take some matter in a particular state (solid, liquid, or gas), with a particular density, and divide it in two, the intensive property (in this case density) remains the same. Intensities and intensive properties cannot be added but averaged.

This is not just relevant for thermodynamics but also for setting the conditions or atmosphere for becoming different. Zones of intensity for an ethics of becoming would resemble the building of a threshold. These thresholds would not be defined by spatial limits per se, through extensive properties, but by critical *thresholds*. For ethical-social actors these intensive thresholds are important, because they drive processes.

Diversity, an educational buzzword for the past twenty-five years or more, is something that's traditionally been marked and measured by extensive differences. The differences between people and their cultures from a traditional diversity standpoint are clear identarian markers. And while these markers of difference are important for both practical and socio-historical reasons, traditional conceptions of diversity may indicate only what has already changed in the past. Diversity as extensive difference, such as that describing a distinct cultural identity, does not necessarily tell us about what actually drives or facilitates difference and becoming different.

In 2016 I had the honour of participating in a panel discussion entitled "Rethinking Education for Citizenship" at Haigazian University in Beirut, Lebanon. This was amid heavy fighting in neighbouring Syria and the movement of hundreds of thousands of people into Lebanon (the total number would eventually reach around 1.5 million). I'm not any kind of authority on the Syrian conflict or the migrant populations arising from it. Most of what I know comes from mainstream media, friends, and my host on that memorable trip, Hagop Yacoubian. That conflict, along with the Lebanese civil war, were faintly present over the course of the visit. Talk of these conflicts regularly entered our conversations about how science education could be integral to citizenship education. How were educators supposed to focus on issues of citizenship when a war was raging near the Lebanese border?

The conflict created multiple intensities that influenced the ethical-political questions we were trying to ask. The extensive differences of nationality, religion, class, gender, ethnicity, and political affiliation mattered among the teachers we were working with. But in terms of trying to engage issues of ethical importance, these extensive differences mattered only insofar as they were directly related to the geopolitical and ecological intensities in the region. It would have, in fact, been easier to focus on the extensive aspects of conflict, such as migration patterns, nominal differences of religion and ethnicity; and the geographic borders set by those wielding power, which in the case of Syria include European colonial powers. That is, it would have been easier to imagine an ethics of boundaries, permissions, quotas, protocols, finance, penalties, and the categories of "them and us." But an ethics that focuses too much on extensive properties may be one reason why ethical solutions to conflicts are so difficult. If only approached from a legal-juridical-majority (identarian) perspective, ethical questions of being and becoming can't be engaged. How might ethics change if educators and their students paid more attention to the intensive trauma of conflict as well as the joys of connection and peace?

Table 6.1 contrasts a few intensive and extensive differences inherent to modern conflicts. The point is not that intensive differences are

Table 6.1. Contrasting extensive and intensive differences of war.

Extensive Differences	Intensive Differences
Nominal cultural, linguistic, ethnic, religious, and political affiliations	Experiences of trauma and safety
National borders set by colonial and geopolitical powers	The building of solidarity
Numbers of casualties and migrants	Impacts of war on ecological and social landscapes

more important but that *both* intensive and extensive differences are vital considerations for solutions to conflict and ethical-political issues. Obviously, these differences are interrelated and only a suggestive beginning, but they point to this forgotten intensive dimension.

When I facilitated a teaching workshop to discuss "socioscientific" issues with teachers across Beirut, both extensive and intensive differences guided our discussions. The garbage crisis of 2016 was used as an example of a local socioscientific issue that involved multiple stakeholders; these included government officials, neighbourhood organizations, health officials, and nonhuman actors such as decomposers and scavengers.[28] However, I soon found out that the teachers were somewhat distressed at the prospect of discussing this issue because of the different political and religious affiliations among teachers and students in Beirut. Many teachers in that room had a specific relationship to the garbage crisis based on their ethnic-religious-political group identity. In short, those extensive differences stultified discussions about the crisis because, as it was patiently explained to me, some teachers were uncomfortable confronting other teachers' positions. So, besides the extensive differences between teachers, the intensive differences, how they felt about the garbage crisis and the new solidarities they wanted to form, were also important to engaging the crisis. At the end of the workshop there was a mix of solidarity, frustration, and desire to find a solution. The war in Syria spilled into our conversations because talking about the garbage strike, the right to clean water, and disease-free living is directly related to the fact that, at the time, public schools in Lebanon were accommodating over two hundred thousand Syrian refugee children.

Educators might consider how these intensive differences and thresholds, along with the practical considerations of numbers, affiliations, and borders, have intensities of their own. Obviously, it would be a mistake to think that intensive and extensive differences can be easily separated. Once intensities pass productive thresholds of change these changes can be labelled and then become identifiable as extensive differences.

Become Minor!

Becoming minority can be viewed as a subversion of the majority because it requires subtracting some part of the self that prevents becoming. Setting up spaces for becoming minor through education means that, on a basic level, teachers and schools shouldn't demand that particular languages, cultures, and expressions of gender and sexuality be the only ways to exist in our shared world. The possibilities for becoming (minor) are directly related to our discussion of assemblages and schooling. Tightly bound and rigid assemblages don't give enough room for movement or deterritorialization. They reterritorialize things, like different ways of thinking and acting that try to escape these confines. The creation of different ways of being is vital to surviving the Anthropocene. Schools that don't enable this becoming may be implicated as part of the problem regardless of how badly we need to train people for careers. An ethics of becoming (minor) through education is an ontological and material concern; it cannot be addressed without deep consideration of how nonhuman and nonliving things are in the world.

In their book *Kafka: Toward a Minor Literature*, Deleuze and Guattari take up the political fiction of Franz Kafka, whose stories revolve around the confines of twentieth-century bureaucracy, the rigid use of language and culture, and the subsequent alienation resulting from institutional coercion and control.[29] In Kafka's novel *The Trial*, the protagonist Joseph K is charged with a crime. But K cannot determine what aspect of the law, or which corresponding bureau, has actually been defied.[30] The irony is that none of the bureaus or their agents really know either. Kafka's fiction is better thought of as a series of assemblages that "do things" rather than a series of significations. It is a text assemblage with many exits and entrances – perhaps suggesting that literature and politics are "doorways" even when the powers that be don't allow people to see them as such.

The implication for educators is that often the possible "entrances and exits" of things, of social institutions, knowledge, art, or environments, are not absolute. At any point an entire apparatus of control might not understand what it's doing. There's always room for thought and flight within a classroom because totalizing power is impossible. A door, a line of flight, can potentially be created anywhere – even when we are up against a brick wall like Joseph K. To put it in the language of assemblages, any assemblage can be loosened, decoded, and reconnected. Thus it's always only one or two steps away from some sort of deterritorialization. For educators, a big source of hope comes from knowing that a different way of being, thinking, acting, and writing is always possible.

An Ethics beyond Humans (Thus Far)

At this point it might be useful to review some of the points made about an ethics that moves beyond human subjectivity to consider nonhumans. Such an ethics involves ontological exploration of what's possible and how we might become (different and minor). Ethics, as a set of relations or acts of becoming, emerges in assemblages of material and discursive components, and therefore changes with an infinite number of ecological and social contexts. So, what are some of the ideas about an ethics beyond human subjectivity that educators might move forward with? So far, part 2 of this book has made the following general points:

1 Ethics as different ways of being continually emerges. Just like difference continually emerges biologically, geologically, and socially. Human life, like all life, is always in a state of becoming different.[31]
2 Although ethics is essential to education and human existence it does not just involve humans but the wider ecological and material world. Assemblages are one way of conceiving these world(s).
3 Ethics involves ontological consideration of "how things are." How things exist, how they might continue to exist, and how new ways of being are enabled are urgent ethical questions.
4 Ethics is immanent to every assemblage. When working with the concept of assemblages, educators should avoid working with things that cannot be networked into assemblages as material or discursive parts.
5 Ethics comprises experimentation with how entities and their capacities interface. Ethical experimentation is one response to biopower, which already dictates lines of appropriate ethical response.
6 Ethics cannot be solely located in a human subject or subjects – but neither does it reside within any one part of an assemblage. Ethics emerges in assemblages with varying histories, capacities, and scales.
7 Ethics from a sociomaterial perspective is measured by its enabling and nurturing capacity. According to Spinoza, ethics should

be evaluated by how it works to enhance our powers or diminish them.
8 Ethical powers are enhanced by positive and just relations with the nonhuman inhabitants of the world here and now. There is no external transcendent authority for ethics.

For Elizabeth Grosz, ethics will always be an all-encompassing, uncertain aspect of life. As Grosz puts it: "The question of ethics is how can I be worthy of the events that await me, how can I enter into events that sweep me up, pre-exist me, or that I cannot control?"[32] The ethics outlined by assemblages are affirmative in that they work to enhance what bodies, including nonhuman and nonliving bodies, can do in assembly with each other. For Grosz, the act of living and becoming is art, because inventing an ethos or a way of living in assembly with others requires imagination and creativity.

A material ethics of becoming calls on educators and students to seek ways of being that do not yet exist. It is at this boundary between aesthetics and ethics that this chapter on assemblages, and our use of Deleuze and Guattari's work, ends. The next chapter explores how education might consider the aesthetic dimension when it comes to thinking differently about our shared worlds.

7 Aesthetics and Environmentality

Art is thought from the future. Thought we cannot explicitly think at present. Thought we may not think or speak at all. If we want thought different from the present, then we must veer toward art.

– Timothy Morton[1]

According to that map in the preface we've come a long way in our discussion of ethics and education. Some might say we've gone too far! But sometimes teachers need to intentionally change their surroundings, to seek strange ideas. While part 1 focused on ethical subjectivity and reflexivity, part 2 has, so far, focused on a sociomaterial ethics of becoming different. Part 2 is reaching for an ethics that exceeds human subjectivity. Ethics is something that emerges within material-discursive assemblages, something that exceeds human-human relations. An ethics that takes nonhuman entities into account is more appropriate for the extinctions and social inequalities of the Anthropocene. Changing how we live in the world, who we might become, and how we exist in relation with nonhuman and nonliving entities involves social, political, ecological, and cultural change. However, changing how we live ethically also involves fundamental changes at the level of *aesthetics*.

As with ethics, it's best to approach a complex topic like aesthetics in a simple way. Aesthetics comprises that which can be sensed – heard, felt, seen, tasted, and so on. Along with what can be sensed, aesthetics also includes what is *sensible*. Educational research and practice have paid little attention to aesthetics outside arts education and educational philosophy.[2] The aesthetic dimension is a crucial consideration for ethics because it mediates the possible encounters necessary for becoming different. Aesthetics becomes more important when ethics becomes less about moral edicts and more about nurturing different relations with the world and its inhabitants. This chapter continues to explore ethics through explorations in ontology, or "how things are." Since reality is often strange and more complex than it appears it's necessary to examine the aesthetic dimension as an essential part of ethics in the Anthropocene. While aesthetics is easy to understand in a general sense it's still a hard subject to wrap your head around. It consists of everything noticeable or sensible, but also entails the how, what, and why something comes to our attention. Aesthetics is not just important for artists and interior decorators – it's also important for those involved in social, political, and ethical change.

To think about aesthetics, I'll be relying on the thought of Jacques Rancière and Timothy Morton. Timothy Morton's work was introduced to me by Valerie Triggs, a sensational artist and professor at the University of Regina. When she told me that her course on the Anthropocene and Feminism didn't attract a single student I was convinced that she was doing something right (like not compromising on a course title!). After that, I regularly tried to find out what she was reading and why. Sometimes the best reasons were random ones: "I found this book in the recycling." The ideas Valerie introduced cast things like ethics and environmental justice as "not-yet thought" or "not-yet assembled." That is, consisting of what Morton calls "thought from the future."[3] Besides considering nonhumans, an ethics for the Anthropocene needs to draw on a more sensuous and pleasurable reality, one that outcompetes consumerism. Cultivation of an interest in art and aesthetics is sorely needed among science educators to effect the kind of social and ecological transformation needed today.[4]

The shape this chapter will take is as follows. First, I'll discuss the importance of aesthetics using the work of philosopher Jacques Rancière and some examples from science fiction. Science fiction and potentially all art expand what is sensible, and therefore what is ethically and politically possible. After that, I will move into aspects of Timothy Morton's "dark" ecological thinking, a mode of thought which cultivates a sensitivity to the aesthetic dimension, and its implications for ethics and education.

Politics and the "Sensible"

One of the questions I'd periodically ask Valerie was "What exactly *is* the aesthetic?" Valerie would then do something like throw her hands up and say, "Who knows!?" Through our discussions Valerie and I came to agree on three points. First, a simple definition suffices as a beginning: we could say that aesthetics involves everything seen and sensed.

Second, aesthetics also involves a domain of causality and possibility, and if one tries to think through these it often becomes overwhelming and debilitating. It's difficult to grasp the aesthetic precisely because it encompasses everything. Valerie and I agreed on one final thing, that one of the only things people can do is hope to have experiences that allow them to become aware of the aesthetic fabric of experience and reality. That is, to be able to say "All right! I'm having quite an experience!" in one way or another.

Art provokes an encounter with the aesthetic. Labour, too, is an aesthetic experience as far as it involves those intense moments when we realize that somehow time is passing differently and we are here, now, doing this work. But, as Valerie pointed out to me, this experience is fleeting. Any aesthetic experience can only be grasped momentarily. Art, literature, and environmental education might be the best starting points for sparking student awareness of the aesthetic, and of its domain of possibility and causality. That is, any domain that relies more on sensibility, feeling, and affect, and less on systematic thinking or empiricism. Of course all disciplines and domains rely on all of these things to some extent.

It's easy for educators to embrace platitudes. I've recycled many over the decades. We often feel a special responsibility to try and be on the "right side" of things. Adopting short indisputable soundbites, slogans, or factoids becomes very appealing. One problem with platitudes and soundbites, however, is that they often empty the wonder and complexity from acting, thinking, and creating. Art is often made banal or innocuous with phrases like "Art is everywhere!" or "All art is political!" While art is always co-extensive with politics, art and politics are nonetheless different. Politics, as far as its emancipatory potential goes, involves dissensus in the name of equality. In other words, it's something specific. It's not anything that has to do with a governing apparatus like the military or a legislative body. According to Rancière, art is political when it disrupts the domain of the sensible in the name of equality.[5] When it creates dissensus such that those who didn't count now come to count equally. All art carries this potential to disrupt and be involved in political dissensus.

Chapter 5 opened with a short discussion of Haruki Murakami's fiction, and when I was writing about his work I was unsure of its appropriateness to the important topics at hand. But fiction – what I sometimes call "real books" (to the aggravation of my academic colleagues) – is the main reason I became interested in academic work in the first place. Fiction helps me take the world of ideas more seriously, which makes sense considering that the dividing line between nonfiction and fiction is a socio-historical construction. Stories have the power to ignite everyday experience, and attachments to the wider world need this igniting power. Speaking of the Western tradition, the power of fiction increases dramatically with the introduction of the modern novel. The immanent creative powers of modernity enable "novel" thought to reside in the infinite arrangements of words. With the embrace of fiction texts can more easily deviate from a rigid canon. Modern literature, for all its problems with whiteness, maleness, colonialism, and Anglocentrism, has arguably made it more possible to take a line of flight away from authority and tradition towards becoming different.

Literature nurtures various becomings through its *literarity*: the infinite interplay of text, affect, and meaning. A text is more about what it does than its perceived meaning. There is no necessary a priori to literature. This doesn't mean that modernity is not also problematic and destructive. The controlling forces of modernity have a way of categorizing art and literature, dividing it into set histories, types, and hierarchies. We need to be critical of the way modernity puts things in boxes, and has subsequently used literature as a colonizing force. But we also need to recognize our powers of creation against dominant and destructive ways of living and understanding. Modernity acts as both a constitutive and controlling force simultaneously (see chapter 2). Modern fiction is at its best when it nurtures ethical lines of flight towards a new way of being not "coded" by a majority. It can also work politically to disrupt the domain of the sensible in the name of equality.

Jacques Rancière characterizes the changes brought to art through modernity as the "aesthetic regime."[6] What gets eroded in modernity is the distinction between art and "real" life. Art can arise anywhere "artists" decide (art being another thing that loses some of its a priori qualifications). Yet, for Rancière, art still preserves a unique place in the realm of aesthetic experience. There is still today some distinction between art and non-art. And between art and life. Postmodernism, however, erodes this distinction between art and life. The idea that a candy wrapper could be a piece of art is a quintessential example of a postmodern trope: put anything on the table and "Look ... art!" Yet postmodernism re-establishes the idea that art has no a priori by challenging the categories of modernity. What counts as art remains an unanswerable question in postmodernism.

What does it mean for art, and by extension aesthetic experience, to have no a priori? One implication is that no singular image, such as a religious icon or a classical building, can contain or overcode art and aesthetic experience. Any story can be told in any way by any artist. Rancière's historical analysis of the arts helps us see that art and aesthetic experience can be anything. Rancière's work also helps educators realize that aesthetics is less about beauty and more about possibility. It reveals an essential link between aesthetics, what can be seen and sensed, and politics. This is why attention to aesthetics is vital for sociopolitical transformation – redrawing the lines of the sensible so that those who have not been considered equally can come to be regarded equally. The materials educators use, the way they structure learning, where learning happens, and what is evoked comprise the conditions of ethical and political possibility.[7] It's never just about what an educator says or the content of a class.

Politics always comes with an aesthetics that casts its possibilities. A workers' strike will have its picket signs, aspirational slogans, arrangements of bodies in solidarity (picket lines), and empty work sites that all help set the stage for a different, more equitable, collective agreement. An aesthetic that recasts what can be sensed or imagined enables a redrawing of the socio-political order. Octavia Butler's science fiction, for example, helps create new sensibilities for exploring oppressive power relations through the sexuality/sexualization of Black women as cast by/through the institutions of slavery and white supremacy.[8] A change in what can be seen and sensed always accompanies political change. This aesthetic space, which is at once a more-than-human space, gives the first semblance of socio-political possibility. Politics and aesthetics are therefore co-extensive – which means that details matter because they quite often *are* the change. Fiction can be political because of the material circumstances (actual or virtual) that bleed through its imagery allow it to recast what is possible or thinkable. Indigenous and Black science fiction and futurisms offer educators a way to shift what is visible and thinkable if white supremacy and colonialism were to disappear.[9] Political change, along with the ethical ways of being that accompany it, involves remaking and reimagining the social and material fabric of daily life.[10]

There's always a particular aesthetics at play in the pedagogies, environments, and communications of everyday educational life. Some of this is already visible or sensible in the everyday experience of students – from chemistry labs to city parks. Yet it's often the case that pedagogies that disrupt things like Eurocentrism, capitalism, white supremacy, or patriarchy are not recognized as equally legitimate or deemed a waste of time.[11] It is up to the artist, or educator-as-artist, to paint a different landscape. Rancière puts it this way:

> What the artist does is weave a new sensory fabric by tearing percepts and affects out of the perceptions and affections that constitute the fabric

of ordinary experience ... human beings are tied together by a certain sensory fabric ... a certain distribution of the sensible, which defines their way of being together and politics is about the transformation of the sensory fabric of "being together" ... The artistic "voice of the people" is the voice of the people to come.[12]

A huge task for educators looking to nurture just collective futures is to find ways to transgress the boundaries of the sensible.[13] Deliberately turning to art, fiction, affect, and aesthetics, especially in fields that have tended to consider these unworthy of serious attention, is one way to shift what is thinkable and doable in education. Helping students imagine another world arguably does more to shift ecological awareness than yet another lesson about what individuals can do to reduce their carbon footprint in a capitalist economy.

Fiction reimagines relationships between bodies and shared space. A certain kind of equality emerges when signs and sentences are freed on a page that potentially anyone could read – which is why open access is essential. Fiction doesn't just recast the lines of a community; it also recasts what counts as a story. It often breaks free of those compulsory attachments to singular stories, for example those held in place by fundamentalist religious institutions that would ban or censor books. And although fiction often communicates a certain view or aspiration for a society it is simultaneously not beholden to the social order or strata of the day. Art and fiction today are less about social order and divine representation and more about heterogeneity and change. For Rancière, art determines its own specificity to its process and production, unlike in the past when more importance was placed on reproducing a religious order and symbolism. This doesn't mean that dubious things like colonialism and heteronormativity don't influence, or even dominate, art and its modes of creation today. The point is that art carries a heterogeneous power that allows it to take a line of flight away from the social order of the day (strata). This means that any "rules" that arise for making or thinking about art will eventually be transgressed. Art today has this uncanny ability of pulling the rug out from under whatever intelligibility existed before. And in this way – as Valerie Triggs insists – it gives us momentary access to that causal aesthetic dimension.

Another crucial point to make about art and modernity is that it's not just art that changes over time. Life in relation to art also changes. This happens when people become freer to live differently due to realizations or changes that may occur through aesthetic experiences.[14] Art, perhaps especially fiction, asks two powerful questions: What can be experienced in the world and who might experience it? The perspectives of writers other than middle-class white males are thus essential for ecological survival, racial justice, and truth and reconciliation with Indigenous peoples. Having a limited canon of literature, which purposely limits the aesthetic horizon, only impoverishes our shared worlds.

For Rancière, politics first plays out virtually beyond already known roles, procedures, and distributions, helping students and educators to imagine a community not bound to one historical, social, or ecological moment.[15] To imagine just beyond what is sensible or thinkable.[16] A novel or poem or song is more about what it makes students think and less about how important we educators think it is. In this way, it would be a huge mistake to assume that Margaret Atwood's writing is more interesting and relevant than student fiction. Especially if the overall goal of fiction is to stretch imagination. Instead of overly praising a piece of fiction for its perceived significance and erudition, educators might instead turn towards the larger horizon of literarity, that infinite plane of thought that fiction inspires in students. One big lesson of art and fiction – one that *Harold and the Purple Crayon* illustrates (discussed in chapter 5) – is that there's virtually an infinite number of relations possible between signs and things, between language and light. And likewise, a big ethical lesson for educators is that ethical becoming, a line of flight, is always possible.

Science Fictions and Strange Fabulations

Donna Haraway calls on all strange and wonderful beings to "stay with the trouble" in times of ecological precarity.[17] This involves (re)telling multispecies stories – and telling many older stories differently. Haraway refers to the weaving of science fiction, scientific fact, speculative fabulations, speculative feminism, and futurisms as *string figures* (SF).[18] String figures are an appeal to the unruly ways stories about our world need to be (re)told. As Haraway explains, "SF is storytelling and fact telling; it is the patterning of possible worlds and possible times, material-semiotic worlds, gone, here, and yet to come."[19] Haraway's writing invokes a multiplicitous "we." A we-as-muck or we-as-earth-humus kind of collective. Where new worlds decompose and recompose in relations of loving care. Haraway invokes the notion of kin to break down the organic/inorganic dichotomy and include all beings that connect through lines of descent and possibility, from sea urchins to pigeons to pieces of string. Indeed, Haraway's work provokes a visceral encounter with the aesthetic dimension.[20] According to Haraway we're all cyborgs – posthuman beings who transgress the artificial boundaries between the human and nonhuman. Haraway's cyborgs share the planet with the "Chthonic ones" – unwieldy and persistent creatures who revel in the muck and create worlds yet to come.[21] These beings, perhaps us, tell science fiction stories about living and dying in compromised and contaminated worlds. Teachers and students just have to find them, (re)create them, and listen.

In my science and environmental education classes I try to make sure science fiction makes a memorable appearance. There's a lot to say about this genre, but the number one reason I find it useful is for its dystopic, utopic, anti-colonial and anti-capitalist imaginary. It actually *is* possible to imagine worlds without white supremacy or economic exploitation. And it's important for students to not only know this but picture it themselves. The "ah-ha!" moment comes when students make that leap back to the present and realize that the world, no matter how "stuck" it seems, is historically contingent and changeable. It would be helpful to go through a few examples of science fiction that potentially disrupt the domain of the sensible through their otherworldly fabrications. The three pieces are *Binti: The Complete Trilogy*, by Nnedi Okorafor; the short film *Wakening*, written by Tony Elliot and directed by Danis Goulet; and *Psychopompolis*, by Erin Jane Nelson. What I hope to show is how each work makes a significant break with what's sensible and thinkable.

Wakening *(Danis Goulet/Tony Elliot)*

Wakening, a short film by Danis Goulet (director) and Tony Elliot (writer), was a highlight of the 2013 Toronto International Film Festival.[22] It was inspired, in part, by the grassroots Indigenous activist movement Idle No More.[23] The film could be said to be part of growing movement known as Indigenous futurisms – art which imagines various futures for Indigenous peoples and their kin with vivid connections to the past and present. Indigenous futurisms extend the past into the future while offering insightful commentary on the lived present. They also retell past stories, sacred or otherwise, in different ways in order to make them "live" in/with the present. Indigenous futurisms disrupt a normative sense of futurity based on settler colonialism. They show that what has been deeply inscribed in everyday discourse as permanent, like the taken-for-granted idea that white settlers will continue to dominate or exist in North American, can change. For centuries white settlers mistakenly thought First Nations people would eventually disappear. What seems permanent can change.

Wakening illustrates what life has been like for First Nations, Metis, and Inuit peoples in Canada since European colonization by depicting

Figure 7.1. A depiction of Toronto occupied by a late twenty-third-century imperial army in the film *Wakening* (shot near present-day Yonge-Dundas Square). Still from ViDDYWELL FiLMS (2013).

a twenty-third-century imperial power terrorizing and invading the city of Toronto (see figure 7.1). The colonizing force has confined the remaining Indigenous and non-Indigenous people of the city to a literal theatre of images that plays nonstop propaganda (the film was shot in the Elgin and Winter Garden Theatres in Toronto). The protagonist, a Cree hero/trickster figure called Weesageechak, is searching for the spiritual creature *Weetigo* to aid the resistance to this new colonizing force.

Goulet makes the future clash and cohere with the past and present, for example, by blaring racist language from Canada's Indian Act over loudspeakers in the streets of dystopian Toronto. The merging of past, present, and future helps create a rupture in the sensibility of everyday life today in that occupation and oppression *is* everyday life for many Indigenous people today. *Wakening* invites viewers to "wake up" to how absent the (de)colonial narrative has been in mainstream media and science fiction.

Wakening breaks with the sensible not simply by imagining a different future but by highlighting the truth that colonialism is far from over. There's no real future for humankind until the forces that produce things like settler colonialism are faced collectively and spiritually. And it's not just a critical human consciousness that needs to awaken but a spiritual faith in nonhuman beings.[24] A disruption of the sensible in the name of equality can only happen when space is made for Indigenous voices at all levels of creative production.

When I've shown *Wakening*, and its sequel, *The Hunt*,[25] in teacher education classes the general response is usually, "Cool, but what?" Most students needed to engage in discussion about the way science fictions and futurisms shift what seems possible. They've needed encouragement in making interpretations or comments about the film, a process which sometimes resulted in suggestions for sequels and prequels. This discussion time was valuable and necessary – after all, a whole new world was just presented to them! I've found that film is one of the best ways to reconfigure what can be sensed or thought because its images are readily apparent and visceral.

Psychopompolis *(Erin Jane Nelson)*

Psychopompolis, by Erin Jane Nelson, is a visually stunning multi-piece installation of science fiction currently housed at the Document Gallery in Chicago.[26] The name is fun to say. In Greek, psycho-pomp means "soul guide," and in *Psychopompolis* humans encounter a species that takes on this role. The short piece of fiction included in *Psychopompolis* is an ambivalent narrative of hope and survival.[27] In a post-apocalyptic world where humans fight over scarce resources, bizarre sea creatures take it upon themselves to create new forms of collective life that are both joyful and eerie. Climate change has acidified the oceans, and the response from the cephalopods (octopuses and squids) is to create a life-affirming group intelligence to intercede in the activities of humans. Nelson's strange zoological creatures consist of tentacles, eyes, noses, flowers, brains, and mouths (see figure 7.2). Assemblages of bodies, intelligences, and feelings of care present a collective transformation of the sensible in the midst of ruination by humans.

While human beings in Nelson's world ravage "their own" through war and exclusion zones, a different, more-than-human love grows below the surface of the oceans. A love given by equal beings, those beautiful cephalopods, who today don't count as such. Figure 7.2 is a screen capture of one of Nelson's *Psychopompolis* tapestries.

What comes to the surface is a different kind of beauty, love, and collective existence. This new love and collectivity are not experienced without a kind of strangeness and fear. However, this fear is preferable

150 Ethics as Ontological Exploration

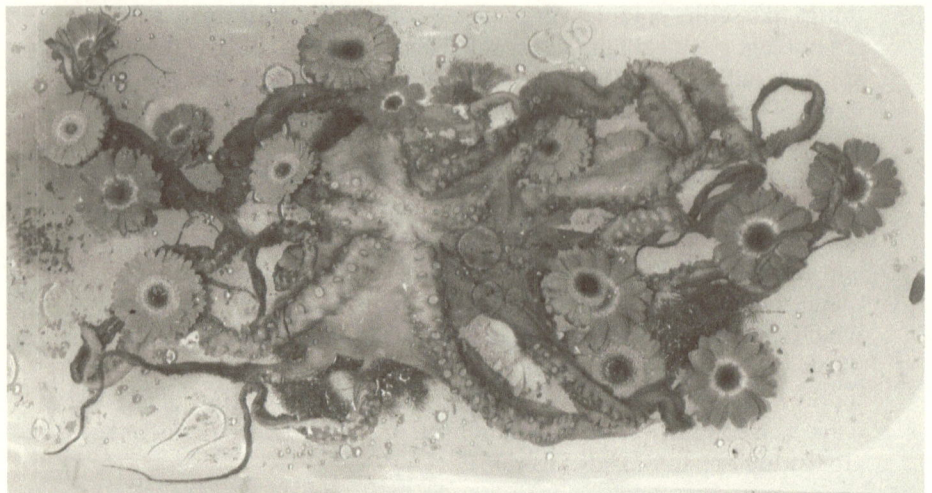

Figure 7.2. Collective life in *Psychopompolis*.

to constant war, deprivation, death, and emptiness. *Psychpompolis* mirrors what many people recognize as an appropriate response to ecological crisis: to (re)experience a wonderful and deep love for the planet and its inhabitants who've shown love for humans all along, in their own ways. Nelson asks an important ethical question in the *Psychopompolis* story: "Why would anyone or anything want to preserve the human species?"[28] Good question. And it's clear that different forms of love and ethics are needed to save countless species from extinction today. Love that can transform the way humans experience empathy, sensory experience, and even their own cognitive processes. *Psychopompolis* shifts our perception of love and agency by stripping intention, aesthetic experience, and love from its anthropocentric prison.

The Binti Trilogy (Nnedi Okorafor)

Nnedi Okorafor's *Binti* trilogy consists of three novels that revolve around young Binti and her lifeworld – an alternative "Africa" thousands of years in the future.[29] The trilogy examines the everyday ethics of family and community life of vastly different interplanetary beings with vastly different histories. This species and the racialized politics of this new Earth and its intergalactic community, while distant, resonate with present-day geopolitics. Binti is a mathematics prodigy of the Himba people, which may or may not be related to the Indigenous Himba peoples of Africa. Binti is on a quest that is both intergalactic and intimately personal, and in this way shows that relations between family, friends, and place are just as important as relations between interplanetary species (in a sense they are one and the same). The worlds depicted by Okorafor bear a striking resemblance to the present in that the war and prejudice between beings, who have much more to share than to fight about, remain nebulous yet surmountable problems. Binti, of her own volition, and pushed by larger forces, is compelled to take a journey of love and sense-making. The question that remains constant throughout the trilogy is, How does someone with both so little and so much power deal with things like interspecies conflict and love?

All three Binti novels outline how some life forms might seek to control others through things like access to knowledge (including a people's own knowledges) and colonization. Okorafor addresses hegemony and colonialism in a way that is accessible to younger readers. A politics of knowledge is brilliantly woven into the story through the prestigious Oomza University, where Binti is confronted with the promise and problems of difference and universalities. Interestingly, through the various racial and ethnic identities and intergenerational migrations there seems to be no entity that could possibly be understood as "white people" – which does not mean there is no embodiment of "whiteness" in the novels. This point is important, because it shows the power of science fiction, and art in general, to virtually redraw the lines of a community. In this case, the idea that white people are automatically guaranteed a futurity when others are not is challenged. Okorafor keeps the reader's mind on an open future and open present simultaneously by flipping the colonial strategy of "whenever it suits, just erase Black, Indigenous, people of colour and their futures." A very clear and necessary disruption to the colonial domain of the sensible is to place African peoples as Earth's hominoid protagonists but in ways that recentre the equality of all beings. This key point of the Binti trilogy is one that is radically democratic and political – a similar positioning could arguably be done with dis/ability, queerness, or nonhumans. That is, there's no more need for white, straight, or neurotypical humans, or humans in general, to be at the centre of our stories about the future.

What I find most pleasurable about the books are the more-than-human characters. More specifically, how they come alive through Binti, who is arguably not really human herself. The integration of the spiritual and material in things like the sacred Himba *Otjize* is particularly interesting. Binti uses this mysterious substance on her body as a medicine and life-giving force; the substance itself has ecological importance because it straddles the living and nonliving in multiple locations of Binti's life. *Otjize* acts as a kind of eternal reminder – a way to recover a lost sensuality. It's this kind of sensing power, an openness to the aesthetic dimension, that's missing from the way some modern humans orient to the planet and its beings.

Science Fiction and Unknowability

Science fiction isn't just for "science nerds" and geeky do-gooders. It's arguably the genre of literature that is most capable of dealing with unknowability, uncanniness, and strange encounters with reality. In this capacity, science fiction serves as a gateway to the final movement of this book, one that grapples with environmental ethics and speculative realism. Most people see science fiction as a creative vision of the future or another world based on the science and social reality of the present. However, literary scholar Brian Willems sees another virtue to science fiction: its unique capacity to outline the ambiguous and unknowable.[30] But why is outlining the unknowable important? One reason is that our shared ecological crisis is itself an uncanny and strange event – something too large and too far-reaching to be fully grasped by science, politics, history, spirituality, or the arts (what Morton calls a *hyperobject*). Only a transdisciplinary approach, like that found in science fiction, can begin to outline some of this unknowability.

Science fiction as a transdisciplinary genre is a unique repository for *dark objects*, objects in a text that resist scientific understanding, future scientific understanding, and even human thought and perception. The contours of dark objects suggest a "world outside" of what humans can sense or think (which is a bit of throwback to the outside of subjectivity discussed in chapter 5). They belong to a world that exists independently of what humans might sense or think about it. With respect to human perception and understanding, dark objects are only theoretically possible since dark objects cannot receive inputs from other objects or systems around them. At least none that humans know about. Their darkness or unknowability is proportional to how detectable their existence is: the more we know about them the more their darkness decreases. The only thing to do in this instance is map their dark contours. Science fiction doesn't just affirm science. It also creates worlds and objects where science "doesn't work." However, this aspect of (some) science fiction also affirms something fundamental about reality. Human knowledge, including scientific knowledge, is predicated on the data we have about things. This knowledge (science) is not to be taken for things in themselves. The presence of objects that resist human perception are important for ecological awareness because they allow us to think outside of anthropocentrism. In other words, ecological awareness requires the ability to think about worlds where humans are not important or necessary.

Science fiction has been more successful than other fantasy genres, in part, because it wields the authority of scientific accuracy as a mode of persuasion.[31] Willems points out that science fiction texts also employ "dark" ambiguous modes of persuasion. Within many of them are moments of inexplicability, the kind that can potentially be explained by science but also that which science can never explain. In other words, situations where humans can only indirectly point at something in an opaque and mysterious way. This kind of "realism" – one that admits that things exist outside human thought and perception – might sufficiently challenge anthropocentrism by restoring the requisite strangeness and wonder to reality. This "speculative" realism, the kind philosopher Graham Harman advocates, assumes that *all* objects have some dark quality to them. This is because something is always lost or "sucked in" (energy, knowability, etc.) when a thing is translated into knowledge or relationships.[32] Pedagogically speaking, embracing this ontological darkness recognizes that there are always recesses of materiality, space, social life, and the mind that are unknowable yet present and "at work" (behind the scenes, so to speak).[33] Derek Ford and Tyson Lewis advocate for a similar kind of unknowability in education – an aesthetic sensibility that is radically open. Such a sensibility would reconnect teachers and students to a heightened sense of participation in collective issues of ethical and political urgency.[34]

This dive into aesthetics and science fiction has been a circuitous way of introducing the relatively new area of philosophical thought called "speculative realisms" that will help guide the final sections of this book. Speculative realisms might be best defined by what they refute. Specifically, they refute the idea that humans can only ever think or perceive things within the correlation between thought and being – between perception and "things in themselves." This idea is known in speculative realism as *correlationism*, which has been part of the dominant Western philosophical view since the eighteenth-century. A primary tenet of correlationism is that a gap exists between things in themselves and knowledge about these things. However, a problem with correlationism is that it relegates all thought and meaning to humans by assuming this gap only exists between humans and everything else. And yet, things existed well before humans were there to think them! This gap exists for all things. Ecological awareness in the

Anthropocene means bending thought and ethics away from anthropocentrism. This means reassessing the idea that humans – their physical being, their thoughts, and their ethics – are essential to this world. In this sense, many modern peoples will need to take strange and winding roads to ecological awareness.

Malfunctioning: A Strange Ethics for the Anthropocene

To be a thing means to malfunction. Beyond relating to other things at all, one's existence is just one continuous mistake.[35]

Timothy Morton

Ecological awareness is not just about alternative energy and electric cars. It encompasses everything from earthworms to electronic equipment – which means we can begin anywhere when teaching about ecological awareness. This should be encouraging for educators who don't see themselves as having much to do with environmentalism or anything ecological. For Timothy Morton, ecological awareness is not about sustainability in terms of finding efficiencies but about becoming aware of unintended consequences. Nothing about the industrial capitalist economies some humans have put in place is sustainable. Ecological awareness means embracing the strangeness of reality. The environmental humanities and the arts offer educators a different take on reality because they enable people to sense things not yet stratified by the social order. That is, they allow teachers and students to sense things that are not totally "thought out" yet. In a way, these thoughts and sensations made possible by the humanities and the arts bring forth what might be called "thought from the future."[36]

All spaces, which include all spaces where education happens, have what Morton calls *environmentality*, or qualities of environment.[37] A wine cellar, prairie valley, and deserted shopping mall are all access points of environmentality for educators. For Morton, humans only really notice things in their environments when they malfunction.[38] Today, the increasing awareness of the disappearance of birds and honeybees, along with the breakdown of atmospheric and economic systems, is directly proportional to how broken they are. Ecological awareness involves noticing things, but often noticing that things aren't functioning quite as expected. It's like the old saying: you don't know what you've got till it's gone (or breaks). The boundary between functioning and malfunctioning is a slippery one. When something is seemingly functioning well a thousand other malfunctions may be happening simultaneously. Human beings will sometimes mask or ignore this malfunctioning, using diversionary concepts like "positive thinking," "personal achievement," "God's plan," and so on.

As we delve deeper into ecological awareness and speculative realisms, some really strange aspects of reality will come to the surface. This is probably typical with any exploration of "how things are" – or how strange and wonderful our shared worlds really are. It may be useful, following Timothy Morton, to start keeping track of these strange aspects of reality.

> *Strange aspect #1. Things often get noticed only when they malfunction.*
> *Strange aspect #2. Everything is constantly malfunctioning.*

Morton's ecological philosophy is critical of those things that prevent the strangeness of reality from breaking through, and in this way takes aim at some of the sacred cows of thought and culture, including the idea of nature itself.

> The environment becomes visible when it malfunctions. You discover radiation in your tissues. You find out you have inhaled some pesticide. But beneath this, it becomes possible to see that the environment is always a kind of "malfunctioning." Furthermore, functioning itself is a kind of malfunctioning. We simply ignore or cover over malfunctioning. The name for this covered over malfunctioning is Nature. But Nature is just a stand-in for the periodic cycling of Earth systems enabled by human agricultural projects of a certain kind designed to minimize diversity and regularize social space. The Fertile Crescent went viral.[39]

The economic systems of the present, built upon ancient human agricultural systems gone viral, have made some humans very rich and powerful and left the rest of the planet incapacitated.[40] These agricultural systems can therefore be seen as a colossal malfunction rather than some quasi-evolutionary stage in human development. The notion of malfunctioning should give educators pause, because for every seamless lesson or curriculum expectation there are millions of malfunctions lurking in the background.

> *Strange aspect #3. Many human systems (not all) are a gigantic malfunction.*

An "ethics of malfunctioning" involves considering functioning and malfunctioning together so that a "functioning" thing would also include (at least hypothetically) its many simultaneous malfunctions. Isn't the existence of corporate CEOs a sort of social-psychotic malfunction?

Are coal-fired power stations not extremely peculiar "carbon" malfunctions? Educators who care and learn from their students understand that even when schooling is functioning it's also malfunctioning. This is another reason why one of the best ethical stances in education is to advocate change all the while understanding that whatever we collectively arrive at will malfunction as well as function. Morton's notion of malfunctioning helps us see that everything we do has many unforeseen consequences, which should compel a kind of pedagogical hesitation.[41]

Strange aspect #4. *There's a gap between a thing and its appearance.*

One of the things Western philosophy has inherited from Kant is the idea that a gap exists between a thing and its appearance. Take, for example, the pen on your desk. Light absorbed and reflected by the pen is interpreted by your eyes and brain as "a pen," but the images in your primary visual cortex are not the pen itself. Neither are measurements of the pen's length, width and height, a twenty-page description of the pen, or the pen's life history the pen itself. Some part of a thing or object, in this case the pen, is always withdrawn or unknowable. In speculative realism great effort is made to try and think outside of correlationism, the idea that humans can only know things through the correlation between thought and being.

This is no easy task, because there can be no direct access to a thing in itself. In this way correlationism says something true about the world. Humans can only know about or access a thing through/in the correlation between what something is and what it appears to be (looks like, sounds like, tastes like, feels like, etc.). However, this "limited access situation" applies to all entities or objects in the world. All things experience only a fraction of another thing – something is always withdrawn or "left in the dark." This is the view of object-oriented ontology (OOO), which is arguably the branch of speculative realisms that best lends itself to ecological thought. Graham Harman's work comprises a good share of the foundational texts for this school of thought.

Speculative realisms, which include OOO, attempt to end the supremacy of human experience in philosophy and thought. They do so, in part, by speculating about how things are when there's no human around to think about them. OOO tries to displace, as much as possible, the importance of human perception or experience over that of the experience of different objects or beings. In this way, it attempts to be a "flat" ontology.[42] Objects that come into some sort of contact always keep parts of themselves withdrawn from each other. This includes humans coming into contact with other humans and other objects. The advantage to thinking in an OOO way is that it allows thought to more easily turn towards how nonhuman things (living or otherwise) experience each other. Chapter 8 will go into more detail about how this is useful when thinking about solidarity with nonhumans.

How educators think with their students doesn't always have to be about how humans experience things. However, as Morton points out, this does not mean our thinking will not to some extent be anthropomorphic.[43] After all, we are humans, doing human-like things with our human brains and hands – that's just how we interact with the world. Just like a pine marten does pine marten-like things with its fur and claws. A pine marten "accessing" a tree by clawing at it is, in a fundamental way, the same as a human accessing a tree by tapping it for maple syrup. In both instances parts of the tree remain "dark" or withdrawn from access. In terms of the tendency of all objects to withdraw from each other, there exists a kind of "equality of access" across objects in which the human mode of access is simply one of many ways of interacting. Indeed, nonhuman beings and objects interact constantly and much more frequently than humans. So why not direct some of our thinking there? OOO maintains that the various modes of interacting with, or accessing, the world are not fundamentally different from the way humans interact with things.

This flatter ontology is essential to ecological awareness for thinkers like Morton. Of course, a fundamental equality with humans and the rest of creation is what Indigenous thought has suggested for millennia. Eurocentric philosophy will have to undergo some radical transformations to catch up. And if it can't, it will very likely need to go.

> ***Strange aspect #5.*** *Humans never have direct or full access to things. Neither does anything else.*
> ***Strange aspect #6.*** *Human thought and perception is just one way of accessing a thing and is equal to other modes of access.*

Opening up environmentality to nonhuman entities means turning attention to the aesthetic dimension – the uncanny powers of mediation, influence, connectivity, and entanglement, not to mention the beauty of all the various assemblages that form in the world. The aesthetic dimension is at once a performative, causal, and political dimension.[44] It helps us think more deeply about things like politics and causality.

From an OOO perspective things are always themselves (real things exist), and yet not quite themselves in that something about them is always withdrawing. The possibility that something will deviate from "being itself" – that is, deviate from the appearance of itself – is present at any juncture. In a way we saw this in chapter 5: the turning inward of the forces that constitute subjectivity creates the conditions for new possibilities. At any point a subject can display, perform, or function in ways that are not itself or what it was supposed to be. Remember Spinoza's ethics: we don't yet know what a body can do! This is why art, philosophy, science, and education are often declared evil. They show us that things are often not what we thought they were. As Morton puts it, thinking needs to get out of the "dotted line" business, because the difference between things and how they appear is always fuzzy.[45]

An ecological ethics needs to increase its range of what counts as a being. The gap between appearance in reality is not just relevant to human perception, for one, because humans are most probably, like almost all species, a temporary entity prone to malfunctioning. There's nothing overly special about human beings compared to alpacas and angiosperms. In this way, we might celebrate entities (including humans) by recognizing malfunctioning as *prior* to functioning. Like the virtual lines of flight contained within Deleuze and Guattari's bodies-without-organs – all entities contain multiple trajectories of malfunctioning and functioning. As educators and students go about realizing the environmentality of everything, their interactions with their surroundings will be funny, wondrous, or weird. Things are much more than what they first appear to be. There is something that's both wonderful and unsettling in thinking about what lurks behind appearances.

The Dark Loop of Ecology

What we get from Morton's thought is that alternative futures are not realizable with the thoughts we are currently thinking. They require thought from the future. If just, sustainable futures depend on different thoughts, then educators have an ethical duty to set the stage for thinking differently. We've arrived again at that fundamental ethical core of education, albeit differently. The intensive calling of educators is largely about enabling others to become different.[46] In this sense, educators are also artists. They facilitate that which can't be thought or said yet. They bring forth thought from the future. There are many ideas about ecology we need to challenge. Some derive from Cartesian coordinates, some from Silicon Valley, and some from monotheisms and their agricultural contexts. Educators need to go deeper than industrialization, because the Anthropocene is arguably an extension of something much deeper and more intricate. It's typical to think of most human beings today as modern, but according to Morton most people today are "Mesopotamians" still caught up within the dream of monocultures and monotheisms.[47]

Morton puts forward a "loop" as a useful ontological form for the Anthropocene. Not a simple loop, such as a positive or negative feedback loop, but a strange loop. A strange loop is when two things that must be separated nonetheless uncannily "loop together."[48] The Anthropocene has strangely looped things together, like geology with politics and progress with evil. Another one of these weird loops has to do with the ethical predicament of being human in the Anthropocene. The future of many species directly depends on human actions – but human actions also brought forth the Anthropocene. I may use my phone to sign a petition fighting the corporate-government push to build pipelines through sacred Indigenous lands (like in the Wet'suwet'en nation) without consultation. But the device that made this possible is the result of destructive precious metal mining and unjust labour conditions. Pressing one's finger to a cell phone screen and scribbling a signature is an insignificant response to the destructive forces facing the planet – the same forces responsible for the iPhone. Yet thousands sign petitions supporting grassroots activism anyway. The point here, though, is the presence of a strange loop. A human being is a geophysical force whose actions matter – yet whose individual actions are extremely insignificant and problematic. There's something uncanny about this loop of ethical intention and complicity. A somewhat dark awareness arises where we realize our actions show care and bring about the ruination of the planet simultaneously. But awareness is all it takes to instil responsibility.[49]

For Morton, one of the reasons why it's so difficult for many people to become ecologically aware today is that "not all of us are ready to feel sufficiently creeped out."[50] While modern humans come to terms with their insignificance in the universe they're also learning that their cultures and political institutions are biological and geological phenomena. The strange contradictions of the Anthropocene demonstrate why an ecological ethics needs to connect with things like Indigenous knowledges and the arts. Looking only to science and technology is highly dangerous. As philosopher Jean-François Lyotard points out, science's powerful methods are all about legitimating empirical data – but these same methods cannot legitimate narratives about science itself. This falls to the narrative knowledges of spirituality, ethics, history, the arts, and social life.[51]

Science shouldn't be the only way we examine, and take pleasure in, reality and "things-in-themselves." Since there's always a gap between appearance and reality, things cannot be reduced to the uses, names, or descriptions humans have for them. For Morton, the more we understand the inexhaustibility of things – that moss growing on trees is as profound as humans having a religious experience – the more we come to realize ecological awareness and responsibility. Ecological survival is fundamentally a problem of being. I'm pretty sure that general sentiment would resonate with most educators.

The final chapter continues our discussion of speculative realisms and ecological awareness, and how they might bring us closer to an ethics of solidarity with nonhumans.

8 Solidarity with Nonhumans

There is an ancient conversation going on between mosses and rocks, poetry to be sure.
— Robin Kimmerer[1]

It seems appropriate that a discussion about ethics and education end with something "radical" or "out there." These, of course, are relative terms. Something that seems radical to a reader with a Eurocentric worldview might seem plain or obvious to an Indigenous reader. The previous chapter discussed how political change and ecological awareness are dependent on the aesthetic dimension. It also discussed how the future relies on thought that's slightly out of reach, yet still within sight.

This chapter continues to explore ethics and education from an ontological perspective, thinking about "how things are," and how this perspective is vital to an environmental ethics for the Anthropocene. Such an ethics means living with ecological disturbance as a way of life under capitalism – an idea that comes from anthropologist and ecological thinker Anna Tsing. I spend the first part of the chapter outlining how disturbance will increasingly come to organize ethical ways of living in the Anthropocene. Finding different ways of living together amid disturbance forms part of the future ethical horizon for teachers. I then follow the line of speculative realisms introduced in chapter 7 through the ideas of Timothy Morton to argue how thinking outside anthropocentrism is necessary for solidarity with nonhumans. While disturbance is a regular part of life on Earth, solidarity is fundamental to being and is readily available. This chapter draws inspiration from the transdisciplinary work of Anna Tsing.[2] Variation, imagination, and innovation are crucial for an ethics of ecological survival.

As chapter 7 noted, the Anthropocene has showed (some) humans just how basic aspects of our reality can and do malfunction. Tsing develops the notion of ecological disturbance on an ontological level; similarly Morton makes malfunctioning a question of existence. In a world marked by ecological disturbance, solidarity with nonhumans becomes a necessary (and overlooked) ethical response. Ethics here is more about becoming-with, something less trapped by anthropocentrism. This last chapter doesn't offer a sober summary or conclusion. Ethics is a shifting terrain that education must follow if it wants to remain relevant. In times of ecological disturbance, educators and students are compelled to think and act in different and seemingly strange ways.

You don't need to be an activist or critical pedagogue to understand solidarity. *Solidarity* simply entails that unmistakeable sense or quality of mutual dependence and unity. Solidarity with nonhumans means fully extending this dependence and unity to our nonhuman kin. With all that's happening in the world today it would be difficult, I think, to reject the idea of codependence as the very basis of life. Using the word solidarity to talk about interdependence and unity with nonhumans might seem strange – but that's only because the term has been unnecessarily limited to humans for so long. Animals and plants have gradually been relegated to a completely different order of things; but maybe they aren't that different at all. Although Indigenous peoples have maintained relations of equality with nonhumans, the Anthropocene and its extinction rates are making such relationships urgent and necessary for modern Western people. Solidarity with nonhumans may also seem strange because a Western education hasn't provided the creative space to think about codependence on a deeper level. As you can see, this chapter, like the last few, is an appeal to rethink fundamental aspects of our shared reality.

Part 1 highlighted a key point that I circle back to here: Being, which involves thinking about how things are (ontology), is fundamentally open to all and cannot be privatized.[3] In this way, disturbance should be thought of as something that affects all beings in the Anthropocene. Even the richest humans are well aware of the need to shield themselves from ecological collapse. Solidarity isn't something exclusive to unions and activist movements. It's a vital part of the symbiotic nature of reality. Educators too often leave thinking about reality to the modern Western sciences, forgetting that some of the most useful ways of making sense of our shared world(s) come from art, philosophy, and Indigenous knowledges.

In the section that follows I use Tsing's anthropological work to illustrate how disturbance recasts collective life in the Anthropocene. In the final section, I follow Timothy Morton's call to open up solidarity to nonhumans as a way of tearing down the walls between humans and the beings with which they share existence. Both sections help set the stage for curious and uncanny explorations into ethics and education. Both point to thoughts yet come.

Eddies of Collective Existence amid Disturbance

Exploring concepts like disturbance is one way to disrupt prescriptive narratives for ethics – which we know to be insufficient given the growing threat of extinctions and widespread inequality. Very often educators and scholars are led to think about ethics with "majority" concepts that don't allow much room for thinking differently.[4] One could argue that many seemingly useful ethical concepts like honour, duty, or even sustainability often come with an expectation of conformity and therefore don't enable ways of being better than the ones already on offer. As stated in the last chapter, educators need to enable different ways of living by radically shifting what Donna Haraway calls "the stories we use to tell stories."[5] These stories will be messy and have moments of ambiguity between times of flourishing and disturbance. They won't just feature one species or one event, but multiplicities that are necessarily incomplete and unfinished.

These kinds of stories resemble what my life-writing colleague Audrey Aamodt thinks of as collective wool-gathering.[6] For Audrey, wool-gathering is a metaphor for always being in the middle of things, and implies that one must go to disparate places to gather stories. The stories of our time, where humans conquer and master their various environments, won't end in victory. However, they will lead to other stories. This is important to remember when environmental collapse triggers in us feelings of hopelessness and sorrow.[7]

Tsing's ethnography *The Mushroom at the End of the World: On the Possibility of Life in Capitalist Ruins* is simultaneously a work of political economy and multispecies ethics. The book outlines a multispecies entanglement of mushrooms, their commodity supply chains, economic migrants, precarious workers, forests, and other nonhuman worlds to see how collective existence might take shape in capitalist ruins. The term "capitalist ruins" implies two things. First, capitalism's addiction to growth has only ruination to offer. Second, this ruination, caused by voracious supply chains that feed on anything that can be commodified and "plugged" into the markets, will increasingly come to (re)organize forms of collective life for the foreseeable future. Tsing recognizes that these stories of ecological disturbance can't be told from one or two vantage points – because stories of ecological collectivity have never belonged to humans exclusively. Disturbance emerges as a creative force in Tsing's work, one that is not just ecological, but psychic, ethical, economic, and political. So how might we think about the role of disturbance in an ethics for the Anthropocene? How might we live with disturbance as an inevitable phenomenon?

It's important to acknowledge that disturbance could mean many things. All disturbances, such as earthquakes, wars, and genetic mutations, alter some kind of expected life pathway. Sometimes they can even be intentional, as in the case of armed conflict and political protest. Disturbances unsettle what's habitual and stable, and in doing so they also unleash intensity and potential. Life is entwined with disturbance; however, in the Anthropocene a rapidly warming planet and ongoing extinctions take disturbance to a whole new level. But disturbance, in itself, is neither bad nor good. Disturbance of the sensible in the name of equality is the essence of radical democracy. Notice how the boundary between what is natural and social doesn't really apply to disturbance as an ontological concept. This is also true for most of the concepts in part 2, such as assemblage, becoming, malfunctioning, rhizome, and line of flight. Our discussion of ethics is still moving slowly away from anthropocentrism, however imperfectly. The ethical work of educators will increasingly take place within this space of natural-social dissolution.

Tsing uses the term assemblage to describe different modes of collective "liveability." She shifts the ethical question of "What modes of life are possible in a given moment and series of relations?" to "How do diverse beings come together to create different forms of liveability in times of disturbance?" Tsing presents us with something more empathetic, less individualistic, and less human-centred. There is no way of life possible without a collective. No new liveability without new collectivity. The details of disturbances matter because they determine whether collective life can grow or diminish. That is, how a disturbance might be potentially "good" or "bad."

Every disturbance has its own history and processes. To get a deeper sense of these, educators should gather as many disparate sources as possible: oral traditions, poems, geological surveys, scientific studies, diagrams, maps, and so on. For Tsing, studying anything begins and ends with diverse *acts of noticing*, which help locate disparate points of connection.[8] Disturbances can be events of great sadness. As when whole biomes change – never to return to their prior state. However, there's never been a "perfect garden" state that precedes disturbance. No perfect community, person, or food web exists. Disturbances also tend to follow each other. Childhood trauma leads to abrupt changes or disruptions in teenage and adult life. Flooding follows large-scale climate disturbance, and conservative political shifts often follow failed social movements. Evaluating a disturbance is contextual and based on the possibilities for living that arise. To some a disturbance may simply be a fortuitous event. Living in a time of ecological precarity and social inequality means paying attention to disturbances as much as it means avoiding them.

With all the historical understanding available to humans today it should be clear that disturbance is a regular part of existence. Humans have mediated disturbances like ice ages for millennia. The difference now is that (some) humans are the cause of grand disturbances like mass extinctions. Finding ways to mediate disturbance alongside our nonhuman kin – mammals, trees, oceans, and grasses – arguably makes up a huge part of the ethical terrain for educators today. Since the effects of disturbances are non-reversable, these effects should be evaluated with care. The variety and ambiguity of disturbance are reminders that a universal ethics is impossible – since any ethics that emerges as a response to disturbance is always socio-historically and ecologically situated. A fascinating aspect of disturbances is that they cannot be placed neatly into one descriptive or ethical category.

Tsing draws from historian Laura Cameron's work to show that disturbances are not just ecological, but psychic and social.[9] Ecological and psychosocial disturbances, in fact, operate in similar ways. Both kinds of disturbance, when a person is traumatized and when an ecosystem becomes severely unsettled result in unpredictable developmental patterns. In a twisted way, disturbances subvert expectations of how the future is supposed to unfold. Disturbances create virtual possibilities for becoming and lines of flight. There is therefore an ever-present ambiguity with disturbance.

A pressing task for educators is to create the conditions for ethical responses to disturbances. As mentioned in part 1, schooling was actually part of the genocide of Indigenous peoples and their nonhuman kin.[10] This genocide set off a social-ecological disturbance of grand proportions, and one that marks the onset of the Anthropocene. The wellness education research of Angela McGinnis and Noel Starblanket responds to this genocidal disturbance by recentring culture-positive Indigenous healing practices.[11] McGinnis and Starblanket draw connections between two interconnected disturbances: the erasure of Indigenous peoples and the extinction of the Lac Lacroix Indigenous pony. The work of these researchers aims to revitalize relations between First Nations peoples, Lac Lacroix ponies, and the spiritual dimensions that connect them. McGinnis and Starblanket's Indigenous healing practices are one example of what healing and pedagogy might look like after disturbance. Education can be both "cause and solution" to disturbances.

What becomes increasingly important is how beings ethically respond to disturbance. This involves paying attention to events before and after a disturbance, as there's an essential temporal (and therefore intensive) component to disturbance. We will never fully know beforehand what disturbance entails and what it will bring forth. A flood may create space for new life and workers' strikes may bring forth new relationships and social institutions. Whether something is "good" or "bad" in the context of disturbance depends on one's perspective. Like Deleuze and Guattari's criterion for ethical becoming(s), it all depends on what life or destruction flows from them. In this sense, the most relevant educational contexts relate to various kinds of disturbances, past and present.

Since disturbances are relational, intensive, ambiguous, and context-specific, educators have an ethical responsibility to ditch prefab answers, concepts, and pedagogies. Disturbances expose what was previously thought to be stable ground, thereby raising the ethical task of nurturing what Tsing calls the "small eddies of interlocking lives in great rivers of disturbance."[12] Tsing asks us to question scalability and the "one scheme fits all" approach to social and ecological life. Ignoring the way things interconnect at various scales makes it impossible to nurture symbiotic relationships with the diverse beings around us, relationships that could also be referred to as solidarity. Exploring solidarity with nonhumans is the final task of this book, and it ends things with a question mark instead of a summary.[13] I'm more interested in starting again than rehashing things. The map at the beginning of the book can act as summary if you need one. There is, however, an afterword that may provide some closure and a new beginning. Now to finish with a call for nonhuman solidarity!

Solidarity with Nonhumans

Solidarity needs to be introduced in schools and universities in transdisciplinary ways. Timothy Morton's work addresses some of the conceptual blocks that limit the way we think about solidarity. For Morton, three basic things keep humans from realizing solidarity with nonhumans. The first involves forms of thinking that emerged alongside systematized agriculture and that benefit only a small number of humans. Morton calls these viral "mono-forms" of thinking *agrilogistics*.[14] The second consists of the controlling apparatuses of modernity, such as capitalism and colonialism, which obscure the inexhaustibility and spectrality of things.[15] The third is Anthropocentric correlationism. Correlationism, which was introduced in chapter 7, holds that humans can only ask questions and realize/access things within the correlation between human thought and being. In other words, what humans can know and think is confined to the gap between appearance and reality. The critique of correlationism's anthropocentrism will guide this discussion of solidarity with nonhumans. This means our final discussion will be ontological in nature.

Despite long-standing efforts to mask the interconnectedness of life, which include the construction of walled cities and conceptual categories that keep humans in and everything else out, no life exists that is not absolutely dependent on others. Take, for example, Holobionts. These are assemblages of "multi-level" organisms living together in the same space, such as cows and their micro-organism digestors. Holobionts demonstrate that often symbiosis is a better way to understand ecology and the interconnectedness of life than something like a phylogenetic tree.[16] Yet modern biology education still insists on viewing the ecological world strictly through species and phyla. Viewing the world as symbiosis is really just another way of calling attention to interdependence. Solidarity is just another name for this symbiosis. And if solidarity is really a form of symbiosis, then we might say that solidarity has come through long periods of evolution. The key ethical question Morton asks is what it might mean to live in symbiotic relation. What does it mean to rely on things? What might it mean to recognize this solidarity?

Morton insists that a certain "rely-on" quality makes up the (inter)connectedness of our shared worlds. This connectedness is what Morton calls the "symbiotic real." This rely-on quality has an uncanny or spectral aspect to it, because it is more than it appears to be. Something is always held back in the relation between how something appears, or how it is accessed, and what it actually is. *In this way every relation is haunted.* So, things like beech forests and cliff formations will always seem ineffable because something about them will remain withdrawn. This rely-on quality, how things are in symbiotic relation, is infinitely variable. Fascinating and queer relationships will inevitably arise because relying-on things has no necessary a priori form. Object-oriented ontology, a branch of speculative realisms that aims (in part) to usher in a post-Kantian school of philosophy, considers the world as composed of objects and their relations. Object-object relations are thereby opened up as a legitimate focus of thought; thus, thought is no longer unnecessarily stuck on human-object or human-human relations. Since all objects can be accessed or grasped in a wide variety of ways (feeling, touching, perceiving, thinking about, etc.), privileging one access mode or one way of being in relation cannot account for the complete reality of that thing. In this way, everything has a kind of spectral aspect to it. Everything is haunted.

Solidarity is really about this relying-on quality, which is part of the codependent nature of virtually everything. To be anything is to be necessarily incomplete (and therefore malfunctioning). In this way, solidarity is fundamental to being. It doesn't require a fist pump or linking arms with another human. Taking a broader approach to solidarity enables modern Western educators and students to more easily involve nonhumans in ethical relationships. Morton argues that most modern people have been cut off from large swaths of the symbiotic real since the advent of systemic agriculture and their monocultures, or what Morton calls the "great severing." The separation of humans from nonhumans, a side-effect of these monocultures, was only deepened by European colonialism and industrialization.

Historically speaking, solidarity has been privatized to humans only. But if solidarity is fundamental to being, we no longer need to think of it as something only humans are capable of. Instead, solidarity is readily available and something every life form needs to survive. We have no choice but to embrace and expand it. In this way, solidarity with nonhumans is also a deeply ethical and spiritual exploration. Nurturing solidarity with animals, rivers, plants, and land is what Indigenous knowledge-keepers and elders, as well as Indigenous scientists, do when they open Western knowledge systems to different ways of knowing and being.[17] And while Indigenous thought is vital for the future, Western ways of thinking need to recast their fundamental concepts and ethical relations, if indeed this dichotomy between Western and other ways of knowing actually exists. Otherwise, large swaths of Western thought will need to be abandoned altogether.

Solidarity with nonhumans would oppose the sharp separation from humans that allows nonhumans to be cast as property. Capitalism and colonialism, like all other controlling forces, rely on alienation – whether it's humans from nonhumans, humans from other humans, nonhumans from nonhumans, or humans from their own agency. Animal rights don't go far enough, because rights are historically tied to property ownership and therefore cycles of alienation. An ethical place for educators to begin is by granting that nonhumans are not fundamentally different from humans. As Morton insists, nonhumans have worlds too, as well as the capacity to share their worlds. The fact that nonhumans have worlds they share with us is easy to grasp because these worlds are full of gaps, the gaps that exist between what something appears to be (how it is touched or thought about) and its being (what a thing actually is). For Morton, a key aspect of worlds is that they don't need a human to think them: "A world doesn't depend on consciousness. It's not about knowing that there is a world. It's about getting on with stuff, going about your doggy, or spidery, or whaley business."[18]

Capitalism effectively masks the spectrality of the world by turning things into slabs of matter that can be exploited and sold. One aspect of capitalist economies, however, does "take advantage" of the spectrality of things. *Commodity fetishism* casts things (things as commodities) as more than they appear. Or more than their use value, that is. Middle-class people don't buy urban jeeps because they need an all-terrain vehicle, but because of the lifestyle image they connote. Commodity fetishism recognizes, albeit in a sick sort of way, that things are more than their appearances by recognizing the socio-economic relations of thing – but again only in terms of what this means in relation to "market value."[19] In this way commodity fetishism never comes close to describing the true inexhaustibility of things – which is why consumerism always fails to deliver real pleasure to people. In the end commodity fetishism doesn't just alienate humans from the use-value of things (replaced by some connotation of what thing is), it also alienates them from the inexhaustibility of what a thing can be. Capitalism effectively locks in only one gap between things: what a thing is and its commodity form. It thereby hides the infinite qualities of things as well as what things might be. Eventually everything becomes some monetary relation between itself and its commodity value. The way capitalism rigidly ties a thing to how it exists as a commodity can be easily seen with dating apps today. These apps market people for intimate relationships according to salary, body type, and one-word interest descriptions (e.g., hiking, reading). The truth is people are infinitely more than commodities.

Marxist economics also limits the infinite qualities of a thing when it defines the use-value of something only in human terms.[20] Morton extends Karl Marx's notion of production by recasting it as anything organisms do, such as eating, resting, foraging, and running.[21] Even essential organisms like algae are not *for* anything. So why, then, do critical Western theoretical concepts, like economic production, remain so tied to human use-value? Morton puts the dire stakes of capitalism this way: "Capitalism implies a substance ontology that sharply divides what things are – 'normal' or 'natural' fixed essences or lumps of matter without qualities – from how they appear, defanging and demystifying things, stripping them of qualities and erasing their data."[22] The pleasure in dismantling capitalism resides in gaining back the infinite spectral quality of things. And the only way we will get rid of capitalism is by having something that's much more pleasurable. For Morton, preserving a world just for humans through efficiency and mere sustainability is not solidarity but a prolonging of the "great severing" and its agricultural-age moralities of good and evil. Only a suspension of capitalism and its values would allow modern Western people to begin to appreciate the infinite and priceless quality of things.

Opening to Nonhuman Worlds

A major sociocultural and geologic event that still influences ethics today is the agricultural revolution that began in the Neolithic era. Since then most humans, save many Indigenous peoples, have become increasingly severed from the space of connectedness, the symbiotic real that is essential for existing. This cutting off' from the symbiotic real coincided with agrilogistics, a reorganization of human social life that severed ecological relationships with nonhumans and established social hierarchies based on land ownership and the ability to stockpile grains.[23] Agrilogistics excludes Indigenous practices of farming that enhance the well-being of large ecosystems, such as cultivating forests, polyculture crop rotation, mixed cropping, and maximizing rainfall.

We don't have to go further than the exile of Adam and Eve from the Garden of Eden to see that people were somewhat aware of this severing. Morton paraphrases the farming ethos of agricultural age religions like this: "... we have to farm now, and farming sucks, it separates us from the beasts and our own life beyond survival (toil and sweat), but we do have to farm."[24] The new walled-off city states of the agrilogistic age excluded those beings that would disrupt their monocrops, monocultures, and monotheisms. Only humans were to have (God-given) access to the order of things! A truth in the book of Genesis is that (some) humans *have* undergone alienation from paradise. This alienation was their connection to nonhuman worlds!

Obviously, privatization has a much older history than modern capitalism. Agrilogistics attributes the privatization of ecological space to some members of one apelike species a few thousand years ago. Morton's description of agrilogistics centres on the establishment of new boundaries:

> Agrilogistics means the logistics of the dominant mode of agriculture that started in Mesopotamia and other parts of the world (Africa, Asia, the Americas) around 10 000 B.C.E. Agrilogistics has an underlying logic

to do with survival: Neolithic humans needed to survive (mild) global warming, and so settled in fixed communities that became cities, in order to store grain and plan for the future. They began to draw distinctions between the human and nonhuman realms – what fits inside the boundary, and what exists outside of it – that continue to this day. Very soon after the agrilogistic program began, all kinds of phenomena we associate with life in general showed up, in particular patriarchy and social stratification, various kinds of caste systems.[25]

For Morton, the ethics of agrilogistics is bad for humans and nonhumans alike. We can think of the Anthropocene as a set of viral agrilogistics programs left running for thousands of years. The presence of agrilogistics is why Indigenous thought is so relevant to non-Indigenous people today – it doesn't accept this severing of the human and nonhuman. The viral quality of monocrop agriculture also explains why it's so difficult for non-Indigenous peoples to step outside of agrilogistic space – to let go of the idea that human civilization is a sublime outcome of history or that human survival is the ultimate goal. One can easily see how *specism* follows the same warped and violent logic as white supremacy. Educators and students can challenge human dominance by restoring the infinite spectral quality of things and their mysterious relations. Even if it means looking non-Western, crazy, or foolish.

Solidarity with nonhumans is an ethical and therapeutic response to the disturbances of systemic (mono)agricultures, colonialism, industrialization, and capitalism. It's not necessary for humans to "think" solidarity exists, because it's already part of the real symbiotic world. According to Morton:

> Solidarity is a deeply pleasant, stirring feeling and political state, and it is the cheapest and most readily available because it relies on the basic, default symbolic real. Since solidarity is so cheap and default, it extends to nonhumans automatically.[26]

Protesting in the streets is just one manifestation of the real solidarity that is always available. And solidarity manifests in many ways when it comes to our nonhuman kin. Humans just need to realize that the way they attune to things is not fundamentally different than the way other entities attune.[27]

Education provides the ethical space needed to nurture ecological awareness and diverse forms of solidarity. Our forays into speculative realism show things in the world aren't always caught between human thought and (human) being.[28] Speculative realism is critical of correlationism's hold on Western philosophical enquiry for over two centuries. Since Immanuel Kant introduced concepts of rationalist and empirical philosophy in the eighteenth century, the "correlators," those who can know, decide, or "tell" what things are in that correlation between thought and being, have always been considered to be human (white males if we're getting more specific).[29] Speculative realisms affirm that things exist outside this relation, which implies that things can always be otherwise to what humans think. They, object-oriented ontology especially, also maintain that philosophy should consider nonhuman-nonhuman relations instead of just human-human or human-nonhuman relations. Speculative realisms maintain that things can always be otherwise than they appear to humans because things exist in a strange and lively universe whether humans participate or not.[30]

As mention in chapter 7, correlationism appears to be "true." There is a gap between things and what humans can think or know about them. Modern science is more or less premised on the idea that people do not access phenomena or things directly, but rather only have data that correlates to things. This approach allows scientists to make accurate predictions using this data. But this data is not reality in-itself, though scientists often speak as if it is, thereby confusing their data and viewpoints as reality itself.[31] So correlationism makes sense. How could humans access a thing in itself without considering things like perception, social position, neuronal systems, and language? Correlationism causes a problem, according to Morton and Graham Harman,[32] when it ties philosophy and thought to the gap between appearance and reality *only* as it pertains to humans. Nonhuman entities also experience this ontological gap between appearance and reality – which is one of the things that makes reality spectral and infinite. There's no good reason to think our world contains one species of primate that does all the deciding, accessing, world-making, or correlating. Morton summarizes it this way:

> Correlationism is true: you can't grasp things in themselves, facts are different than data, and data are different than things. But that doesn't mean that what gets to decide what's real – the correlator, the decider – is more real than those things, whether the decider is the Kantian subject, Hegelian history, Marxist relations of human production, Nietzschean will to power, or Heidegger's flickering lamplight of Dasein.[33]

Solidarity with nonhumans means extending this spectrality, the experience of the appearance-reality gap, to all beings.

Morton describes the gap between things and their appearance as a wavy porous line, and suggests that the symbiotic real "spills" through this line in strange and wondrous ways.[34] I have two autistic teenagers, Luca and Joseph, who demonstrate everyday how this wavy line between things can work. Often Luca and Joseph don't require symbolic meaning to find things fascinating. A new mixture in the kitchen or the coolness of stones become ultra-real and ultra-pleasant for them in a way that goes far beyond the connotative meanings attached to them by other humans. They are more attuned to the worlds of these objects and how the worlds of these objects permeate their worlds. At the same time, the words "phone" and "cinnamon rolls" have high symbolic value. This is just to say that the dividing line between worlds, say the world of the cinnamon roll and the world of Luca, is not clear, and people like Luca get that. Morton likens the dividing line between appearance and reality to a Möbius strip – one never quite gets at one side or the other. This perforated boundary can be observed when we shift orders of magnitude in language. When does a stream become a river? Or a hill a mountain? The boundaries between things are blurry. Which means that worlds overlap and can be shared.

Solidarity becomes easier for educators to imagine when they understand that the boundaries between things are full of holes. This is something caring educators have always understood: everything eventually exceeds the expectations people have for them. These educators often stand apart from those who try to fit the world into boxes. My world never totally belongs to me. It's a shared world, and some parts always remain withdrawn. This permeable aspect of being helps make solidarity, as an essential rely-on quality of existence, readily available. Educators need to ask what historical, material, and ideological barriers keep us from exploring solidarity with nonhumans. The absurd rejection of animal and plant consciousness or sentience in Western thought is just one such barrier. Even a mainstream view of animal and plant sentience recognizes that many nonhuman beings have the ability to feel, perceive, and experience subjectivity – which is basically a full definition of sentience. While this chapter doesn't address plant and animal sentience, exploration of this topic only makes solidarity with nonhumans more urgent.

Ecological crisis is now forcing (some) humans to open up their world and their ethics to nonhumans, awakening a necessary awareness of the mutual dependence of all living things. Educators might consider that nonhumans also experience the world through the gap between appearance and reality. They too are correlators and meaning makers. When they encounter each other, as well as humans, they only have access to a few aspects of another thing. Fundamentally, they're no different than we are, and therefore no less special. Correlationism as a philosophical outlook has an ironic relationship to our ecological crisis: "At the very moment at which philosophy says you can't directly access the real, humans are drilling down ever deeper into it, and the two phenomena are deeply intertwined. Correlationism is true, but disastrous if restricted to humans only."[35]

The root problem is anthropocentrism, which is as much a philosophical problem as it is a spiritual and historical one. Humans can no longer afford to think that they're more legitimate and important as meaning makers, deciders, or "accessor" beings of the world. That is, they are not more important than the things they access, think about, or study. This is one of the things a less anthropocentric ethic of solidarity needs to realize: nonhuman entities have access to the gap between appearance and reality just like humans do, because the lines between worlds are perforated and wavy. Once we accept this fundamental similarity, and make nonhuman beings a part of everyday ethics, solidarity with nonhumans becomes more possible.

Education as an Ethical Call to Solidarity

Since solidarity is part of the symbiotic fabric of reality, exploring it can happen in any classroom or field of study. While it might be easier to imagine solidarity with whales than with turkey vultures, all life forms are worthy of reverence and connection. You don't need an education in social history to show solidarity (though it doesn't hurt). Educators can begin this ethical work under the premise that solidarity is foundational to being in the world and indispensable to creating and sharing worlds in common. A lot of time may be needed for non-Indigenous people to fully appreciate the symbiotic and inexhaustible dimensions of nonhumans.[36] A turn to Indigenous ways of living may be the best option, but until this happens it would be very problematic to leave Western systems of thought unchanged. The kind of education that insists humans exist on an entirely different order than beavers and elm trees is antithetical to an ethics for the Anthropocene. Historically speaking, the humanities and social sciences – two fields that guide education – have designated anything outside the human social world as generally unworthy of in-depth consideration. But the Anthropocene has brought that period to a close, not by virtue but by necessity.

Since all entities rely on each other, we can say that everything is inherently incomplete and dis/abled. And this widespread dis/ability focuses our attention on the ever-present gap between how things appear and what they actually are. This means that everything in the world shares a fundamental unity, and the wonder of the world(s) can never be exhausted. Educators create the conditions for solidarity when they grant nonhumans equal status as entities that access the gap between appearance and reality.[37] Educators might attune their pedagogies to account for the fact that no one mode of access to a thing such as water – either tasting water, measuring its temperature, swimming in it – ever exhausts what water is. Likewise, kissing a seashell, drawing it, studying its symmetry, or blowing air into its entrance does not exhaust what a seashell is. Something always remains inaccessible and withdrawn. The ways of accessing something are never the thing in itself – and who better than children to expand this kind of understanding about our nonhuman kin?[38] How might we ethically approach the nonhuman world with our students, knowing that nonhumans are fundamentally equal?

It seems a bit crazy to conclude with the idea that the way a stick insect accesses the world is as important as the way a school administrator does. This is probably because educational studies and social theory didn't prepare my generation to engage anthropocentrism. As Morton notes, advocating for our nonhuman kin can often mean being the person nobody wants to sit beside in class.

> The person who would do that isn't the person you would want to be if you're trained in theory class: some kind of hippie. Of course, in reality race, gender and environmentality are deeply entwined, as the strong correlationist New Leftist will admit when it becomes tactically necessary to talk about the environment as, for instance, a discursively (in the Foucauldian sense) feature of social space. But this sidesteps the elephant in the room – the literal elephant in the room. Social space is always already construed as human.[39]

It's often risky for a professional educator to challenge anthropocentrism. To insist that a fundamental rely-on quality unites frogs, pelicans, humans, and lakes is to risk sounding naive and hokey. But true solidarity means having and sharing something in common. An education that makes this rely-on quality apparent will help construct a new ethics for the Anthropocene, whatever this ends up looking like.

Educators must provide ways of exploring ethical relationships with nonhumans that are wondrous and inexhaustible, even when such relationships are trivialized as child's play. Moving beyond anthropocentrism is possible because of the ubiquitous nature of solidarity and the permeability of things and their worlds. It's time for educators to let go of their ego.[40] Morton assures us that this kind of letting go is always possible:

176 Ethics as Ontological Exploration

How come I can have an experience that is beyond my ego? Because I'm not completely me! I am full of holes because I am like everything else, a living, breathing malfunction made up of all kinds of things that aren't me, that misbehave constantly ... I am shimmering.[41]

An education for the commons allows insects, atmospheres, and books to keep their infinite qualities. It affirms a solidarity that is ontologically foundational. And isn't it always the case that something that escapes our limited thinking becomes the very thing that draws us, and our students, back to the mysterious aspects of our shared reality? Ending on this thought makes me smile. Education, since its very core is ethics, needs to leave room for those things we have yet to understand or even sense. I find it fitting that the final chapter of this book ends in a bit of mystery.

Afterword: Monstrous Flesh and Possibility

These Irish crows make a lot of noise. I think they're telling me I'm done for now. If there's one thing I'd like to leave the reader with it's that education is full of open-ended possibility. My original plan for this afterword was to list the many things I'd forgotten or ignored in the book. But that list is way too long. When I completed the first draft I was convinced I'd leave Saskatchewan (Treaty 4) for Europe and stay there for a few decades. But it turned out this was not what my family and I wanted. As a result, this book was written in the midst of transition between places, in a liminal space. It was not written for the Irish educational context nor was it explicitly mainly for the Canadian context. This was especially clear to me when hundreds of unmarked mass graves of Indigenous children were discovered on old Indian residential school sites in the spring of 2021. It's best to look at this book as a collection of thoughts. Some of which may get others thinking about ethics and education. So maybe it's best to conclude with a positive thought or two. Something uplifting.

Following a path in education, or in life, means making decisions about where you should go, who you should work with, and how you should spend your time. Inevitably, students, friends, and colleagues will ask you questions like these: Should I become or remain a teacher? Should I study something different, like film or bugs? Should I live in a place like Shanghai or Kildare? Is this job, with all its suffering, really worth it? One of the things I've learned in my journey so far is that it's important to keep these choices as open as possible. While this book is really an appeal to a kind of openness, this openness is always accompanied by contingency and constraint. Maybe the only choice you have is to live in a bog or along the Yangtse river. Maybe no job in a capitalist economy can really be fulfilling. The point being that constraints, and disturbances, inevitably shape all choices. While most constraints will be unwanted, and often unjust, some of them also bring a certain ineffability. Something unpredictable has presented itself and now you must follow it.

Chapter 1 opened by explaining how an element of randomness plays a role in how life unfolds on earth. It also made the point that the same is true for writing. What we write about is trapped between constraint and things like desire and choice. I was fortunate to have this book reviewed by three knowledgeable education scholars. One of them suggested I end by discussing the "flesh of the multitude," a phrase used by Hardt and Negri in their book *Multitude*.[1] I never would have chosen to end this way. But following this random contingency, something that came from elsewhere feels right.

The section on Spinoza's ethics in chapter 5 was added after the first draft was written, but it seems that this tiny part of the book actually matters a lot. Spinoza arguably provides the ethical frame for much of this book, as interpreted through theorists like Deleuze and Guattari. Spinoza also shows up in Hardt and Negri's conception of the multitude and its monstrous flesh. The multitude is a concept that gets at a fundamental tension between ethics and politics – a tension that permeates this book and isn't going to be resolved anytime soon. Spinoza's ethics come down to the potentials of the body. In the sense of the multitude, of multiplicities, Spinoza's body of infinite potential can also be thought of as one multitudinous flesh. Just like a body is composed of many distinct individual parts that act as a composite, the multitude is composed of a plurality that doesn't form one unitary hierarchical body, but one monstrous multitudinous flesh.[2]

When educators go searching for an ethics that seeks justice and equality, they need to not look to an empty past form but instead to this infinite potential of the multitude and its flesh. At once individual (it's about you, and me too) and collective (it's not about you or me at all). This flesh is a common living substance of unformed potential where the task becomes learning what this flesh can do.[3] *Our powers cannot be fully contained. Educators know this intensely.* They know the collective power and potential of their students exceeds them, the school, the government, and anything that would try to curtail them. These powers are monstrous in that they always eventually exceed the confines of traditional ways of being. Educators should seek to be in solidarity with the beautiful monsters they encounter every day in the world. The ones remaking it.

Notes

Preface

1 In *What Is Philosophy?* Deleuze and Guattari distinguish philosophy as the creation of concepts. However, these concepts work differently than concepts in disciplines like science or marketing.
2 Orr, *Earth in Mind*.
3 Rancière not only challenges the role of the teacher as controlling explicator, but implicates these teachers in the reproduction of inequality. Rancière, *The Ignorant Schoolmaster*.
4 See Zheng, "A Performative History of STEM Crisis Discourse."
5 Noel Gough kindly offered some reassurance about language and accessibility when I was preparing the final manuscript; he also recommended I consult the work of Patti Lather. See Lather, "Troubling Clarity."
6 Sean McEvenue's work demonstrates how biblical truth is best viewed as poetic truth, of which the expectancy of the text forms a part. See McEvenue, *Interpreting the Pentateuch*.
7 Foucault, "Authorship."
8 Texts can be seen as dynamic assemblages or "machines" that create lines of possibility (flight). See Deleuze and Guattari, *A Thousand Plateaus*, 91–6.
9 Since texts are manifestations of material histories, getting started may be a matter of first lining things up in a rough sequence. See Jameson, "Wallace Stevens."
10 Kurt Vonnegut's novel *Breakfast of Champions* moved me to use drawings when writing because they are simultaneously non-discursive and discursive. Vonnegut, in a moment of protest and disgust, breaks the surface of the page by inserting a simple picture of an asshole with five lines and a dot. The effect is multiple: the breaking of the text on the page causes the reader to think about the gravity of American cultural and historical myths (there are other drawings, too) in a visceral (ontic) way. Provoking

thought is the primary goal; conveying a specific meaning is secondary. All educators understand there is something "more" happening when children (and adults?) play with paint, paper, and pencils – why not adults? See Vonnegut, *Breakfast of Champions*.
11 See Gough and Sellers, "Changing Planes."

1 (Un)Disciplined: Education as an Open Work

1. See Gould, *Wonderful Life*, 320.
2. Gould's work is an example of how scientists can be involved in rethinking our ethical relationships to the world around us.
3. See Eco, *The Open Work*, 14.
4. Some would argue that love is one of the lost elements of Paulo Freire's work. See Darder, *Reinventing Paulo Freire*.
5. The ontological outlook of *Empire* (the book) has been very influential to part 1 of this book. See Hardt and Negri, *Empire*.
6. For a discussion on how private property rights relates directly to race and education see Ladson-Billings and Tate, "Toward a Critical Race Theory of Education," 30.
7. An essay that captures the ambiguity of "enlightenment" (which is different than modernity) is Foucault's *What Is Enlightenment?* A basic idea being that it is not necessary to be for or against enlightenment or modernity.
8. See Grosz, *The Incorporeal*.
9. See Gosh, *The Great Derangement*.
10. See *Snowpiercer* and *The Hunger Games*.
11. See Jameson, *An American Utopia*.
12. Although semiotics has understood the latent meanings of symbols since Marx, the basic idea is laid out by Marx in *Capital*.
13. Mari J. Matsuda's technique of always asking "another" critical question is helpful. So, when exploring issues of racism, ask "where is the homophobia in this issue?" And when exploring issues of heteronormativity ask "Where is the racism in this issue?" See Matsuda, "Beside My Sister," 1183.
14. See Crutzen, "The 'Anthropocene.'"
15. See Davis and Turpin, *Art in the Anthropocene*.
16. For a discussion of Anthropogenic signatures and the criteria for assigning a new geological epoch see Lewis and Maslin, "Defining the Anthropocene."
17. See Morton, *Hyperobjects*.
18. See Shotwell, *Against Purity*.
19. Although the phrase "always already is overused in critical theory-based scholarship, to ask after how an individual is disciplined in multiple ways

always happens after the fact. See the work of Judith Butler, most notably "Contingent Foundations."
20 See Miller, *Shingwauk's Vision*. For a more accessible account of residential schools see Neissen, *Shattering the Silence*.
21 The etymology of discipline goes far back, coming from the Latin *disciplinus* for student, or the Old French *descepline*, which referred to suffering.
22 See Foucault, *Discipline and Punish*.
23 Although the later volumes of the *History of Sexuality* are more succinct, Foucault's lectures at this time outline some of his thinking regarding his research transition. See Foucault, *The Hermeneutics of the Subject*.
24 For a detailed discussion of science's "disciplinary problem" see Stengers, *Another Science Is Possible*.
25 See Foucault, "The Subject and Power."
26 See Lee, Cornell, Gregory, and Fan, "High Suspension Schools." Even in places where data are not collected on suspension rates and race, there are perceptions that students of colour are treated worse than white students. See, for example, Ontario Human Rights Commission, *Disproportionate Impact in Ontario*.
27 Foucault, Michel. *The History of Sexuality*, vol. 1.
28 Curran, "Anatomy of a Crisis."
29 Truth and Reconciliation Commission of Canada (TRC), *Calls to Action*.
30 See, for example, Carrington, "School Climate Strikes."
31 During my PhD studies I published a paper with Heather Sykes that interrogated essentialist views of sexuality and gender in a biology textbook. See Bazzul and Sykes, "The secret Identity of a Biology Textbook." Later in the dissertation work it became apparent that gendered discourses and images in science education are also racialized. See also Marks, *Is Science Racist?*
32 A vivid image of this can be seen in Franz Kafka's short story "In the Penal Colony," where a machine inscribes the law on disciplined bodies.
33 See Wallace, "The Paradox of Un/making Science People."
34 See Solly, "DNA Pioneer James Watson Loses Honorary Titles."
35 See Lyotard, *The Postmodern Condition*.
36 Kuhn was not arguing that all scientific knowledge is socially constructed. He believed in the methods and rigour of the modern Western sciences. See Kuhn, *The Structure of Scientific Revolutions*.
37 Foucault's essay "Discourse on Language" discusses Gregor Mendel's experiments on heredity and how acceptance by the scientific community was necessary before his knowledge on genetics would be considered as "in the true." Truth and power are co-extensive irrespective if something is actually true or not (it just needs to be considered true). See Foucault, *The Archaeology of Knowledge*.

38 A compelling account of the material conditions of racial and class inequality can be found in Kozol, *Savage Inequalities*.
39 *Awake!* is one of the magazines published by The Watchtower and Tract Society. The content of these magazines ranges from doctrinal pieces to current events and science stories. See https://www.jw.org/en/library/magazines/.
40 Jehovah's Witnesses and political regimes are not unique in their ability to control conduct. For example, James Joyce's short story *The Sisters* shows how the Catholic Church has governed the emotional and aspiration life of communities for centuries.
41 Homi Bhabha's work shows how the discourses and structures of colonialism constitute different subjectivities in the colonized and colonizer. For example, the same school resource can make white or straight identities feel affirmed, and nonconforming or "othered" peoples as abhorrent or unwelcome. See Bhabha, *The Location of Culture*.
42 See David. "Education Policy as an Act of White Supremacy."
43 Jay Lemke calls out science for its political conservatism based on the way it engages students. See Lemke, "The Secret Identity of Science Education."
44 This means politics can never be finished. See Rancière, *Dissensus*.
45 On some of the difficulties of granting rights in order to protect a river in New Zealand, see, for example: https://www.theguardian.com/world/2019/nov/30/saving-the-whanganui-can-personhood-rescue-a-river.
46 See Butler, "What Is Critique?," 310.
47 See Kanu and Glorr, "'Currere' to the Rescue?," 106. Also see Edward Said's work on critical intellectuals from which they draw: Said, *Representations of the Intellectual*.
48 See especially Althusser, "Philosophy as a Revolutionary Weapon," 3.
49 For Barthes, right-wing ideological speech has specific features that allow it to be detected. See Barthes, *Mythologies*.
50 See Badiou, *Infinite Thought*.
51 See Wilson, *Consilience*.

2 Multiplicity and the Commons

1 See Hardt and Negri. *Commonwealth*, 181.
2 See Rose, "The Politics of Life Itself."
3 See specifically their seminal work *Empire*.
4 See Means, Ford, and Slater, *Educational Commons*. More specifically, see Bazzul and Tolbert, "Reassembling the Natural and Social Commons."
5 See Ford, *Politics and Pedagogy*.

6. Ibid., 2–3.
7. For a more in-depth and creative description of an apparatus see Agamben, *"What Is an Apparatus?"*
8. See Foucault, "The Subject and Power," 781.
9. See Kirchgasler, "Strange Precipitate."
10. See Canguilhem, "The Living and Its Milieu."
11. See Thorpe, "Political Theory in Science and Technology Studies."
12. Murphy's work goes beyond Foucault's (both are engaged in this book) in that it focuses more on twentieth-century economic and political questions, such as racial inequalities. See Murphy, *The Economization of Life*.
13. Ibid., 8.
14. See Yusoff, *A Billion Black Anthropocenes*.
15. For Foucault individuals and populations are two sides of the same coin (or two poles) of governance. See Foucault, *The History of Sexuality*, vol. 1, 139.
16. Even vital knowledge about environmental concerns is not free of power, ideology, and politics. See, for instance, Fortun, *Biopolitics and the Informating of Environmentalism*.
17. See Stoler, *Race and the Education of Desire*.
18. Hardt and Negri call this altermodernity. See *Commonwealth*. 101–18.
19. See Lewis, "Biopolitical Utopianism."
20. See Thomas Lemke's overview of biopolitics, where many meanings of biopolitics are given consideration: Lemke and Casper, *Biopolitics*.
21. See Bazzul, *Ethics and Science Education*.
22. See Bazzul, "Tracing 'Ethical Subjectivities.'"
23. A basic example being the reports delivered by the United Nations Intergovernmental Panel on Climate Change. https://www.ipcc.ch/assessment-report/ar6/.
24. For an expansive view of the commons and education see Means, Ford, and Slater, *Educational Commons in Theory and Practice*.
25. See Stefanovich, Roman, and Jones, "Too Many First Nations Lack Clean Drinking Water," 2.
26. See Harvey, *Rebel Cities*, 70.
27. The cultural and social organizations that have historically governed the commons are emphasized in this seminal work: Ostrom, *Governing the Commons*.
28. See Moore, *Capitalism in the Web of Life*.
29. See Jasanoff, "Taking Life."
30. On Freire and love see Antonia Darder's *Freire and Education*. Also see Michael Hardt's critique of hierarchy in Hardt, "The Militancy of Theory."
31. See Haraway's speculative fabulations in Haraway, *Staying with the Trouble*. Anna L. Tsing makes the point that the stories used to teach us about

humans and animals keep humans separate from nonhumans. See Tsing and Bazzul, *A Feral Atlas*.
32. Even in COVID's early days we saw a rapid increase in the net worth of the very rich: "America's Billionaire Wealth Jumps by over Half a Trillion during COVID-19 Pandemic." *New York Times*, 4 June 2020, https://www.nytimes.com/reuters/2020/06/04/business/04reuters-health-coronavirus-billionaires.html.
33. See Henderson and Hursh, "Economics and Education for Human Flourishing."
34. See Russell, "Whose Better?"
35. A fascinating example of this is the battle over India's national science narrative, where Hindu nationalist, postcolonial, and communitarian versions of science and society all vie to become the sanctioned story of India and science. See Chadha, "Towards an Informed Science Criticism." For a follow-up on this discussion as it relates to science education see also Raveendran, *Conceptualizing Critical Science Education*.
36. See, for example, this think-tank policy document: Atkinson and Mayo, "Refueling the US Innovation Economy."
37. Clayton Pierce ties larger controlling forces of white supremacy and (bio)capitalism with science education in the following book: Pierce, *Education in the Age of Biocapitalism*.
38. See Butler, *The Psychic Life of Power*.
39. The most useful theory here is Althusser's take on interpellation and how the law creates subjects by its larger grammars. See Althusser, "Ideology and Ideological State Apparatuses."
40. See Butler, "What Is Critique?," 310.
41. The death of Coulton Boushie in 2016 redoubled efforts to change a legal system mired in settler colonialism. See Tasha Hubbard's 2019 documentary *Nîpawistamâsowin: We Will Stand Up*.

3 Education Needs Politics and Imagination

1. See Buchanan, *Fredric Jameson*, 131.
2. The original paper this chapter is based on is slated to be published in the journal *Critical Education* in 2022 under creative commons licensing.
3. The Teaching Council in Ireland for example commits its teachers to the promotion of social justice. See *Code of Professional Conduct for Teachers*.
4. Jacques Rancière's thesis on politics is helpful because it distinguishes politics as emancipation from politics as the exercising of power and governance. See Corcoran and Rancière, *Dissensus*.
5. For me, this is another instance where the "post" label in postcritical is another ironic modernist tendency to label and structure. Many critical

schools of thought represent the intimate connections and embodiments bound up in critique. However, it is easy to take the general point of post-criticality as an enrichment of criticality, just like it's easy to take postmodernity as enrichment of modernity.

6 Elizabeth Grosz makes a strong case that all materiality is bound up with an ideality that must be taken seriously – a point that most educators would surely agree with. See Grosz, *The Incorporeal*.
7 Concepts like immanence, the virtual, and their infinite planes can all be found in the work of Gilles Deleuze and Félix Guattari and are discussed in more detail throughout this book. See especially Deleuze and Guattari, *A Thousand Plateaus*.
8 Deleuze and Guattari differentiate philosophy from science and art by distinguishing how these disciplines operate on different planes. To me it's more useful to see them operating on the same immanent plane of reality (though operating differently). For a fuller discussion see Deleuze and Guattari, *What Is Philosophy?*
9 See *A Thousand Plateaus*, 213.
10 It's important to understand what represents a challenge to the visibility of the community or what counts. Many things are counted in a community – just not equally or on equal grounds. See also Rancière, *Disagreement*.
11 See Deleuze and Guattari, *What Is Philosophy?*, chapter 1 ("What Is a Concept?") and chapter 2 ("The Plane of Immanence").
12 See Ford and Lewis, "On the Freedom to Be Opaque Monsters."
13 In science education Elizabeth McKinley encapsulates this phenomenon of hybridity and racialized identity in productive ways for educators. See McKinley, "Brown Bodies, White Coats."
14 Jodi Dean discusses a more expansive vision of communism that retains some of the effective aspects of past communisms, while infusing the concept with new imagination. See Dean, *The Communist Horizon*.
15 Ibid., 11.
16 Ibid., 16.
17 Slavoj Žižek is similarly nostalgic for social democratic bureaucracy, arguing that access to electricity, health care, and clean environments requires a large and relatively seamless entity – a state – that, while alienating, nonetheless would allow people to lead a somewhat non-alienating local life. See Žižek, "Slavoj Žižek en el CBA."
18 See De Lissovoy, Means, and Saltman, *Toward a New Common School Movement*.
19 Elsewhere I discuss this relationship between science education, ideology, and neoliberalism in reference to how science is cast for students as a competitive enterprise. See Bazzul, "Neoliberal Ideology."
20 See Means, "Jacques Rancière."

21 Rooney, "Symptomatic Reading," 137.
22 See Deleuze and Parnet, *Dialogues II*, 10.
23 I specifically remember a conversation about new materialisms with science education professor Matthew Weinstein at the American Educational Research Association Meeting (AERA) in San Antonio, Texas. We agreed that if science education is to embrace justice it's important to ask what our philosophical theories have to offer in terms of politics and emancipation.
24 Foucault, from my reading, would be wary of anyone saying that one should be absolutely against or for certain complex theoretical, historical developments (like modernity). Or more accurately, that we don't have to be forced into a position about being absolutely for or against social realities that have many ambiguities.
25 See Jameson, *Marxism and Form*, chapter 5.
26 See Buchanan, *Fredric Jameson*.
27 See Anker and Felski, *Critique and Postcritique*.
28 See Rooney, "Symptomatic Reading," 128.
29 See Haraway, *The Haraway Reader*, 83.
30 To use Deleuze's words. See Deleuze, "Postscript on the Societies of Control," 4.
31 See Todd, "An Indigenous Feminist's Take."
32 See Haraway, "A Cyborg Manifesto."
33 See Barad, "Diffracting Diffraction."
34 In discussing object-oriented ontology, Graham Harman wants a philosophy that works with science, but that still has the freedom to explore new problems. Interview with Graham Harman by Jon Coburn.
35 See Grosz, *The Incorporeal*, 13.

4 Ethics and Subjectivity: The Vital Terrain of Education

1 Murakami's fiction works with a vision of the self that is self-contained and somewhat independent from its surroundings. However, like chapter 4 of this book, his work also advocates a "breaking out" of the self. This entails a more traditional idea of understanding the self, but also attunement to those aspects of the surrounding world that are uncertain, uncanny, and bigger than the self. As such Murakami's fiction cracks open reality on a personal and global level. See, for example, Murakami, *Kafka on the Shore*. (Quote is from chapter 3.)
2 See Bannerji, *The Dark Side of the Nation*. See also Anderson, *Imagined Communities*.
3 Individuation in psychology was first written about a hundred years ago by Carl Jung. See Jung, *Psychological Types*.

4 This book does not engage Levinas's work, which may seem like an unfortunate limitation. The best defence I have for this that his work contains a kind of humanism (finding ethics in the eyes of another human) that didn't seem to fit into this book. See, for example, Levinas, *Totality and Infinity*.
5 See Faubion, *An Anthropology of Ethics*, 55.
6 See Ermine, "The Ethical Space of Engagement," 193.
7 See Donald, "Forts, Curriculum, and Ethical Relationality."
8 See Blades, "Levinas and an Ethics for Science Education."
9 I was encouraged in reading the first sentence of Elizabeth Grosz's *The Incorporeal* because the it states that ethics concerns "what is to be done." It was affirming to see a leading philosopher put forward a very simple definition for ethics. However, our efforts to expand and specify ethics are always partial.
10 See Slater and Griggs, "Standardization and Subjection."
11 Indeed neoliberalism's use of the self-improvement discourse is pervasive. See, for example, Han, *The Burnout Society*.
12 See Mattingly, "Two Virtue Ethics," 177–8.
13 See Wain, "Chapter 11: Foucault."
14 See hooks, "Yearning."
15 In volume 2 of the *History of Sexuality* Foucault makes a decisive break with the volume 1 by going into another time and social context (Greco-Roman antiquity). In doing this Foucault is able shed some the influence of previous analyses and begin a different exploration of ethics and subjectivity. The second and third volumes centre on ethics and auto-poiesis or ethical self-creation, though they cover different time periods and outline a different ethics. I started reading volume 4 as I book was completing this book. See Foucault, *The History of Sexuality*, vols. 2 and 3.
16 The separation of justice and truth does indeed make more sense when we consider the Bible. This book doesn't ask its reader to consider whether its ethical systems conform to a view of truth extraneous to the Bible itself. For Foucault's treatment of truth and justice in antiquity see Foucault, *Wrong-doing, Truth-telling*.
17 Ibid., 29.
18 From my understanding it is the consensus of modern secular religious scholars that the biblical account of the Israelite enslavement in Egypt is, like most foundational myths, largely fictional.
19 For more on the notion of *parrhesia* see Foucault, *The Hermeneutics of the Subject*.
20 See also this set of lectures by Foucault where he further develops a classical sense of ethical reflexivity and self-governance: Foucault, Davidson, and Burchell, *The Courage of Truth*.

21 These concepts seem to be formulated from conversations with Foucault at Berkeley in 1983. See Foucault, *On the Genealogy of Ethics*.
22 *Ascesis* was taken up in the Christian tradition as training the mind to focus on God. Foucault's use of the word seems to be more general. See Foucault, *On the Genealogy of Ethics*, 137.
23 While 2SLGBTQI+ individuals are still violently oppressed, straight people also suffer from this violence. Foucault's thinking is useful here, because the stakes of things like gay rights struggles are so that people in general (including straight people) can have new types of loving relationships. See Foucault, "Friendship as a Way of Life."
24 See Foucault, *On the Genealogy of Ethics*, 256.
25 Judith Butler's work develops this idea of a subject's vulnerability to enter into a power relationship and how one comes to see certain ways of being as normative, the key point being that a subject is always already vulnerable to the call of power (to varying degrees). Exploring this vulnerability is important when thinking about other ways of being. See Butler, *Senses of the Subject*.
26 See MacPherson, "Student Participation in Anti-pipeline Rally."
27 Lazzarato, "From Biopower to Biopolitics." See also, for example, Davies, Bronwyn, and Bansel, "Neoliberalism and Education." For a good explanation of neoliberalism from a historical perspective see Foucault's seminal lectures: Foucault and Senellart, "The Birth of Biopolitics." See also Dumas, "My Brother as 'Problem.'"
28 It is interesting to read Pierre Bourdieu's work on ideology, culture, and class, which gives an explanation of how these advantages (and by extension white supremacy) are woven into everyday ideology. See Eagleton and Bourdieu, *Doxa and Common Life*. Also see Bourdieu, *On Television*.
29 See Žižek, *Living in the End Times*, 52.
30 Rancière seems convinced that a turn to ethics exclusively is a very bad idea. His assessment should give educators pause, because it means our work must be politically engaged/informed to make a difference. See Rancière, "The Ethical Turn of Aesthetics and Politics."
31 For an example of an episode that depoliticizes ethics see "The Trolley Problem"; this is not to say that the episode doesn't do a good job with some basic ethical questions. See *The Good Place*.

Part Two: Ethics as Ontological Exploration

1 Elizabeth Grosz is discussing the bidirectional aspect of Gilbert Simondon's *Ethics*. Often ethics pulls us in two (or more) completely different directions. See Grosz, *The Incorporeal*, 201. See also Bazzul, "Ethics, Subjectivity, and Sociomaterial Assemblages."

5 Outside the Subject of Ethics

1. In other words, any sense of self is dependent on a (material) outside of self. See Deleuze, *Foucault*, 105.
2. Ibid.
3. The story of Harold and the purple crayon is required reading in my family. See Johnson, Jordan, and Levi, *Harold and the Purple Crayon*. I was also pleased to read about the authors' progressive political statements. See Nel, "Never Overlook the Art of the Seemingly Simple."
4. The will is not a straightforward aspect of human nature (as the debates on free will would have it), but something that emerges within a social and moral order. The will can affirm a subject in a particular social order, or it can be used to render them immoral. See Ahmed, *Willful Subjects*.
5. Deleuze, *Foucault*, 101.
6. I very much dislike the term the phrase "working within and against" as it seems like a justification for doing or thinking nothing about systemic violence. However, the phrase does make a clear point about the nature of resistance.
7. Judith Butler discusses the difficulty of coming to terms with "a self," along with the compulsion or desire to do so. See Butler, *Giving an Account of Oneself*.
8. Deleuze. *Foucault*, 123.
9. See Deleuze, *Spinoza*.
10. Ibid., 4–5.
11. See specifically *Ethics*, part 3, movement 2, in Spinoza, *A Spinoza Reader*.
12. Deleuze, *Spinoza*, 17.
13. Ibid., 22.
14. Ibid., 41.
15. See Nietzsche, *The Gay Science*, 300.
16. Deleuze and Guattari go into great detail about the attributes of rhizomes. See Deleuze and Guattari, *A Thousand Plateaus*, 9.
17. Ibid., 3.
18. See the explanation offered by Sui Van, "Velut arbor ævo."
19. See Gough and Sellers, *Changing Planes*.
20. See Deleuze, *Difference and Repetition*, specifically the chapter "Image of Thought."
21. Deleuze and Guattari, *A Thousand Plateaus*, 6.
22. See Grande, *Red Pedagogy*, 112.
23. See Tuck, "Breaking Up with Deleuze."
24. See Coulthard, *Red Skin, White Masks*, especially chapters 1 and 3.
25. Although not directly about curriculum (in a Western sense), this lecture is one that students have appreciated in both Ireland and Canada. See Little Bear, "Big Thinking-Leroy Little Bear."

26 As my colleague Audrey Aamodt says, becomings are always multiple (even when the grammar is not).
27 The clearest discussion of becoming minor is in Deleuze and Guattari's book on Franz Kafka's work. See Deleuze and Guattari, *Kafka*.
28 Ngui, *Bubble Nut Pictures*.

6 Assemblages and the Emergence of Difference

1 See Bolaño, *2666*, 430.
2 Centring nonhumans and materiality is a real struggle in education. In science education see Milne and Scantlebury, *Material Practice and Materiality*.
3 I have found the readings of John Mohawk most helpful in my teaching, especially the ethic of living with future generations in mind. See Mohawk and Barreiro, *Thinking in Indian*.
4 See DeLanda, "Interview with Manuel DeLanda," 43.
5 This chapter draws heavily from Manuel Delanda's reading of Deleuze and Guattari in their book *Assemblage Theory*.
6 See DeLanda, *Intensive Science and Virtual Philosophy*, 2.
7 See Barthes, *Mythologies*. I also wrote a short book chapter about how Barthes's *Mythologies* relates to education. See Bazzul, "Becoming a 'Mythologist.'"
8 See Gough and Sellers, *Changing Planes*, 104.
9 For further reference, check out Noel Gough's work, which uses Deleuzian concepts like "flows" and "planes" in an accessible way. See, for instance, Gough, "Changing Planes."
10 See Deleuze, *Spinoza*, 122–3.
11 The use of the word "might" instead of "should" is a shift in language for part 2. Not only does ethics involve "what should be done?" it also involves seeking lines of possibility for becoming different (what might I become?). It does not erase the importance of the first question, but rather the two exist alongside each other.
12 See Barad and Kleinman, "Intra-actions."
13 Barad's masterwork helps explain the fine nuance of entanglement. See Barad, *Meeting the Universe Halfway*.
14 See Barad, "Diffracting Diffraction."
15 See Zembylas, "The Contribution of Non-representational Theories in Education."
16 In chapter 1 of *Assemblage Theory* Delanda lays out an anti-totalizing philosophy for assemblages.
17 See Grosz, *The Incorporeal*, 151.

18 Territory here doesn't refer to property or land, but is employed to subvert things like categorization and ownership. Having said this, the term remains controversial because of the continued struggle for land by Indigenous groups. Deleuze and Guattari have encountered other problems with their use of language, "becoming-woman" for example. Overall, it's best to ask whether these concepts are productive or not.
19 For a more in-depth discussion of assemblages and education, which includes the points made here but in more detail, see Bazzul and Kayumova, "Toward a Social Ontology for Science Education."
20 Delanda, *Intensive Science*, 2.
21 It's not that rigid assemblages and free-flowing assemblages have some set of ethical values. It's that in societies of control and dominance students and teachers should seek to enable lines of flight and rhizomatic connection. See Deleuze, "Postscript on the Societies of Control."
22 See Deleuze, *Difference and Repetition*.
23 See DeLanda, *Intensive Science*, 60–75.
24 Deleuze and Guattari, *A Thousand Plateaus*, 59–60.
25 See Donald, "Indigenous Métissage."
26 For an intricate explanation of the codependence of deterritorialization and reterritorialization (which also extends to rhizome and tree) see Deleuze and Guattari, *A Thousand Plateaus*, 10.
27 The image is also used in Bazzul and Santavicca, "Diagramming Assemblages of Sex/Gender."
28 See a comic description of the strike here: Habib, "River of Garbage."
29 See Deleuze, *Kafka*.
30 See Kafka, *The Trial*.
31 A point made by Tamsin Lorraine in her book on Deleuze and Guattari's ethics. See Lorraine, *Deleuze and Guattari's Immanent Ethics*.
32 Grosz, *The Incorporeal*, 151.

7 Aesthetics and Environmentality

1 Morton, *Dark Ecology*, 1.
2 I say forgotten because one of John Dewey's books from the 1930s, *Art and Experience*, did ground education in aesthetic experience. This help pave the way for an education that immersed students in the world, not rows of desks and chalk. See Dewey, *Art as Experience*. More recently education scholars have seized on the political potential of aesthetics and education: see Lewis, *The Esthetics of Education*.
3 Morton, *Dark Ecology*, 2.

4 Save this volume: Bellocchi, Quigley, and Otrel-Cass, *Exploring Emotions*. See especially the thinking of Steve Alsop in in "Encountering Science Education's Capacity."
5 Rancière's political theories always draw from the realm of aesthetics and experience. See Rancière, *Dissensus*.
6 My approach to aesthetics in this chapter largely follows Rancière's in his work on aesthetics and politics. See Rancière, *The Politics of Aesthetics*.
7 See the discussion on aesthetics and possibilities in science education in Tolbert and Bazzul, "Aesthetics, String Figures, and the Politics of the Visible."
8 For example, Octavia Butler challenges racist stereotypes in *Kindred*.
9 Rebecca Roanhorse's *Trail of Lightning* imagines a world where Indigenous people (continue to) survive colonialism.
10 See Lewis, "Jacques Rancière's Aesthetic Regime."
11 Countries like Ireland face the problem of aesthetics and education when it comes to testing culture. COVID-19 has exposed the limits of testing to provide equitable access to education, and when the test is taken away Irish teachers are collectively unable to conceive of assessments to replace the test. It's essentially a problem of exposure.
12 Rancière, *Aesthetics*, 3–4.
13 bell hooks sets the stage for transgressive teaching by relating the intensely personal with the political. hooks's book *Teaching to Transgress* is one of the most transformative reads for teachers.
14 For a lucid explanation of Rancière's historical regimes of art see Tanke, "What Is the Aesthetic Regime?"
15 Rancière goes to great lengths to make politics, a very specific process of disruption in the name of equality, co-extensive with everything under the sun. See Rancière, *Dissensus*.
16 The double meaning of "sensible" works well here, that is, beyond what can be sensed and what is common sense.
17 See Haraway, *Staying with the Trouble*.
18 Ibid., 2.
19 Ibid., 31.
20 I am thinking specifically of Haraway's chapter on "tentacular" thinking (to think as if you had tentacles), and how it involves a sensibility that's immediately multiple, wonderful, and uncomfortable. See Haraway, *Staying with the Trouble*.
21 Ibid., 2.
22 See *Wakening*.
23 See the documentary interview with Goulet about Indigenous futurisms: *This Is Worldtown*.
24 For a thoughtful analysis of *Wakening* see Monani, "Feeling and Healing Eco-social Catastrophe."

25 *The Hunt*.
26 My plans to see the gallery fell through when the COVID-19 pandemic hit. My plan was to stop off in Chicago on the way to Toronto in June 2020 (to catch our flights to Ireland). Unfortunately, the border was shut at the time.
27 See http://psychopompopolis.net.
28 Ibid.
29 See Okorafor, *Binti*.
30 See Willems, "Speculative Realism and Science Fiction."
31 See Miéville, "Cognition as Ideology."
32 Graham Harman's view of object-oriented ontology is hard to take in at first. One reason for this is the way Harman dispenses with the qualifications philosophers often have to do to say anything about reality. This seems intentional in Harman's writing. See Harman, *Bells and Whistles*.
33 See, for example, Jessie Beier's work on black holes and unknowability in science education: Beier, *Tracing a Blackhole*.
34 See Ford and Lewis, "On the Freedom to Be Opaque Monsters," 102.
35 See Morton, *Mal-functioning*, 105.
36 See Morton, *Dark Ecology*, 1.
37 Morton, *Mal-functioning*, 97.
38 Timothy Morton draws from Martin Heidegger and Graham Harman for his conception of malfunctioning. First, from Heidegger's discussion of a "tool," we don't notice a tool that's functioning, only the ones that are malfunctioning. Second, things get noticed *as* they perform this being – with some of this being always being withdrawn. Through Heidegger and Harman, Morton is able to put forward the "malfunction" as a viable ontological-ecological theory of "things." See Harman, *Tool-Being*. See also Heidegger, *Being and Time*.
39 Ibid., 111–12.
40 The criticisms of systemic agriculture exclude sustainable agriculture practices such as those practised by Indigenous peoples for centuries.
41 Hesitations that begin with abundance, even when it comes to things like malfunctions and dark ecologies. See Wallace, "The Paradox of Un/making Science People."
42 See Harman, *Object-Oriented Ontology*.
43 See Morton, *Being Ecological*.
44 See Morton, *Realist Magic*.
45 Morton, *Mal-functioning*, 112.
46 Both parts 1 and 2 insist that ethics is central to education. Part 1 argues that ethical subjectivity is central to education – moving someone from one way of being to a better one. This act is intensive because it resides at the nexus of control and resistance or (bio)power. Part 2 argues that educators,

in keeping with their intensive ethical calling, facilitate becoming different in wider relation to the material world. Both are necessary responses to a dying planet.
47 What Morton calls "agrilogistics," which we will touch on in chapter 8. See Morton, *Dark Ecology*.
48 Another strange loop goes back to our Foucault/Deleuze loop (fold) of subjectivity – a line that crosses itself, enfolding an "inside" out of an "outside." The inside potentially becomes different than what constituted it.
49 Morton, *Dark Ecology*, 8–9.
50 Ibid., 12.
51 See Lyotard, *The Postmodern Condition*, 7–14.

8 Solidarity with Nonhumans

1 See Kimmerer, *Gathering Moss*.
2 Tsing's work is a huge inspiration for this chapter, and also for chapter 1. See Tsing, *The Mushroom at the End of the World*.
3 A shared ontology is the basis for Hardt and Negri's interrelated concepts of the common(s) and multiplicities. See specifically Hardt and Negri, *Commonwealth*, specifically part 1, "Republic (and the Multitude of the Poor)."
4 As chapter 5 suggests, ethics, finding different ways of being in the world, involves becoming minor. In this way, it may also involve using minority concepts like disturbance.
5 See Haraway, "It Matters What Stories Tell Stories."
6 Audrey Aamodt's work tangles personal writing with ethics in open-ended ways. See Aamodt, *Becomings-Unsettled*. See also Aamodt and Bazzul, "In the Middle of Treaty Walking."
7 Sharon Todd's work considers climate sorrow an integral part of our aesthetic encounters with the world. See Todd, "Creating Aesthetic Encounters of the World."
8 Tsing, *Mushroom at the End of the World*, 37.
9 See Cameron, "Histories of Disturbance."
10 See Miller, *Residential Schools and Reconciliation*.
11 See Snowshoe and Starblanket, "Eyininiw Mistatimwak." (Snowshoe was Angela McGinnis's former surname.)
12 Tsing, *Mushroom at the End of World*, 187–90.
13 This section is very similar to an essay I wrote at the time I was writing this book's ending. I see speculative realisms as a relevant topic to the work on ontology and ethics. See Bazzul, "Solidarity with Nonhumans."
14 The way to view agrilogistics is to see it as a series of "viral programs" run amok. Many problems today are because the result of deep beliefs and

ways of conducting everyday life that have these logics running in the background. See Morton, *Dark Ecology*, 84.
15 The rest of this chapter draws heavily from Morton's book *Humankind*, which attempts to open social theories, like Marxism, to nonhuman solidarity.
16 Two interesting pieces worth noting are Margulis and Fester, *Symbiosis as a Source of Evolutionary Innovation*, and Gilbert, "Holobiont by Birth."
17 See especially the work of Robin Kimmerer, which informs a lot of the environment/science education in Saskatchewan: Kimmerer, *Braiding Sweetgrass*.
18 Morton, *Humankind*, 92.
19 Ibid., 63.
20 Ibid., 26.
21 Morton works through this point using the following text: Marx, *Notes on Adolph Wagner's "Lehrbuch der politischen Ökonomie."*
22 Morton, *Humankind*, 63.
23 Morton, *Dark Ecology*, 42–6.
24 Morton, *Humankind*, 147.
25 Morton, *Being Ecological*, 50.
26 Morton, *Humankind*, 19.
27 This idea that humans have no special access to reality or entities in the world comes, in part, from Graham Harman's object-oriented ontology. Morton also draws from literary theory as well as from Marxism.
28 Quentin Meillassoux's work challenges the view that, since Kant, human thought is trapped between the correlation of human consciousness and what exists (being). One of the things Meillassoux asks is what philosophy has to say about things that existed and will continue to exist without humans around to think them. See Meillassoux, *After Finitude*.
29 For Kant, this is the transcendental subject, and throughout modernity this "correlator" changes to things like human power relations (Foucault), human economic relations (Marx), etc. See Morton, *Humankind*, 7–9.
30 To get more insight into the recent development of speculative realisms and object-oriented ontology see Harman, *Towards Speculative Realism*.
31 This actually makes sense for scientists to do on a practical level. First, doing science doesn't require a nuanced philosophical view of science. Second, it's much easier grammatically to refer to things in themselves, which also goes for day-to-day conversation about things in themselves.
32 See Harman, *Towards Speculative Realism*.
33 Ibid., 52.
34 Morton, *Humankind*, 14. See also Lyotard, *Discourse, Figure*.
35 Ibid., 17.

36 Blair Stonechild's lucid descriptions of aspects of Indigenous spirituality show how integral nonhumans are to spiritual and collective life. See Stonechild, *The Knowledge Seeker*.
37 Jane Bennet's work *Vibrant Matter* would seem a good text to pair with speculative realisms in establishing nonhuman entities in meaning-making and relations of solidarity.
38 As an example of a similar ontological shift in education see Taylor and Pacini-Ketchabaw, *The Common Worlds of Children and Animals*.
39 Morton, *Humankind*, 11.
40 Teaching in a country like Ireland has reminded me that teachers and professors hold very tightly to their status and ego. Modern systems of education continue to reward educators who present themselves as the beginning and end of all answers.
41 Morton, *Humankind*, 88.

Afterword

1 See Hardt and Negri, *Multitude*.
2 Ibid., 190.
3 Ibid., 191.

Bibliography

Aamodt, Audrey. *Becomings-Unsettled? (Un) Braiding Settler-Treaty Life Writing.* PhD diss., University of Regina, 2020.
Aamodt, Audrey, and Jesse Bazzul. "In the Middle of Treaty Walking: Entangling Truth, Ethics, and the Risky Narratives of Two Settler(Colonial)s." In *Critical Voices in Science Education Research*, 179–87. Dordrecht: Springer, 2019.
Agamben, Giorgio. *"What Is an Apparatus"? and Other Essays.* Redwood City, CA: Stanford University Press, 2009.
Ahmed, Sara. *Willful Subjects.* Durham, NC: Duke University Press, 2014.
Alsop, Steve. "Encountering Science Education's Capacity to Affect and Be Affected." *Cultural Studies of Science Education* 11, no. 3 (2016): 551–65.
Althusser, Louis. "Philosophy as a Revolutionary Weapon." *New Left Review* 64 (1970).
Althusser, Louis. "Ideology and Ideological State Apparatuses." *In Literary Theory: An Anthology*, edited by J. Rivkin and M. Ryan, 294–304. Malden, MA: Blackwell, 1998.
Anderson, Benedict. *Imagined Communities: Reflections on the Origin and Spread of Nationalism.* New York: Verso Books, 2006.
Anker, Elizabeth S., and Rita Felski eds. *Critique and postcritique.* Durham, NC: Duke University Press, 2017.
Atkinson, R., and M. Mayo. "Refueling the US Innovation Eeconomy: Fresh Approaches to Science, Technology, Engineering and Mathematics (STEM) Education. Information Technology and Innovation Foundation. https://www.itif.org/files/2010-refueling-innovation-economy.pdf.
Badiou, Alain. *Infinite Thought: Truth and the Return to Philosophy.* London: Bloomsbury, 2014.
Bannerji, Himani. *The Dark Side of the Nation: Essays on Multiculturalism, Nationalism and Gender.* Toronto: Canadian Scholars Press, 2000.
Barad, Karen. *Meeting the Universe Halfway: Quantum Physics and the Entanglement of Matter and Meaning.* Durham, NC: Duke University Press, 2007.

Barad, Karen. "Diffracting Diffraction: Cutting Together-Apart." *Parallax* 20, no. 3 (2014): 168–87.

Barad, Karen, and Adam Kleinman. "Intra-actions." Interview by Adam Kleinman. *Mousse* 34 (2012): 76–81.

Barthes, Roland. *Mythologies*. Paris: Éditions du Seuil, 2015.

Bazzul, Jesse. "Neoliberal Ideology, Global Capitalism, and Science Education: Engaging the Question of Subjectivity." *Cultural Studies of Science Education* 7, no. 4 (2012): 1001–20.

Bazzul, Jesse. "Becoming a 'Mythologist': Barthes' Mythologies and Education." In *International Handbook of Semiotics*, edited by P. Trifonas, 1155–68. Dordrecht: Springer, 2015.

Bazzul, J. "Tracing 'Ethical subjectivities' in Science Education: How Biology Textbooks Can Frame Ethico-Political Choices for Students". *Research in Science Education* 45, no. 1 (2015): 23–40.

Bazzul, J. *Ethics and Science Education: How Subjectivity Matters*. New York: Springer International Publishing, 2016.

Bazzul, Jesse. "Ethics, Subjectivity, and Sociomaterial Assemblages: Two Important Directions and Methodological Tensions." *Studies in Philosophy and Education* 37, no. 5 (2018): 467–80.

Bazzul, Jesse. "Solidarity with Nonhumans as an Ontological Struggle." *Educational Philosophy and Theory* (2020): 1–10.

Bazzul, Jesse, and Shakhnoza Kayumova. "Toward a Social Ontology for Science Education: Introducing Deleuze and Guattari's Assemblages." *Educational Philosophy and Theory* 48, no. 3 (2016): 284–99.

Bazzul, Jesse, and Nicholas Santavicca. "Diagramming Assemblages of Sex/Gender and Sexuality as Environmental Education." *Journal of Environmental Education* 48, no. 1 (2017): 56–66.

Bazzul, Jesse, and Heather Sykes. "The Secret Identity of a Biology Textbook: Straight and Naturally Sexed." *Cultural Studies of Science Education* 6, no. 2 (2011): 265–86.

Bazzul, Jesse, and Sara Tolbert. "Reassembling the Natural and Social Commons." In *Educational Commons in Theory and Practice*, edited by Alex Means, Derek Ford, and Graham Slater, 55–73. New York: Palgrave Macmillan, 2017.

Beier, J. "Tracing a Black Hole: Probing Cosmic Darkness in Anthropocenic Times." In *Reimagining Science Education in the Anthropocene*, edited by Maria Wallace, Jesse Bazzul, Marc Higgins, and Sara Tolbert, 35–52. New York: Palgrave Macmillan, 2021.

Bellocchi, Alberto, Cassie Quigley, and Kathrin Otrel-Cass, eds. *Exploring Emotions, Aesthetics and Wellbeing in Science Education Research*. New York: Springer, 2016.

Bennett, Jane. *Vibrant Matter: A Political Ecology of Things*. Durham, NC: Duke University Press, 2010.
Bhabha, Homi K. *The Location of Culture*. Abingdon, UK; New York: Routledge, 2012.
Blades, David W. "Levinas and an Ethics for Science Education." *Educational Philosophy and Theory* 38, no. 5 (2006): 647–64.
Bolaño, Roberto. *2666*. Milan: Adelphi, 2013.
Bourdieu, P. *On Television*. New York: New Press, 1998.
Buchanan, Ian. *Fredric Jameson: Live Theory*. London: Bloomsbury Publishing, 2006.
Butler, Judith. *The Psychic Life of Power: Theories in Subjection*. Redwood City, CA: Stanford University Press, 1997.
Butler, Judith. "What Is Critique? An Essay on Foucault's Virtue." In *The Judith Butler Reader*, edited by S. Salih and J. Butler, 302–22. Malden: Blackwell. 2004.
Butler, Judith. *Giving an Account of Oneself*. New York: Fordham University Press, 2009.
Butler, Judith. "Contingent Foundations: Feminism and the Question of 'Postmodernism.'" In *Feminists Theorize the Political*, edited by J. Butler and J. Scott, 21–39. Abingdon, UK; New York: Routledge, 2013.
Butler, Judith. *Senses of the Subject*. New York: Fordham University Press, 2015.
Butler, Octavia E. *Kindred*. Boston: Beacon Press, 2003.
Cameron, Laura. "Histories of Disturbance." *Radical History Review* 74 (1999): 5–24.
Canguilhem, Georges. "The Living and Its Milieu." *Grey Room* (2001): 7–31.
Carrington, Damian. "School Climate Strikes: 1.4 Million People Took Part, Say Campaigners." *The Guardian*, 19 March 2019.
Chadha, Gita. "Towards an Informed Science Criticism: The Debate on Science in Post-Independence India." *Culture and the Making of Identity in Contemporary India* (2005): 246–58.
Code of Professional Conduct for Teachers. Updated 2nd edition, 2016. An Chomhairle Mhúinteoireachta –The Teaching Council (2016). https://www.teachingcouncil.ie/en/publications/fitness-to-teach/code-of-professional-conduct-for-teachers1.pdf.
Cole, Peter. *Coyote and Raven Go Canoeing: Coming Home to the Village*. Montreal and Kingston: McGill–Queen's University Press, 2014.
Coulthard, Glen Sean. *Red Skin, White masks: Rejecting the Colonial Politics of Recognition*. Minneapolis: University of Minnesota Press, 2014.
Crutzen, Paul J. "The 'Anthropocene.'" In *Earth System Science in the Anthropocene*, 13–18. Berlin: Springer, 2006.
Curran, Peggy. "Anatomy of a Crisis after 100 Days of Protest." *Montreal Gazette*, 22 May 2012, A6.

Darder, Antonia. *Freire and Education*. Abingdon, UK; New York: Routledge, 2014.

Darder, Antonia. *Reinventing Paulo Freire: A Pedagogy of Love*. Abingdon, UK; New York: Routledge, 2017.

Davies, Bronwyn, and Peter Bansel. "Neoliberalism and Education." *International Journal of Qualitative Studies in Education* 20, no. 3 (2007): 247–59.

Dean, Jodi. *The Communist Horizon*. London: Verso Books, 2012.

DeLanda, Manuel. "Interview with Manuel DeLanda." *New Materialism: Interviews and Cartographies* (2012): 38–47.

DeLanda, Manuel. *Intensive Science and Virtual Philosophy*. London: Bloomsbury Publishing, 2013.

DeLanda, Manuel. *Assemblage Theory*. Edinburgh: Edinburgh University Press, 2016.

Deleuze, Gilles. *Foucault*. Minneapolis: University of Minnesota Press, 1988.

Deleuze, Gilles. *Spinoza: Practical Philosophy*. San Francisco: City Lights Books, 1988.

Deleuze, Gilles. "Postscript on the Societies of Control." *October* 59 (1992): 3–7.

Deleuze, Gilles. *Difference and Repetition*. New York: Columbia University Press, 1994.

Deleuze, Gilles, and Felix Guattari. *Kafka: Toward a Minor Literature*. Minneapolis: University of Minnesota Press, 1986.

Deleuze, Gilles, and Félix Guattari. *A Thousand Plateaus: Capitalism and Schizophrenia*. London: Bloomsbury Publishing, 1988.

Deleuze, Gilles, and Parnet Claire. *Dialogues II*. New York: Columbia University Press, 2007.

De Lissovoy, Noah, Alexander J. Means, and Kenneth J. Saltman. *Toward a New Common School Movement*. Abingdon, UK; New York: Routledge, 2015.

Davis, Heather, and Etienne Turpin. *Art in the Anthropocene: Encounters among Aesthetics, Politics, Environments and Epistemologies*. London: Open Humanities Press, 2015.

Dewey, John. *Art as Experience*. New York: Penguin: 2005.

Donald, Dwayne. "Indigenous Métissage: A Decolonizing Research Sensibility." *International Journal of Qualitative Studies in Education* 25, no. 5 (2012): 533–55.

Donald, D. "Forts, Curriculum, and Ethical Relationality." In *Reconsidering Canadian Curriculum Studies*, edited by N. Ng-A-Fook and J. Rotman, 39–46. New York: Palgrave Macmillan, 2012.

Dumas, Michael J. "My Brother as "Problem": Neoliberal Governmentality and Interventions for Black Young men and Boys." *Educational Policy* 30, no. 1 (2016): 94–113.

Dylan, Bob. "Key West (Philosopher Pirate)." *Rough and Rowdy Ways*. Track 9. Columbia.

Eagleton, T., and P. Bourdieu. "Doxa and Common Life. *New Left Review* 191 (1992): 111–21.

Eco, Umberto. *The Open Work*. Trans. Anna Cancogni. Cambridge, MA: Harvard University Press, 1989.

Ermine, W. (2007). The Ethical Space of Engagement. *Indigenous Law Journal* 6: 193.

Faubion, James D. *An Anthropology of Ethics*. Cambridge: Cambridge University Press, 2011.

Ford, Derek R. *Politics and Pedagogy in the "Post-truth" Era: Insurgent Philosophy and Praxis*. London: Bloomsbury Publishing, 2018.

Ford, Derek R., and Tyson E. Lewis. "On the Freedom to Be Opaque Monsters: Communist Pedagogy, Aesthetics, and the Sublime." *Cultural Politics* 14, no. 1 (2018): 95–108.

Fortun, K. "Biopolitics and the Informating of Environmentalism." In *Lively Capital: Biotechnologies, Ethics, and Governance in Global Markets*, edited by K. Rajan, 306–28. Durham, NC: Duke University Press, 2012.

Foucault, Michel. "Authorship: What Is an Author?" *Screen* 20, no. 1 (1979): 13–34.

Foucault, Michel. *The History of Sexuality*. Vol. 1, *An Introduction*. New York: Vintage, 1980.

Foucault, Michel. "The Subject and Power." *Critical Inquiry* 8, no. 4 (1982): 777–95.

Foucault, M. "What Is Enlightenment?" In *The Foucault Reader*, edited by Paul Rabinow, 32–50. New York: Pantheon, 1984.

Foucault, Michel. "Friendship as a Way of Life. In *Essential Works of Foucault, 1954–1984*. Vol. 1, *Ethics: Subjectivity and Truth*, edited by Paul Rabinow, 135–41. New York: New Press, 1997.

Foucault, Michel. "On the Genealogy of Ethics: An Overview of a Work in Progress. In *Essential Works of Foucault, 1954–1984*, vol. 1, *Ethics: Subjectivity and Truth*, edited by Paul Rabinow, 253–80. New York: New Press, 1997.

Foucault, Michel. *The Hermeneutics of the Subject: Lectures at the Collège de France 1981–1982*. London: Macmillan, 2005.

Foucault, Michel, and M. Senellart. *The Birth of Biopolitics: Lectures at the Collège de France, 1978–1979*. New York: Picador, 2010.

Foucault, Michel. *The Archaeology of Knowledge and the Discourse on Language*. New York: Vintage, 2010.

Foucault, Michel, A.I. Davidson, and G. Burchell. *The Courage of Truth: The Government of Self and Others II*. Vol. 8, *Lectures at the Collège de France, 1983–1984*. London: Macmillan, 2012.

Foucault, Michel. *Discipline and Punish: The Birth of the Prison*. New York: Vintage, 2012.

Foucault, Michel. *The History of Sexuality*. Vol. 2, *The Use of Pleasure*. New York: Vintage, 2012.

Foucault, Michel. *The History of Sexuality*. Vol. 3, *The Care of the Self*. New York: Vintage, 2012.

Foucault, Michel. *Wrong-doing, Truth-telling: The Function of Avowal in Justice*. Chicago: University of Chicago Press, 2014.

Ghosh, Amitav. *The Great Derangement: Climate Change and the Unthinkable*. London: Penguin, 2018.

Gilbert, S.F. "Holobiont by Birth: Multilineage Individuals as the Concretion of Cooperative Processes." In *Arts of Living on a Damaged Planet: Ghosts and Monsters of the Anthropocene*, edited by A.L. Tsing, N. Bubandt, E. Gan, and H. Swanson, 73–89, Minneapolis: University of Minnesota Press, 2017.

Gillborn, David. "Education Policy as an Act of White Supremacy: Whiteness, Critical Race Theory and Education Reform." *Journal of Education Policy* 20, no. 4 (2005): 485–505.

The Good Place. Season 2, episode 6. NBC, broadcast 19 October 2017. Netflix: https://www.netflix.com/watch/80209705?trackId=200257859.

Gough, Noel. "Changing Planes: Rhizosemiotic Play in Transnational Curriculum Inquiry." *Studies in Philosophy and Education* 26, no. 3 (2007): 279–94.

Gough, N., and W. Sellers. "Changing Planes: Lines of Flight in Transnational Curriculum Inquiry." In *Expanding Curriculum Theory: Dis/positions and Lines of Flight*, edited by William M. Reynolds and Julie A Webber. Abingdon, UK; New York: Routledge, 2016.

Gould, Stephen Jay. *Wonderful Life: The Burgess Shale and the Nature of History*. New York: W.W. Norton, 1990.

Grande, Sandy. *Red Pedagogy: Native American Social and Political Thought*. Lanham, MD: Rowman & Littlefield, 2015.

Grosz, Elizabeth. *The Incorporeal: Ontology, Ethics, and the Limits of Materialism*. New York: Columbia University Press, 2017.

Habib, Battah. "River of Garbage: Parody Drone Video Mocks Beirut's Rubbish Crisis." *The Guardian*, 11 March 2016. https://www.theguardian.com/cities/2016/mar/11/river-garbage-parody-drone-video-mocks-beirut-lebanon-rubbish-crisis.

Han, Byung-Chul. *The Burnout Society*. Redwood City, CA: Stanford University Press, 2015.

Haraway, Donna. "A Cyborg Manifesto: Science, Technology, and Socialist-Feminism in the Late 20th Century." *The International Handbook of Virtual Learning Environments*, edited by Joel Weiss et al., 116–58. Dordrecht: Springer, 2006.

Haraway, Donna J. *Staying with the Trouble: Making Kin in the Chthulucene*. Durham, NC: Duke University Press, 2016.

Haraway, Donna. "It Matters What Stories Tell Stories; It Matters Whose Stories Tell Stories." *a/b: Auto/Biography Studies* 34, no. 3 (2019): 565–75.

Hardt, Michael. "The Militancy of Theory." *South Atlantic Quarterly* 110, no. 1 (2011): 19–35.
Hardt, Michael, and Antonio Negri. *Empire*. Cambridge: MA: Harvard University Press, 2000.
Hardt, M., and A. Negri. *Multitude: War and Democracy in the Age of Empire*. New York: Penguin Press.
Hardt, Michael, and Antonio Negri. *Commonwealth*. Cambridge, MA: Harvard University Press, 2009.
Harman, G. *Tool-Being: Heidegger and the Metaphysics of Objects*. Peru, IL: Open Court Publishing, 2002.
Harman, Graham. *Towards Speculative Realism: Essays and Lectures*. Winchester, UK: John Hunt, 2010.
Harman, G. *Bells and Whistles: More Speculative Realism*. Winchester, UK: John Hunt, 2013.
Harman, G. Interview by Jon Cogburn, 2015. Accessed 31 January 2019 from https://euppublishingblog.com/2015/09/10/an-interview-with-graham-Harman/.
Harman, Graham. *Object-Oriented Ontology: A New Theory of Everything*. London: Penguin, 2018.
Harvey, David. *Rebel Cities: From the Right to the City to the Urban Revolution*. London: Verso Books, 2012.
Henderson, Joseph A., and David W. Hursh. "Economics and Education for Human Flourishing: Wendell Berry and the Oikonomic Alternative to Neoliberalism." *Educational Studies* 50, no. 2 (2014): 167–86.
Heidegger, Martin. *Being and Time*. Albany, SUNY Press, 2010.
hooks, bell. *Teaching to Transgress*. Abingdon, UK; New York: Routledge, 2014.
hooks, bell. *Yearning: Race, Gender, and Cultural Politics*. Abingdon, UK; New York: Routledge, 2014.
Hubbard, Tasha. *Nîpawistamâsowin: We Will Stand Up*. Downstream Documentary Productions. 2019.
The Hunger Games. Directed by Gary Ross. Lionsgate. 2012.
The Hunt. Directed by Danis Goulet. Viddywell Films, 2017. CFC (Canadian Film Centre). Accessed 12 February 2019 from https://www.dropbox.com/s/vm17j4fl00ujci9/The%20Hunt-%20Final_mono360.mp4?dl=0.
Jameson, F. *Marxism and Form: Twentieth-Century Dialectical Theories of Literature*. Princeton, NJ: Princeton University Press, 1974.
Jameson, Fredric. "Wallace Stevens." *New Orleans Review* 11, no. 1 (1984): 10–19.
Jameson, Fredric. *An American Utopia: Dual Power and the Universal Army*. London: Verso Books, 2016.
Jasanoff, Sheila. "Taking Life: Private Rights in Public Nature." In *Lively Capital: Biotechnologies, Ethics, and Governance in Global Markets*, edited by Kaushik Sunder Rajan, 155–83. Durham, NC: Duke University Press, 2012.

Johnson, Crockett, Owen Jordan, and Paul Alan Levi. *Harold and the Purple Crayon*. New York: Harper & Row, 1955.

Jung, Carl Gustav. *Psychological Types*. Abingdon, UK; New York: Routledge, 2014.

Kafka, Franz. *In the Penal Colony*. London: Penguin, 2011.

Kafka, Franz. *The Trial*. Irvine, CA: Xist Publishing, 2015.

Kanu, Y., and M. Glorr. "'Currere' to the Rescue? Teachers as 'Amateur Intellectuals' in a Knowledge Society." *Journal of the Canadian Association for Curriculum Studies* 4, no. 2 (2006).

Kirchgasler, Kathryn L. "Strange Precipitate: How Interest in Science Produces Different Kinds of Students." In *STEM of Desire*, edited by Will Letts and Steve Fifield, 191–208. Leiden: Brill Sense, 2019.

Kimmerer, Robin Wall. *Braiding Sweetgrass: Indigenous Wisdom, Scientific Knowledge and the Teachings of Plants*. Minneapolis: Milkweed Editions, 2013.

Kimmerer, Robin Wall. *Gathering Moss: A Natural and Cultural History of Mosses*. London: Penguin, 2021.

Kozol, Jonathan. *Savage Inequalities: Children in America's Schools*. New York: Broadway Books, 2012.

Kuhn, Thomas S. *The Structure of Scientific Revolutions*. Chicago: University of Chicago Press, 1996.

Ladson-Billings, Gloria, and William F. Tate. "Toward a Critical Race Theory of Education." In *Critical Race Theory in Education: All God's Children Got a Song*. Abingdon, UK; New York: Routledge, 2006.

Lather, Patti. "Troubling Clarity: The Politics of Accessible Language." *Harvard Educational Review* 66, no. 3 (1996): 525–46.

Lazzarato, Maurizio. "From Biopower to Biopolitics." *Pli: The Warwick Journal of Philosophy* 13, no. 8 (2002): 1–6.

Lee, T., D. Cornell, A. Gregory, and X. Fan. "High Suspension Schools and Dropout Rates for Black and White Students." *Education and Treatment of Children* 34, no. 2 (2011): 167–92.

Lemke, Jay. "The Secret Identity of Science Education: Masculine and Politically Conservative?" *Cultural Studies of Science Education* 6, no. 2 (2011): 287–92.

Lemke, Thomas, Monica J. Casper, and Lisa Jean Moore. *Biopolitics: An Advanced Introduction*. New York: NYU Press, 2011.

Levinas, Emmanuel. *Totality and Infinity: An Essay on Exteriority*. Berlin: Springer Science & Business Media, 1979.

Lewis, Simon L., and Mark A. Maslin. "Defining the Anthropocene." *Nature* 519 (March 2015): 171–80.

Lewis, Tyson. "Biopolitical Utopianism in Educational Theory." *Educational Philosophy and Theory* 39, no. 7 (2007): 683–702.

Lewis, Tyson E. *The Aesthetics of Education: Theatre, Curiosity, and Politics in the Work of Jacques Rancière and Paulo Freire*. New York: Bloomsbury, 2012.

Lewis, T.E. "Jacques Rancière's Aesthetic Regime and Democratic Education." *Journal of Aesthetic Education* 47 (2013): 49–70.
Little Bear, Leroy. "Big Thinking-Leroy Little Bear: Blackfoot Metaphysics 'Waiting in the Wings.'" Congress of the Humanities and Social Sciences, Calgary, 2016. https://www.youtube.com/watch?v=o_txPA8CiA4.
Lorraine, Tamsin. *Deleuze and Guattari's Immanent Ethics: Theory, Subjectivity, and Duration.* Albany: SUNY Press, 2011.
Lyotard, Jean-François. *The Postmodern Condition: A Report on Knowledge.* Minneapolis: University of Minnesota Press, 1984.
Lyotard, Jean-François. *Discourse, Figure.* Minneapolis: University of Minnesota Press, 2011.
MacPherson, A. "Student Participation in Anti-pipeline Rally a 'Significant Concern': Greater Saskatoon Catholic Schools." *Saskatoon Star Phoenix*, 31 October 2016. http://thestarphoenix.com/news/local-news/student-participation-in-anti-pipeline-rally-a-significant-concern-greater-saskatoon-catholic-schools.
Margulis, Lynn, and René Fester, eds. *Symbiosis as a Source of Evolutionary Innovation: Speciation and Morphogenesis.* Cambridge, MA: MIT Press, 1991.
Marks, Jonathan. *Is Science Racist?* Hoboken, NJ: John Wiley & Sons, 2017.
Marx, Karl. *Notes on Adolph Wagner's "Lehrbuch der politischen Ökonomie."* Vol. 1, 2nd ed. (1879). Accessed 2 August 2019 from https://www.marxists.org/archive/marx/works/1881/01/wagner.htm.
Marx, Karl. *Capital.* Vol. 1. Progress Publishers. https://www.marxists.org/archive/marx/works/download/pdf/Capital-Volume-I.pdf.
Matsuda, Mari J. "Beside My Sister, Facing the Enemy: Legal Theory out of Coalition." *Stanford Legal Review* 43 (1990).
Mattingly, Cheryl. "Two Virtue Ethics and the Anthropology of Morality." *Anthropological Theory* 12, no. 2 (2012): 161–84.
McEvenue, Sean. *Interpreting the Pentateuch.* Collegeville: MN: Liturgical Press, 1990.
McKinley, Elizabeth. "Brown Bodies, White Coats: Postcolonialism, Maori Women and Science." *Discourse: Studies in the Cultural Politics of Education* 26, no. 4 (2005): 481–96.
Means, Alexander. "Jacques Rancière, Education, and the Art of Citizenship." *Review of Education, Pedagogy, and Cultural Studies* 33, no. 1 (2011): 28–47.
Means, Alexander J., Derek R. Ford, and Graham B. Slater, eds. *Educational Commons in Theory and Practice: Global Pedagogy and Politics.* New York: Springer, 2017.
Meillassoux, Q. *After Finitude: An Essay on the Necessity of Contingency.* London: Bloomsbury Publishing, 2010.

Miéville, China. "Cognition as Ideology: A Dialectic of SF Theory." In *Red Planets: Marxism and Science Fiction*, edited by Mark Bould and China Meiville, 231–48. Middletown, CT: Wesleyan University Press, 2009.

Miller, J.R. *Shingwauk's Vision: A History of Native Residential Schools*. Toronto: University of Toronto Press, 1996.

Miller, James Rodger. *Residential Schools and Reconciliation: Canada Confronts Its History*. Toronto: University of Toronto Press, 2017.

Milne, Catherine, and Kathryn Scantlebury, eds. *Material Practice and Materiality: Too Long Ignored in Science Education*. Cham: Springer International Publishing, 2019.

Mohawk, John, and Barreiro, José. *Thinking in Indian: A John Mohawk Reader*. Wheat Ridge, CO: Fulcrum Publishing, 2010.

Monani, Salma. "Feeling and Healing Eco-social Catastrophe: The 'Horrific' Slipstream of Danis Goulet's Wakening." *Paradoxa* 28, no. 1 (2016).

Moore, Jason W. *Capitalism in the Web of Life: Ecology and the Accumulation of Capital*. London: Verso Books, 2015.

Morton, Timothy. "Mal-functioning." *The Yearbook of Comparative Literature* 58 (2012): 95–114.

Morton, Timothy. *Hyperobjects: Philosophy and Ecology after the End of the World*. Minneapolis: University of Minnesota Press, 2013.

Morton, Timothy. *Realist Magic: Objects, Ontology, Causality*. London: Open Humanities Press, 2013.

Morton, Timothy. *Dark Ecology: For a Logic of Future Coexistence*. New York: Columbia University Press, 2016.

Morton, Timothy. *Humankind: Solidarity with Non-human People*. London: Verso Books, 2017.

Morton, Timothy. *Being Ecological*. Cambridge, MA: MIT Press, 2018.

Murakami, Haruki. *Kafka on the Shore*. New York: Vintage, 2006.

Murphy, Michelle. *The Economization of Life*. Durham, NC: Duke University Press, 2017.

Nel, Philip. "Never Overlook the Art of the Seemingly Simple: Crockett Johnson and the Politics of the Purple Crayon." *Children's Literature* 29, no. 1 (2001): 142–74.

Ngui, Marc. *Bubble Nut Pictures: A Thousand Plateaus*. http://www.bumblenut.com/drawing/art/plateaus/index.shtml.

Nietzsche, Friedrich Wilhelm. *The Gay Science: With a Prelude in German Rhymes and an Appendix of Songs*. New York: Vintage, 1974.

Okorafor, Nnedi. *Binti: The Complete Trilogy*. New York: DAW Books, 2019.

Ontario Human Rights Commission. *Disproportionate Impact in Ontario* (no date). http://www.ohrc.on.ca/en/ontario-safe-schools-act-school-discipline-and-discrimination/vii-disproportionate-impact-ontario.

Orr, David W. *Earth in Mind: On Education, Environment, and the Human Prospect*. Washington, DC: Island Press, 2004.
Ostrom, Elinor. *Governing the Commons: The Evolution of Institutions for Collective Action*. Cambridge: Cambridge University Press, 1990.
Pierce, Clayton. *Education in the Age of Biocapitalism: Optimizing Educational Life for a Flat World*. New York: Springer, 2012.
Rancière, Jacques. *The Ignorant Schoolmaster: Five Lessons in Intellectual Emancipation*. Redwood City, CA: Stanford University Press, 1991.
Rancière, Jacques. *Disagreement: Politics and Philosophy*. Minneapolis: University of Minnesota Press, 1999.
Rancière, Jacques. "The Ethical Turn of Aesthetics and Politics." *Critical Horizons* 7, no. 1 (2006): 1–20.
Rancière, Jacques. *The Politics of Aesthetics*. London: Bloomsbury, 2013.
Rancière, Jacques. *Dissensus: On Politics and Aesthetics*. London: Bloomsbury, 2015.
Raveendran, Aswathy. *Conceptualizing Critical Science Education Using Socioscientific Issues*. PhD diss., Tata Institute of Fundamental Research, Mumbai, 2016.
Roanhorse, Rebecca. *Trail of Lightning*. New York: Simon and Schuster, 2018.
Rooney, E. "Symptomatic Reading Is a Problem of Form." In *Critique and Postcritique*, edited by E. Anker and R. Felski, 136–48. Durham, NC: Duke University Press, 2017.
Rose, Nikolas. "The Politics of Life Itself." *Theory, Culture & Society* 18, no. 6 (2001): 1–30.
Russell, Joshua. "Whose Better? (Re)orientating a Queer Ecopedagogy." *Canadian Journal of Environmental Education* 18 (2013): 11–26.
Said, Edward W. *Representations of the Intellectual*. New York: Vintage, 2012.
Shotwell, Alexis. *Against Purity: Living Ethically in Compromised Times*. Minneapolis: University of Minnesota Press, 2016.
Slater, Graham B., and C. Bradford Griggs. "Standardization and Subjection: An Autonomist Critique of Neoliberal School Reform." *Review of Education, Pedagogy, and Cultural Studies* 37, no. 5 (2015): 438–59.
Snowpiercer. Directed by Bong Joon Ho. Moho Films, 2013.
Snowshoe, Angela, and Noel V. Starblanket. "Eyininiw Mistatimwak: The Role of the Lac La Croix Indigenous Pony for First Nations Youth Mental Wellness." *Journal of Indigenous Wellbeing* 2, no. 2 (2016): 60–76.
Solly, Melan. "DNA Pioneer James Watson Loses Honorary Titles over Racist Comments." *Smithsonian Magazine*, 15 January 2019. https://www.smithsonianmag.com/smart-news/dna-pioneer-james-watson-loses-honorary-titles-over-racist-comments-180971266/.
Spinoza, Benedict de. *A Spinoza Reader: The Ethics and Other Works*. Princeton, NJ: Princeton University Press, 1994.

Stefanovich, O., K. Roman, and J.P. Jones. "Too Many First Nations Lack Clean Drinking Water and It's Ottawa's Fault, Says Auditor General. *Canadian Broadcasting Corporation*, 21 February 2021. https://www.cbc.ca/news/politics/auditor-general-reports-2021-1.5927572.

Stengers, Isabelle. *Another Science Is Possible: A Manifesto for Slow Science*. Hoboken, NJ: John Wiley & Sons, 2018.

Stoler, Ann Laura. *Race and the Education of Desire: Foucault's History of Sexuality and the Colonial Order of Things*. Durham, NC: Duke University Press, 1995.

Stonechild, Blair. *The Knowledge Seeker: Embracing Indigenous Spirituality*. Regina: University of Regina Press, 2016.

Sui Van, Nadia. "*Velut arbor ævo*: The Meaning of U of T's Motto." *University of Toronto Magazine*, 3 January 2018. https://magazine.utoronto.ca/campus/history/velut-arbor-aevo-university-of-toronto-motto-coat-of-arms-nadia-siu-van/.

Tanke, Joseph J. "What Is the Aesthetic Regime?" *Parrhesia* 12 (2011): 71–81.

Taylor, Affrica, and Veronica Pacini-Ketchabaw. *The Common Worlds of Children and Animals: Relational Ethics for Entangled Lives*. Abingdon, UK: New York: Routledge, 2018.

This Is Worldtown. Spotlight: Danis Goulet on Indigenous Futurism in Film. http://thisisworldtown.com/indigenous-media-makers-spotlight-ft-danis-goulet/.

Thorpe, C. "Political Theory in Science and Technology Studies." In *The Handbook of Science and Technology Studies*, edited by E. Hackett., O. Amsterdamska, M. Lynch, and J. Wajcman, 63–82. Cambridge, MA: MIT Press, 2008.

Todd, Sharon. "Creating Aesthetic Encounters of the World, or Teaching in the Presence of Climate Sorrow." *Journal of Philosophy of Education* (2020). DOI:10.1111/1467-9752.12478.

Todd, Zoe. "An Indigenous Feminist's Take on the Ontological Turn: 'Ontology' Is Just Another Word for Colonialism." *Journal of Historical Sociology* 29, no. 1 (2016): 4–22.

Tolbert, Sara, and Jesse Bazzul. "Aesthetics, String Figures, and the Politics of the Visible in Science and Education." *Journal of Curriculum and Pedagogy* 17, no. 1 (2020): 82–98.

Truth and Reconciliation Commission of Canada (TRC). *Calls to Action* (2015). http://trc.ca/assets/pdf/Calls_to_Action_English2.pdf.

Tsing, Anna Lowenhaupt. *The Mushroom at the End of the World: On the Possibility of Life in Capitalist Ruins*. Princeton, NJ: Princeton University Press, 2015.

Tsing, A., and J. Bazzul. "A Feral Atlas for the Anthropocene: An Interview with Anna L. Tsing." In *Science Education in the Anthropocene*, edited by

M. Wallace, J. Bazzul, M. Higgins, and S. Tolbert. New York: Palgrave Macmillan, 2021.

Tuck, Eve. "Breaking Up with Deleuze: Desire and Valuing the Irreconcilable." *International Journal of Qualitative Studies in Education* 23, no. 5 (2010): 635–50.

Vonnegut, K. *Breakfast of Champions*. New York: Random House, 2009.

Wain, Kenneth. "Chapter 11: Foucault: The Ethics of Self-Creation and the Future of Education." *Counterpoints* 292 (2007): 163–80.

Wakening. Directed by Danis Goulet. Performed by Sarah Podemski and Gail Maurice. ViddyWell Films, 2013. https://www.youtube.com/watch?v=bbmi2ff3MBk. Accessed 10 September 2018.

Wallace, Maria F.G. "The Paradox of Un/making Science People: Practicing Ethico-Political Hesitations in Science Education." *Cultural Studies of Science Education* 13, no. 4 (2018): 1049–60.

Willems, Brian Daniel. "Speculative Realism and Science Fiction." In *Speculative Realism and Science Fiction*. Edinburgh: Edinburgh University Press, 2022.

Wilson, Edward O. *Consilience: The Unity of Knowledge*. New York: Vintage, 1999.

Yusoff, Kathryn. *A Billion Black Anthropocenes or None*. Minneapolis: University of Minnesota Press. 2018.

Zembylas, Michalinos. "The Contribution of Non-representational Theories in Education: Some Affective, Ethical and Political Implications." *Studies in Philosophy and Education* 36, no. 4 (2017): 393–407.

Zheng, Lei. "A Performative History of STEM Crisis Discourse: The Co-constitution of Crisis Sensibility and Systems Analysis around 1970." *Discourse: Studies in the Cultural Politics of Education* 42, no. 3 (2021): 337–52.

Žižek, Slavoj. *Living in the End Times*. London: Verso, 2011.

Žižek, S. Slavoj. "Žižek en el CBA: Alegato a favor de un socialismo burocrático." Círculo de Bellas Artes (2017). https://www.youtube.com/watch?v=4qMqVI25kPk.

Index

Aamodt, Audrey, 14, 163, 190n26, 194n6
aesthetics, 11, 24, 30, 62, 68, 138–46, 150–3, 157, 161, 188n30, 191n2, 195nn5–12
agrilogistics, 166, 170–1, 194n47
Ahmed, Sara, 98, 189n4
alienation, 73, 137, 168, 170
Althusser, Louis, 58, 68–9, 85, 182n48, 184n39
Anthropocene: anthropocentrism, 100, 171; epoch, 12, 55–6, 76, 93–4, 109, 112, 137, 180nn14–16; and ethics, 131, 140–1, 154, 158–65, 174–5, 183n16; overview, 22–5; plane of emergence, 121
anthropocentrism, 7–8, 101; ethics and ontology, 100, 115, 117, 119, 125, 134, 153, 161–4, 167, 174–5; human rights, 23; humanism, 67; subjectivity, 94
antiquation (of theory), 61, 66, 69–70
apparatus (*Dispositif*): dissensus, 142; modernity, 166; schooling and power, 31–2, 34, 43–4, 48, 50, 64, 78, 183n7; subjectivity and self-creation, 85, 129
arborescent, 109, 112–14, 131

art(s), in the anthropocene, 6, 23; art and aesthetics, 141–7, 150–9; art and labour, 62; art and politics, 67; art and self-creation, 85, 139; artists, 68; as composition, 105; of governance, 47; and John Dewey, 191n2; philosophy of, 185n8, 192n14
ascesis, 84, 188
assemblages, 7, 13, 107, 111, 149; ethics 104, 140, 191n21; livability, 164; overview, 117–39, 190n5, 191n19; scale, 31, 167; texts, 179n8

Barad, Karen, 71, 123, 190nn12–14
Barthes, Roland, 41, 119, 182n49, 190n7
becoming, 28, 62, 165–6; becoming different, 50–1, 57, 85, 94, 100–2, 110, 112–15, 134–5, 140, 143, 194–5n46; becoming ethical, 15–16, 74, 125, 138–9, 146; becoming (minor), 129–32, 137, 162, 190n11, 191nn18, 26–7, 194nn4, 6
Bible, 8, 18, 37, 79, 130, 187n16
Binti Trilogy, 147, 150–2, 193n29
biopolitics, 49, 54, 61, 183nn18, 20, 188n27
Blades, David, 75, 187n8

bodies: assemblages, 133, 139, 149; bodies without organs, 104, 114–15, 158; and power, 11, 18, 31–3, 35–6, 39, 43–4, 48, 52, 95, 102, 181n32, 185n13; power (of), 144–5

Butler, Judith, 40–1, 58–9, 99, 180–1n19, 182n46, 184nn38, 40, 188n25, 189n7

Butler, Octavia, 99, 192n8

capitalism, 10, 11, 13, 27–8, 65, 74–5, 104, 111, 145, 154, 177, 180n12; and culture, 42; and ecology, 54–6, 161, 168–70; growth of capital, 19, 43, 46, 51, 128–9, 133, 163; human capital, 5, 56–8, 184n37; privatization, 22

Christianity, 37–8, 49, 78, 80, 83, 110, 130, 188n22

climate change, 18, 21–2, 34, 55, 68, 84, 88, 149, 165; climate sorrow, 194n7; climate strikes, 45–6, 126, 181n30, 183n23

Cole, Peter, 13

colonialism, 9, 11, 18–20, 24–6, 30, 44, 68, 78, 85, 143–5, 151, 184nn35, 41; colonial powers, 29, 31, 34, 46–8, 53, 59, 80, 88, 135–6, 148–9; and environment, 51, 168, 171; settler colonialism, 12, 64, 111–12, 192n9

common(s), 5–6, 9, 12, 19–20, 63, 66, 71–2, 77, 109, 112, 131, 174–6, 178, 182n4, 194n3; overview of the commons, 43, 49–57

communism(s), 38, 65, 185n14

commodity fetishism, 22, 69

conduct, 5, 17, 19, 25–35, 43–9, 51, 57, 76, 82, 85–8, 95, 98–9, 125–6, 182n40

correlationism, 2, 153, 156, 167, 172–4

Coulthard, Glen, 111, 189n24

COVID-19, 29, 117, 133, 184n32, 192n11, 193n26

critique, 29, 58, 61, 64–6, 70, 111, 167, 182n46, 183n30, 184n40, 185–6n5

curriculum, 9–10, 18, 49, 65, 112, 155, 189n25; and discourse, 33, 102

dark ecology, 141, 152–3, 156–9

Delanda, Manuel, 70, 117–19, 123, 190n5

Deleuze, Gilles, 10, 67, 69, 93, 100, 110, 126, 129–30, 132, 137, 158, 166, 179n1, 185nn7–8, 189n16, 190n27, 191nn19, 26; assemblages, 117–18; criticism of, 110–12; immanent planes, 63–4, 120; rhizomes, 106–7, 113–14; on Spinoza, 103–4, 178; and subjectivity, 93–9, 102

democracy, 63, 80, 164

desire, 19, 33, 48, 54, 81, 84, 98, 130, 178, 189n5; captured by interests, 21–2, 57, 111; for communal living, 65–6, 72

deterritorialization, 126, 132–3, 137–8, 191n26

dialectical method, 68

difference, 2, 4–5, 40, 48, 62, 110, 115, 151; and the commons, 51–2, 56; emergence of, 17, 43, 71–2, 101, 103, 120–1, 123, 128–31; intensive and extensive, 134–7

discipline: fields of study, 4–6, 17–18, 24, 35, 37, 58, 69, 76, 82, 89, 94, 101, 117, 119–21, 142, 179n1, 185n8; power and subjectivity, 25–9, 35, 39, 41, 44–5, 47, 65, 181nn21, 32

discourse, 9, 70, 99, 102, 119, 147, 181n31, 187n11; and assemblages, 122, 133; and power, 33, 37, 44, 47, 50, 58–9, 68, 76, 95, 182n41

dissensus, 61, 63–5, 67, 142, 192n15

disturbance, 25, 161–6, 171, 177, 194n4
Donald, Dwayne, 19, 78, 80, 87, 131

empire, 19–20, 22, 46, 48, 180n5
enclosure, 53, 55, 72
environmentality, 154, 157–8, 175
epistemology, 24, 40, 65, 71, 101
equality, 4, 6, 55–6, 145, 151, 157, 162, 178; radical democracy, 40–1, 61, 63–4, 66–7, 71, 142–3, 149, 164, 192n15; space of, 79–80
Ermine, Willie, 75, 187n6
ethics: and education, 2–7, 9–12, 15–18, 21–2, 25–7, 40, 44, 140–1, 193–4n6; differentiation, 48, 110; emergent material ethics, 112–17, 120–1, 123, 125–6, 128–35, 138–9, 155, 161–6, 174–80, 188n1; Indigenous ethics, 78, 162; issues, 36–7, 50, 136; and politics, 43, 61–3, 69–72, 86–9, 188nn30–1; relationality, 46, 51, 56, 168, 180n2, 190n3; as resistance, 20, 45, 106, 146; responsibility, 30, 55, 187n9; self-creation, 29, 35, 49, 98–102, 187n15, 194n6; Spinoza's ethics, 103–5, 158; subjectivity, 28, 31–3, 41–2, 57–60, 74–85, 93–7
evil, 40, 104, 158–9, 170
exteriority, and subjectivity, 94–5, 97–8, 124

Faubion, James, 75
fiction, 24, 73–4, 137, 142–3, 186n1, 187n18; science fiction, 48, 144–9, 151–3
fidelity, 6, 19, 36, 39, 41–2, 66
Foucault, Michel, 27, 67, 180n7, 181n23, 183nn12, 15, 186n24, 187nn15–16, 20, 188nn21–4, 27; Deleuze on, 94–6, 99–100; ethics, 75–85; power, 29–33, 44–5, 69

freedom, 4, 22, 45, 54, 59, 83–5, 94–5, 97, 109, 186n34; and mastery, 35; to speak truth, 77, 80; within assemblages, 126–8
futurisms (Indigenous and Black), 144, 146–7, 149, 192n23

Gough, Noel, 12, 107–8, 179n5, 190n9
Gould, Stephen J., 15–16, 20, 52, 180n1
Goulet, Danis, 147–8, 192n23
Grande, Sandy, 111, 189n22
Grosz, Elizabeth, 20, 63, 91, 125, 139, 185n6, 187n9, 188n1
Guattari, Felix, 9, 93–4, 126, 129, 132, 139, 158, 166, 178, 179n1, 185nn7–8, 189n16, 190n27 (ch. 5), 190n5 (ch. 6), 191nn18, 26; assemblages, 117–18; criticisms of, 110–12; immanent planes, 63–4, 120; rhizomes, 106–7, 113–14; on Spinoza, 103–4, 178

Haraway, Donna, 70–1, 146–7, 163, 183n31, 192n20
Hardt, M., and A. Negri, 19, 43, 46, 48–9, 54, 178, 180n5, 194n3
Harman, Graham, 153, 156, 172, 186n34, 193nn32, 38, 195n27
hooks, bell, 77, 187n14, 192n13
hyperobjects, 24, 52

ideality, 63, 71, 185n6
identity, 4, 17, 20, 26, 35, 88, 123, 136, 156; and discipline, 27, 31, 33, 45, 95–6, 98, 182n41; fluidity, 111; gender, 77, 181n31; intersectional, 52, 185n13; minoritarian, 110, 112–14, 132; ossified, 101; performance, 59
ideology, 77, 104, 188n28; (neo) liberal, 65, 86, 185n19; and power, 37, 39, 41, 69, 183n16

immanence, 10, 20, 48–9, 67, 97, 100, 104, 106, 118, 130, 132, 138, 143; planes of, 63, 121–2, 125, 185nn7–8; Spinoza's notion of, 69
Indigenous, 6, 18, 21, 29, 41, 51, 78, 111, 116–17, 146, 159, 161–2, 177, 191n18; activism, 86–7; colonization, 24, 26, 39, 53–4, 59, 85, 151, 165; futurisms, 144, 147–9, 192n9; Indigenous ways of knowing, 5, 11, 70, 75, 112, 117, 157, 168, 170–1, 174, 193nn36, 40; treaties, 1
intersectionality, 52, 113
interiority, and subjectivity, 94–5
interpellation, 184n39
intra-action, 123

Jasonoff, Sheila, 55
Jameson, Fredric, 11, 21, 61, 68–9, 179n9

Kant, Immanuel, 101, 156, 167, 172, 195n28
Kirchgasler, Kathryn, 47

labour (aesthetic), 17, 19, 38, 57, 62, 66, 71, 129, 142, 159
Laidlaw, James, 84
language, 26–7, 30, 38, 67, 70, 131, 137–8, 148, 172–3, 181n37; intelligibility, 8, 179n5; and light, 100–3, 126, 146, 191n18
law, 20, 31, 37, 130; nonhuman rights, 40; privatization, 55–6; and subjectivity, 45, 58, 84–5, 137, 181n32, 184n39
Lazzarato, Maurizio, 86, 188n27
left (political), 5–6, 19, 64–5, 69, 175
lines of flight, 105–7, 110–14, 126, 132, 137, 143, 145–6, 164

literarity, 143, 146
loop (strange), 158–9, 194n48
love, 8, 19, 21, 25, 42, 66, 88, 98, 111, 134, 149, 149–51, 180n4, 183n30

macro-micro: assemblages, 118–19, 128, 133; politics, 30–1, 33, 63–4
majority, 11, 27, 39, 79, 112–14, 132, 135, 137, 143, 163
malfunctioning, 116, 154–8, 161–2, 164, 168, 176, 193nn38, 41
materiality, 9, 11, 60, 63, 66, 70, 100, 102, 125–7, 185n6, 190n2
minority, 110, 114, 137, 194
Marx(ism), 29, 67–9, 71, 129, 172, 180n12, 195n15
McEvenue, Sean, 10, 179n6
McGinnis, Angela, 165, 194n11
Moore, Jason, 54
morality, 17, 21, 30, 36–8, 41, 79, 83–5, 88, 98–9, 104, 106, 112, 123, 130, 140, 170, 189n4
more-than-human, 56, 115, 144, 149, 151
Morton, Timothy, 24, 140–1, 152, 154–62, 166–73, 175, 193n38, 194nn47–8, 194–5n14, 195nn15, 27–9
multiplicity, 6, 20, 52, 83, 111–12, 125, 131–2
multispecies, 19, 106, 123, 125, 146, 163
multitude, 51–2, 55, 71, 78, 94, 178, 194n3
Murakami, Haruki, 73–4, 142, 186

nationalisms, 19, 29
Nelson, Erin Jane, 147, 149–50
neoliberalism, 36, 56, 58, 86, 115, 185n19, 187n11, 188n27
nonhumans, 3, 19, 25–6, 28, 36, 39, 55–6, 60, 70–3, 78, 81, 86, 116, 119, 141, 151, 157; solidarity with,

160–3, 166–8, 170–5, 183–4n31, 190n2, 196n36

object-oriented ontology (OOO), 156, 167, 172, 186n34, 193n32, 195nn27, 30
Okorafor, Nnedi, 147, 150–1
ontology, 43, 54, 70–1, 83, 102, 109, 117–20, 129, 138, 141, 156–7, 162, 164, 167, 169, 172, 180n5, 186n34, 191n19, 193n32, 194n3, 195nn27, 30, 196n38; the commons, 51, 54; critique, 111; dark-speculative, 153, 159, 193n38; and difference, 130–1; ontological planes, 120–1, 127; ontological turn, 7

parrhesia, 79–80, 187n19
part of no part, 62–3
Pierce, Clayton, 58, 184n37
pleasure, 5, 12, 22, 62, 78, 106, 159, 169–70
posthuman, 61, 66–7, 92, 146
poststructuralism, 7, 61–2, 66–7, 69, 111, 123
power, 65–6, 68, 86, 144; biopower, 12, 19–20, 43–52, 56–9, 76, 83–5, 87, 115; of creation, 9, 63, 69, 71–2, 97, 101–6, 125, 129–32, 135–9, 143, 145, 152, 157, 178; discipline, 25–41, 100, 188n25; freedom, 77–80, 109–12; relations, 3–4, 54, 99, 193n46, 195n29
privatization, 22, 53–4, 170
Psychopompolis, 147, 149–50, 193n27
punishment, 32, 80, 84, 103, 128, 181n22

queer(ing), 40, 56, 133, 151; relationships, 17, 167; youth, 29

racism, 5, 25, 37, 47, 59, 119, 180n13
Rancière, Jacques, 61–4, 87, 141–6, 179n3, 182n41, 184n4, 185n10, 188nn30–1, 192nn5–6, 10, 13, 15
realisms, 120, 122–3; magical, 74; scientific, 17, 65; speculative, 52, 153, 156, 160–1, 167, 171–2, 194n13, 195n13, 196n37
relationality, 78, 83, 125, 131, 187n7
relations of self, 2, 57, 59, 80–4, 94, 99–101
religion, 52, 58, 84, 135, 170
responsibility, 4, 12–13, 15–16, 23, 30, 39, 42–3, 45, 48, 50, 55, 57, 59, 77, 81, 83, 101, 103, 123, 142, 160, 166
reterritorialization, 133, 191
rhizome, 3, 105–9, 112–13, 115, 126, 189n16, 191n26
Russell, Joshua, 56, 184n3

Saskatchewan, 1, 8, 45, 59, 116, 177, 195n17
science, 3, 10–11, 14, 16–17, 24, 27–8, 36–7, 39, 46–8, 50, 55, 57, 59, 63, 65, 71, 73, 116–17, 119–20, 158–9, 162, 172, 174, 179n1, 181n24, 184n35, 185n8, 186n34; science education, 62, 75, 101, 135, 182n43, 184n37, 185n13, 186n23; science fiction, 144, 146–9, 151 3
Sellers, Warren, 10, 107–8
sharing, 4–5, 51–2, 54, 65, 174–5,
sociomaterial, 96, 102, 11, 115, 117, 120, 130, 138, 149, 188n1
solidarity, 12, 51, 62, 81, 86, 110, 136, 144, 157, 160–2, 166–8, 170–6, 178, 195n15, 196n37
spectral(ity), 167–72
Spinoza, Baruch, 49, 69, 103–5, 109, 138, 158, 178, 189n11

spiritual, 4–5, 13, 23–4, 35, 55, 75, 116, 121, 131, 148–9, 151–2, 159, 165, 168, 174, 196n36
Starblanket, Noel, 165, 194n11
strata, 95–8, 100, 102–5, 110, 115, 128–9, 131, 145
strategic zone, 96–7, 102
string figures, 146, 192n7
subjectivity, 2, 6, 11, 17, 32, 45, 57–8, 60, 74, 76, 77, 82, 89, 93–103, 105, 112, 114–15, 138, 140, 152, 158, 173, 187n15, 193n46, 194n48
superstructure, 68–9, 131, 167
symbiosis, 119, 128, 131–2, 162, 166–7, 171, 195n16; symbiotic real, 168–72, 174

Todd, Sharon, 194n7
Todd, Zoe, 70
transcendence, 49, 69, 97–8, 104, 118, 120, 122–3, 130, 132, 130, 139, 195n29

transdisciplinary, 2, 5–6, 9, 28, 76, 119, 122, 126, 152, 161
Triggs, Valerie, 141–2, 144–5
truth, 17–18, 34, 37–8, 42, 44–5, 69; and colonialism, 58, 72, 146, 148, 181n29; and love, 42; religious, 8, 84, 170, 179n6; truth and justice 78–80, 187nn16, 20
Tsing, Anna, 161–6, 183–4n31, 194n2
Tuck, Eve, 111, 189n23

uncanny, 11, 22, 38, 57, 74, 115, 145, 152, 157, 159, 163, 167, 186n1

Wakening (science fiction film), 147–9
Wallace, Maria (F.G.), 36, 193n41
white supremacy, 3, 5, 8, 19, 30, 39, 64, 68, 76, 88, 109, 112, 144, 147, 171, 182nn41–2, 184n37, 188n28

Žižek, Slavoj, 1–2, 87, 185n17

www.ingramcontent.com/pod-product-compliance
Lightning Source LLC
Chambersburg PA
CBHW030317080526
44584CB00012B/597